Nell Gwynne

Nell Gwynne

Graham Hopkins

Robson Books

First published in Great Britain in 2000 by Robson Books, 10 Blenheim Court, Brewery Road, London N7 9NT

A member of the Chrysalis Group plc

British Library Cataloguing in Publication Data
A catalogue record for this title is available from the British Library

ISBN 1 86105 370 3

Typeset by FiSH Books, London
Printed and bound in Great Britain by Creative Print & Design (Wales), Ebbw Vale

Contents

For Kathryn Stone
Her Book

Acknowledgements

Quite simply this book would not have been published without the tireless energy, support, creativity and belief of Kathryn Stone (sending the manuscript to publishers in an orange crate with oranges was truly inspired). My love and thanks to you.

I would also like to pay tribute to the support, kindness and encouragement given to me by His Grace the Duke of St Albans (who also kindly agreed to write the Foreword) and Nell Gwynne's family historian Peter Beauclerk-Dewar. I'm particularly grateful for being granted access to the Crofton Croker collection and for the duke's permission to reproduce a number of unique and unpublished prints from that collection. Peter Beauclerk Dewar also commented on the draft manuscript and suggested some thoughtful and helpful lines of inquiry.

I would also like to thank Commander J A Holt, MBE, the club secretary of the Army & Navy Club for permission to view its collection of papers, warrants, receipts and memorabilia, and to the club's archivist Major Jack Triggs who gave up so much time to ensure I got all the information I needed.

There are some excellent collections of Nelly-related material in the United States. Unable to afford to see them first-hand I am hugely grateful for the time, electronic and more traditional correspondence and copying of manuscripts that the following people generously donated: Christine Nelson, curator of Literary and Historical manuscripts at the Pierpont Morgan Library, New York; Elva Griffith, Rare Books and Manuscripts, State University of Ohio; and Elizabeth Hopkin, assistant registrar, Columbus Museum of Art. Other American-based source materials were kindly provided by Marc Greitens, curatorial assistant, Osborn Collection Beinecke Library, Yale University; Lisa Libby at the Huntington Library; Brian Welch, Widener Library, Harvard College Library; and Eleanor S Hyun, administrative assistant at the Metroplitan Museum of Art, New York.

Closer to home, I'd like to thank Sue Hubbard at the Hereford Record Office and particularly local historian John Harnden who carried out sterling research work on Nelly's links to Hereford. Also to Miss J Williams, librarian, the Cathedral Library, Hereford.

Back on our travels again, I would like to thank Daniel Rebours for the wide-ranging research he conducted in Paris in trying to uncover information about the death of Nelly's second son, James. Linked to this I would also like to thank Catherine Cunard, documentaliste, Mediatheque de l'Institut Français du Royaume-Uni, and Luis Amigues, director des archives, Ministère des Affaires Étrangères. Thanks also to Eva Karlsson, Department of Photos and Rights, at Statens Konstmuseer, Sweden, and Eilis Ni Dhuibhne at the National Library of Ireland.

English universities, libraries, archives, record offices and others have, as expected, provided great help. In particular I would like to thank Oliver Pickering, senior assistant librarian at the Brotherton Library, Leeds University, who unearthed an exciting scrapbook of Nelly memorabilia which had, to date, evaded all Nelly's biographers. Others to whom I am very grateful include: Ms M Simms, Mark Lawrence, Mark Priddey and Elizabeth A Finn at the Oxfordshire County Council Archives; Karin Brown, assistant librarian at the Shakespeare Centre; Guy Holborn, librarian at Lincoln's Inn; Adrian Blunt, librarian, Inner Temple; Sarah Edmondson, archivist at the Berkshire Record Office; William Young, custodian of the archives at St Martin-in-the-Fields; Miss Rachel Watson, county archivist for Northamptonshire County Council, and Peter Moyse, historical photographer; Michael Webb at the Bodleian Library, Oxford University; Mrs A Fitzsimons, assistant Pepys Librarian, Magdalene College, Cambridge; Betty Beesley, secretary to Works of Art Committee, Garrick Club, London; Revd Canon John Rogan, archivist, Bristol Cathedral; Dr J R Gurney, curatorial officer, Historical Manuscripts Commission; Richard Mangan, administrator, Mander & Mitchenson Theatre Collection; Brett Dolman, superintendent, Manuscripts Reading Room, British Library; Roy Gillett, president of the Astrological Association of Great Britain; Thomas Woodcock, College of Arms; Stephen Rabson, group information manager, P&O, 79 Pall Mall; Jackie Keating and Bill O'Keefe, Bank of England; and Philip Winterbottom, archive manager, Royal Bank of Scotland.

And I haven't finished yet. I would like to thank individuals who have read drafts, provided advice, help, support or who just kept asking how things were going. These include Marcus Woolley, Craig and Loz Marston, Eric Davis, Jo Hopkins, Ian and Mark Hopkins, Frances Rostron, Edward Kenny, Stephen Hicks, and my dad. Good policy also, methinks, to thank the team at Robson Books: Cheryl Merritt, Lorna Russell and Jeremy Robson for taking the chance and turning my dream into a reality.

Finally, and perhaps above all, I would to thank my mum. I will always love and miss you.

Graham Hopkins

Foreword

This is the fifteenth full biography of Nell Gwynne to have been written quite apart from the many references to her in books about King Charles II, royal mistresses and the theatre. It is a great tribute to her that so many people over three centuries should have wished to devote so much time and effort to her memory.

Back in 1974 when *The House of Nell Gwyn – The Fortunes of The Beauclerk Family 1670–1974* was published, one of its authors and the family historian, Peter Beauclerk-Dewar, had managed to trace some 2,000 living descendants of Nell Gwynne and Charles II, of which I am one. Each one of those descendants will, I am sure, be fascinated to read this sympathetic biography of their ancestress of whom they can be justly proud. More importantly, so too will the public at large, who throughout the centuries have taken Nell Gwynne to their hearts, making her the loved icon that she still is.

Graham Hopkins has not only drawn from, but has correlated and assessed the information given in all these previously published works. Moreover, he has unearthed new seams of unpublished material in the Brotherton Library, Leeds, in addition to Ohio University and the Pierpont Morgan Library, New York, which has added significantly to our knowledge of Nell Gwynne as well as challenging some of the myths. Thus this book is the most comprehensive work of its kind to have been written – yet written with objectivity and sympathy, if that is not a contradiction in terms. It is both scholarly and readable, and I commend it as a proud great-great-great-great-great-great-grandson.

His Grace the Duke of St Albans

The natural children of Charles II

Mother	Children
Lucy Walter or Barlow (1630–58)	James Crofts, (1649–85), created Duke of Monmouth in 1663
Elizabeth Killigrew, Lady Shannon (born c1662)	Charles Fitzroy (c1651–84)
Catherine Pegge, Lady Green	Charles Fitzcharles – known as 'Don Carlos' – (1657–80) created Earl of Plymouth in 1675 Catherine Fitzcharles (born 1658)
Barbara Palmer (nee Villiers), Countess Castlemaine, Duchess of Cleveland (1640–1709)	Anne Palmer (1661–1722), Countess of Sussex Charles Fitzroy, (1662–1730), created Duke of Southampton 1675 and became first Duke of Cleveland 1709 Henry Fitzroy (1663–90), created the Duke of Grafton 1709 Charlotte Fitzroy (1664–1718), Countess of Lichfield George Fitzroy (1665–1716), created Duke of Northumberland 1683
Mary 'Moll' Davis	Mary Tudor (c1668–1726)
Eleanor 'Nell' Gwynne (c1642–1687)	Charles Beauclerk (1670–1726), created Duke of St Albans 1684 James Beauclerk (1671–1680)
Louise Renee de Penancoet de Keroualle, Duchess of Portsmouth (1648–1734)	Charles Lennox (1672–1723), created Duke of Richmond 1675

Introduction

Her story is romance itself.

W J MacQueen-Pope,

For Nell Gwynne has become, inalienably, a figure
of romance.

John Drinkwater

It is difficult to account for the popularity of certain
historical characters, and we can only accept it as a fact that,
while large numbers of distinguished men and women are
completely forgotten, the whole world knows Nell Gwynne.

H B Wheatley,

Why does the whole world know Nell Gwynne? Ask almost anybody,
even those with no interest in history, and they will probably say
something about her being the one with the oranges or being a king's
mistress. And even if they get the king wrong, they know her name (even
though no one is quite sure how to spell it). She has become one of
England's best-loved icons.

One or two snap that she is tiresome and crude, but historians have
been, on the whole, kind to Nelly. They see her as harmless light relief.
To them she's vivacious, disarmingly vulgar, a picaresque heroine, saucy,
piquant, petite, winsome, kind-hearted, beautifully shaped, good-
natured, generous, a merry minx and universally popular.

Her story is of an extraordinary woman in a remarkable time. She epitomises the classic rags-to-riches story: the poor girl who fell in love with a king, but who never forgot the place or the people whence she came. The affection we hold for her is all the sweeter because she was mistress to one of Britain's most popular monarchs. Restored to the throne after the austere rule of the Commonwealth ('the dark days of Oliver'), Charles II's reign was characterised by the social boom of alehouse, theatre, sport and gambling. It was the time of events known to every school child: the Plague, the Great Fire of London, the princes being found in the Tower and Colonel Blood's failed attempt to steal the Crown Jewels. It was a reign peopled by Pepys, Evelyn, Newton, Halley, Dryden, Purcell, Bunyan, Milton, Wren, Lely and Kneller. Set in such flourishing and dizzying times, you have an irresistible and timeless romance between the merry monarch and pretty, witty Nell.

Charles had other mistresses but they have passed largely unmourned and unremembered. Nelly was different. She only dabbled in politics when she needed to, for the others it was the purpose of their being. Although Nelly was extravagant, she never came close to the grasping greed of her rivals. She was also loyal to Charles (who was anything but to her) and loved him dearly as a man, while the others in his bed clearly kept one eye on his crown. She was kind, caring and charitable. Famously pretty, she became the leading comedy actress of her day, dancing and singing herself into the hearts of the people. She was the darling strumpet of the crowd.

Indeed, it was her ability to make people laugh with her wit, humour and a delicious line in mimicry, that is perhaps her most endearing talent. In a court of educated dukes and earls, the illiterate one-time street urchin hawking fish around Covent Garden confidently held her own. Indeed they courted her. Her house at Pall Mall became the meeting place for the so-called 'merry gang' – the court's finest wits, drinkers and socialites, who also happened to be some of the most important politicians of the day.

She set fashions in clothes and hairstyles. She was – along with the other mistresses – the subject of much gossip and rumour. Indeed, it is difficult for us today to sift through the wealth of anecdotal evidence to pick out the real Nelly from the mythical one. Hard because even the most outrageous stories are believable because they sound just like Nelly.

She was also a mother, giving birth to two of Charles II's

acknowledged 13 natural children, all of whom were with his mistresses. His queen, Catherine of Braganza, was unable to have children. Nelly's eldest son, Charles Beauclerk, would become the first duke of St Albans. Today's duke is her descendant.

At her funeral, at St Martin-in-the-Fields, the crowds packed the church and the surrounding areas in their thousands. Nelly had asked the rector, Dr Thomas Tenison, to speak her funeral sermon. Despite threats from the Church's hierarchy that to speak at the funeral of a 'whore' would damage his clerical career, he did so. In the end it did him little harm as he would become archbishop of Canterbury. But that such an ambitious and promising cleric would risk his career to preach at her funeral shows the magical effect she had on people.

Her story is romance itself: the common-born orange-selling actress and the king. Both had the common touch – he found it and she never lost it. This book tells the story of her life and times. It tries to explain why the whole world knows Nell Gwynne.

— 1 —

First Appearance

I sing the story of a scoundrel lass
Rais'd from a Dung-hill to a King's embrace.
'The Lady of Pleasure', anonymous, c.1687

Eleanor 'Nell' Gwynne was born at 6 am on 2 February 1650. Or so all her historians have agreed since Peter Cunningham formally opened the industry with the first serious biography in 1852. She may well have been, but the evidence, as with most of Nell's early life, is far from certain. The precision of the time and date of her birth is, for someone who came from such poverty, odd in itself. But the faith, blindly granted, to such precision is based on one piece of evidence: Nell's supposed horoscope.

It is perhaps not surprising that historians treasure every little piece of contemporary evidence, but this little treasure appears not to have been questioned in any way. A closer look reveals that it might well be tarnished.

The horoscope sits in Oxford University's Bodleian Library, part of the Ashmole collection. Nell's biographers have variously ascribed the casting of the horoscope as the work of Ashmole himself, his mentor and teacher William Lilly, and to a Dr Dee, a pupil of Lilly. But is likely to have been the work of Ashmole himself. Elias Ashmole himself (1617–92) was certainly a contemporary of Nell and may well have met her. They had a mutual acquaintance in trusty William Chiffinch who was, in effect, Charles II's private secretary. Ashmole's diary entry for 9 February 1681 runs thus:

> Mr William Chiffinch (Closet keeper to ye King) dyned at my house: and then told me that his Nephew Tho: Chiffinch (son to Tho: Chiffinch my most worthy friend) dyed the weeke before.

It was his most worthy friend, Thomas Chiffinch,who presented him to Charles II. Charles even appointed Ashmole Windsor Herald – which would suggest that the king thought highly of him. However, what is remarkable for such a name-dropper as Ashmole is that in his diaries there is not a mention of Nell Gwynne, a meeting, or her horoscope.[1] And this for the most famous woman of the time.

The actual horoscope also causes concern. It is the only chart that does not contain the name of the person on it. The name 'Nel Gwyn' is written beneath it, as if in afterthought. While the chart and Nell's name appear to be in the same hand, it is noticeable that the capital 'N' and 'G' of Nell's name are different to those on the charts on the same page. The chart is also noticeable because of the '*Nata* — ' (Latin for 'place of birth') where the person's name is on other charts, which can only mean that the place of birth is unknown. This is concerning because charts need to be based somewhere. It is also strange that someone would know that they were born at six o'clock in the morning on 2 February 1650 (and perhaps even know it to be a Saturday), but not actually know or recall *where* the happy event took place. None of the other horoscopes on the page spell out the place of birth – so why does its absence have prominence on Nell's supposed horoscope?

Nell's biographers have been appeased from any doubt they may have held by the fact that this horoscope captures the essence of her almost perfectly. One reading runs:

> In the sign of Aries, which is believed to show personality, the Sun, Venus, Mercury, and Mars – the two latter in conjunction – were all in the ascendant, denoting charm, sociability, sexual attractiveness, self confidence and quick wit, whilst in the Moon being in the same date in the sign of Cancer and therefore in her greatest dignity, is held to indicate popularity.[2]

The president of the Astrological Association of Great Britain concurs that the reading of Nell's chart fits in with what we know about her.[3] The chart describes 'a woman who was essentially sensual and giving in her work, emotions and beliefs; rough and determined, yet lovable, independent and unconventional in her personality; because of her sexuality likely to be thought the "worst" of in a very public way.'

The only other date that has been offered up for Nell's possible birth puts her eight years back to 'about 1642'. This came from 'The Manager's Note Book', published in 1838 in *The New Monthly Magazine and Humorist*.[4] No evidence is actually given to substantiate this date, and the article also includes other information which is at best doubtful and at worst plain wrong. None the less, as the story of her life unravels, 1642 or something near it, seems more likely. The date is also preferred by *Highfill's Biographical of…Stage Personnel in London 1660–1800*[5] and is presumably the reason Nell's picture is captioned '*c*. 1642–87' in London's Theatre Museum.

Even if the horoscope is true, it offers no help in determining where Nell was born. Tradition, rather than historical fact, has thrown up three contenders: London, Oxford and Hereford. Nell's biographers have tended to prefer London, recognise Hereford but dismiss Oxford.

Oxford's claim is undoubtedly the weakest. It hinges almost entirely on the conjecture that Nell's first son, Charles Beauclerk, granted the titles of Earl of Burford and Baron Headington in 1676, was created such out of respect for Nell's birthplace: the two towns being close to Oxford.

However, Charles II regularly visited Oxford and often Nell would accompany him, especially for the horse-racing on Burford Downs, where Charles also enjoyed hawking.[6] Undoubtedly, good memories of the area for both parents would have had some influence on the decision. Charles might also have held affection for Burford as it was the site of a Levellers' mutiny against Cromwell in 1649.[7] Other supporting evidence for Oxford includes a manuscript note by the antiquarian and genealogist, Charles Kirkpatrick Sharpe:

> When I went first to Oxford, Dr John Ireland, an antiquary, assured me that Nelly was born in Oxford. He named the parish, but I have forgot it. It is certain that two of her sons' titles – Headington and Burford – were taken from Oxfordshire localities.

A stronger and sadder connection is that Nell's father may well have died in an Oxford gaol. The satire *A Panegyric*, written in 1681, and usually (but wrongly) attributed to John Wilmot, Earl of Rochester, contains the following lines:

From Oxford prison many did she free,
There dy'd her father, and there glory'd she.
In giving others life and liberty
So pious a remembrance still she bore
Ev'n to the fetters that her father wore.

Thus emerges a strong case that her charitable works in memory of her father and her enjoyable times with Charles in the county are the reasons for the Burford and Headington titles, and not a deference to her birthplace. It has also been suggested that Charles was planning to marry Nelly's son to the heiress of the earl of Oxford, and that influenced the choice of titles.[8] It is therefore perhaps safe to say that Oxford was not her birthplace.

Less safely, and despite the consensus among Nell's biographers, we can also question London. The city's claim is strong because Nell certainly spent most of her life there, and is traditionally enhanced by her popular image as the cheeky, chirpy cockney actress. The London theory was first introduced in 1715 by a certain Captain Alexander Smith in his hugely unreliable *The Lives of the Court Beauties*, which was updated a year later and retitled *The Court of Venus*.[9] This must have been the source for the famous actor Thomas Betterton who repeats it in his *History of the English Stage* (although the Nell Gwynne entry was actually written by William Oldys), but which was not published by Edmund Curll until 1741, some 30 years after Betterton's death.

These books state categorically that Nell was born in the slum-filled Cole (or Coal) Yard Alley. This may have derived its name from the storage of coal, but one 'Bassit Cole, Esq' lived nearby in 1646, and it was probably named after him. A 'Cole's Yard' was certainly there in 1676. This lay at the Holborn end of Drury Lane, surviving until 1900 (albeit with a change of name in 1833 to Goldsmith Street, after the Irish writer Oliver Goldsmith), when it was demolished to make way for the Aldwych. In 1720, Strype, who updated John Stow's *Survey of London*, described 'Coal Yard' constituting houses 'not over well inhabited, except some of them noted for the reception of the kinder sort of females'. Hence the conclusion of some biographers that Nelly must have been one such 'kinder sort' in her early years.

It has also been suggested that Nell was born in the Hop Garden – 'a shabby little byway off St Martin's Lane, southwest of Covent Garden'.[10]

The basis for this is the contemporary satire *The Lady of Pleasure*, which is sub-titled *The life of Nelly truly shown from Hopgard'n Cellar to the Throne till into th' grave she tumbled down*. A street called The Hop Gardens exists today. It was originally a 40-acre herb and vegetable garden belonging to the Abbey of St Peter, Westminster (which was once known as the Convent Garden – hence its name today), dating back to at least the twelfth century.

Even if Nell wasn't born in London there can be little doubt that she became at very least an honorary Londoner; her popularity with the people guaranteed her that.

However, the claim that Nell was born in Hereford is strong and unswerving. Unlike London and Oxford, the city of Hereford proudly proclaims Nell her own. For example, the street she was supposedly born in – Pipewell Street (later Pipe Lane) – was renamed Gwynne Street in 1855. Awash with circumstantial evidence, the claims are loud, if not clear.

The cornerstone of the tradition is that Nell's grandson (the seventh son of the first duke of St Albans), Dr James Beauclerk, was bishop of Hereford for 40 years, until his death at the age of 85 in 1787. It has been argued that had the devout, noble bishop not believed it to be true, he would have dismissed the claim – which he clearly did not. Indeed it has also been said by 'aged persons in that city that the bishop used to admit the truth of the tradition'.[11] Unfortunately, the cornerstone isn't too well laid – relying as it does on such anecdotal cement. The good bishop seemingly hasn't written on the matter.

The grounds of the bishop's palace ran up to what is now Gwynne Street and the bishop's appointment has been revered as a sort of 'coming home'. However, correspondence held in the British Library shows that the 40 years spent at Hereford were not entirely by choice. The bishop recommended himself for consideration of other vacant bishoprics (including London, Durham and Worcester – the latter when he heard that the then incumbent was 'dangerously ill and that there is little probability of his recovery') and for the post of 'Clerk of the Closett'.[12]

It has been suggested that lord Beauclerk also knocked down the house bringing the site into the episcopal gardens. A scrapbook of Nell Gwynne memorabilia held at the Brotherton Library, Leeds University, includes a letter from what looks like a Mr E G Wright to a Mr W R Whitmore, dated 12 October 1839. Mr Wright conjectures that Nell 'was born in Pipe Lane but I believe there is no registry of her birth; it has always been said, when her grandson Lord James Beauclerk became Bishop of Hereford, he bought the house in which she was born, pulled it down, and took the grounds within the palace precincts, which I think very probable.' The deeds for the houses, deposited by the ecclesiastical commissioners in the Hereford Record Office, show that the buildings were owned by the church. So, it was possible for the palace to subsume the property. However, it is now clear that the house was demolished between 1858 and 1859 – many years after the death of Nell's grandson. *The London Illustrated News*, on 1 August 1885, commented shrewdly that the tourist would be far more interested in seeing the actual cottage than a plaque commemorating the site.

In 1859, an enterprising local man was advertising the following: 'Nell Gwynne's birthplace: A good stereoscopic view of the birthplace of Nell Gwynne which has recently been taken down – may be had of Mr W M Gethen, High Town, Hereford, by enclosing 13 postage stamps; or 19 stamps for a coloured view.'

In 1883, it was reported that the then bishop, Dr James Atlay, had consented to 'the fixing of a memorial tablet in honour of Nell Gwynne on the outer face of the garden wall, so as to mark what is alleged to have been the house in which the royal favourite was born'.[13] Indeed, despite the Victorian interest in the story of Nell Gwynne, it would still appear to be a brave move by any member of the clergy, let alone a bishop, to promote the birthplace of such a notorious courtesan. Unless, of course, there was a convincing historical reason to do so. The noble gesture was somewhat sullied by the wording that proved historical accuracy was perhaps not high on the agenda after all. The plaque read: 'Site of the Birthplace of NELL GWYNNE. Founder of Chelsea Hospital and Mother of First Duke of St Albans. Born 1650. Died 1691.' Nell actually died in 1687 and her role in the foundation of the Chelsea Hospital is uncertain. Following vandalism, the original rectangular plaque marking the site of the Gwynne cottage was replaced with the present (and now correct) circular one, although the reference to Chelsea Hospital remains.

Intriguingly, the database of the Astrological Association of Great Britain has a chart for Nell. This chart times Nell's birth at 6 hours, 10 minutes and 52 seconds (the precision of the timing suggests that an astrologer has considered other reliably dated events in her life) on 12 February 1650.[14] It also records Hereford as the place of birth. However, the source is not referenced and one has to assume that the astrologer was aware of Hereford's claim rather than conclude that the information available on the original horoscope signals Hereford as her birthplace. Apparently, whether she was born there or in Oxford or London, would make only a minor difference to the general character analysis of the chart.

Hereford's historians have promoted the city as Nell's birthplace. John Price in 1796, said that 'Nell Gwynne...was born near Wyebridge.'[15] John Duncombe, eight years later, wrote that a 'shorter communication from the bridge to the cathedral was formerly called Pipe-well-street, now abbreviated into Pipe-lane; and it attaches as much celebrity as can be acquired by having given birth to *Mrs Eleanor Gwynne*, the celebrated favourite of Charles II.'[16] Jones's *Handbook of Hereford*, in 1856, commented that 'branching eastward, at the lowest point of Bridge Street, is a narrow thoroughfare...now designated Gwynne Street...There seems to be some doubt as to whether the exact house was not taken down some years ago; but a building at the rear of the Royal Oak Inn is usually pointed out as the place.' John Hutchinson, in 1890, continued the tradition: '...the balance of testimony, to say nothing of the weight of tradition, still inclines to show that she first saw the light in the city of Hereford, in a cottage in the narrow street now bearing her name...'[17] The *Hereford Times* on 25 May 1895 ran a feature on Nell in its 'Some Old Hereford Worthies' series. And it's not just the local historians who are convinced. W P Courtenay, in the *National Biography*, states that 'historians accept the tradition that she was born in a house in Pipe Well Lane,' even though most of Nell's biographers are less sure.

Much is made of Gwynne (in all its variants) being a Welsh name, with at least one contemporary suggesting that her father was from Wales. Nehemiah Wharton, writing in 1643, as part of the besieging Commonwealth army said that many people in Hereford spoke Welsh.[18] It could even be suggested that some of Nell's striking characteristics – her wit, singing voice and red hair are Celtic traits. Gwynne has also been touted as a popular name in Herefordshire, thus improving the chances that she might have come from there. Gwynne is a Welsh name, and the River Wye which flows serenely through Hereford was once known to the Welsh as 'Gwy' which could account for the common-ness of the name. If, of course such common-ness were true at the time. Unlikely as it seems, the name does not appear to have been that widespread – and is absent from all surviving records.

Whether Nell was born in 1642 or 1650 she was born into a country fractured by civil war. Parish, manorial and court records around this time were not well kept, and even those that were have not survived well. Of course, a baptismal record would settle the when and where debate. However, Hereford records show that if Nell was born there it could not have been before 22 April 1635, or between 25 March 1638 and 15 May 1640, or possibly not in 1647 onwards. This means that she could not have been born in Hereford in 1650, but could have been between 1640 and 1647, which allows 1642 as a possibility.

Another piece of circumstantial evidence that has stirred up debate is one that can finally be put to rest. It has long been considered that the organ in Hereford Cathedral, built by Renatus Harris in 1686, was donated by Charles II. The gift, it was argued, was in recognition of the city that provided the king with his beloved mistress. A romantic notion that is sadly misplaced, not least because Charles died a year before it was built. The king, even when alive, paid not a penny towards the organ. It was paid for by public subscription as the Catalogue of Benefactors testifies.[19]

Another unsubstantiated tradition is that Nell donated the windows at the east end of the choir aisles at Bristol Cathedral. It derived from the fact that a notice declaring that she had done so was for some time hanging in the cathedral itself and Horace Walpole may well have seen the notice. He wrote: 'The cathedral is very neat, and has pretty tombs, besides two windows of painted glass, given by Mrs Ellen Gwyn.'[20] If this was the case why Bristol if not because of the West Country link? However, it seems again not to be the case. The heraldry of the windows indicates that the windows were donated by Dean Henry Glenham. As Glenham was dean between 1660 and 1667, this effectively rules out any link with Nell who only became the king's mistress towards the end of 1667 and who certainly would not have been in any financial position to afford such a donation until much later. Incidentally, Glenham was uncle to Barbara Villiers, Lady Castlemaine, the king's main mistress at that time. Pepys describes Glenham as 'a drunken, swearing rascal, and a scandal to the Church.'[21] Perhaps no wonder that people preferred to believe it was Nell, rather than Glenham, who donated the windows – a disreputable dean upstaged by an immoral actress.

None the less, Hereford has a proud historical link with the stage. The actor and theatre manager David Garrick (1717–79) was born in The Angel Inn, Widemarsh Street, Hereford. Garrick organised a Shakespeare Jubilee at Stratford-upon-Avon in 1769 which, despite not actually featuring any of Shakespeare's work, was so successful that it essentially raised the curtain on the industry we have today. Garrick himself believed that he and Nell shared the same city of birth. There would be something satisfying to know that the city that gave England arguably its greatest actor also gave the country arguably its most famous actress. The theatrical connection is not spent there either. Sarah Siddons (1755–1831), who has been called the 'finest English actress of all time', had her family home in Church Street, Hereford, although she was actually born in Brecon.

The Hop Garden link, mentioned as part of London's case, is also wheeled out in defence of Hereford: the county being noted for its hop growing. However, locals would refer to hop yards as opposed to hop gardens. Another stretched suggestion concerns the poet and playwright John Dryden. Dryden wrote parts especially for Nell. It was also a Dryden trait to make up the names of his characters, particularly in his heroic tragedies, and he often did so to suit the character being played or the actor playing the part. Nell's first important role is thought to be in Dryden's *The Indian Emperor*. Nell played Cydaria, although the prompter John Downes spelt it Cideria. This could well have been a play on 'cider' – a well-known product of West England. In 1828, the writer T Horton had little doubt about the actress's origins and celebrated the city's most famous daughter in his play *Nell Gwynne, The City of the Wye; or The Red Lands of Herefordshire*.

Although tarnished, the sheer weight of the treasure trove of tradition tips the scales in favour of Hereford. The individual pieces of evidence may well be dulled by doubt but they still out-sparkle their rivals.

— 2 —

The Family

No man alive could ever call her daughter,
For a battalion of armi'd men begot her.

'A Panegyric', anonymous, 1681

Nell's disposition developed despite and not because of her parents and upbringing. Indeed it is testament to her character that she simply survived her childhood. She challenged her desperate times with wit and spirit. Even when she left those times behind, memories of her adversity kept her heart soft and her head hard. A childhood that would destroy the soul of many, fashioned her wit, loyalty and charity – and thus her charm.

Very little is known of her father. Anthony à Wood suggests that he was the son of Edward Gwin, MA, who was installed canon of the fourth stall in Christ Church College, Oxford on 11 May 1614, and who died on 24 August 1624. Wood's pedigree unfortunately does not suggest a first name for Nell's father. Frederick Van Bassen, writing in 1688 (a year after Nell's death) claimed that her father was 'Thomas Gwine, a captain of ane ancient family in Wales'. The Oxfordshire marriage index lists a marriage between a Thomas Guin and Dorothy Davis on 12 January 1643. However, it is known that Nell's mother was called Helena (or Eleanor), and Wood suggests that her birth name was Smith. It has also been suggested that Nell's father's name was James, although evidence is lacking.[1] It is possible that her father was a captain in the Royalist army and was based in Oxford, which was at the outset of the Civil War a city loyal to the king as, indeed, was Hereford. However, he seems to have quickly fallen on hard times and found himself in a debtors' prison where he died.

Unfortunately, the Quarter Sessions records in Oxford relating to the Castle Gaol do not begin until 1687. Records for other prisons in and around Oxford have not survived. The parish register transcript for Oxford St Thomas, which is the parish where the main Oxford prison is located, shows no reference to any Gwynne (in all its variants) being buried there. Interestingly, the parish register for Oxford St Peter-le-Bailey reveals that on 19 November 1643 a Captain Rowland Gwein was buried. It is tempting to think that this may well be Nell's father. The chances must be slight of two Captain Gwynnes dying at around this time, especially since St Peter-le-Bailey parish is next to the St Thomas parish and close to Oxford prison. That there are no entries in the Oxford wills indexes would suggest that Captain Rowland Gwein died destitute as might be expected from an inmate of a debtors'prison. Also, if Rowland was Nell's father, then the latest date for her birth would be around August 1644. However, it is more likely that she would have been born before Rowland's imprisonment. Thus, again, a birth date of 1642 remains possible.

We know more about Nell's mother. Helena, like many of her time and since, was forced to work in brothels, supplementing this with occasional work in the more riotous taverns. She was very overweight and an alcoholic. Indeed, while alcohol was her life it also proved to be her death: she drowned while drunk in 1679. Her death was the subject of many reports. The satire *The Lady of Pleasure* recounts how

> Maid, Punk, and Bawd, full sixty years and more
> Dy'd drunk with brandy in a common shore.

On 5 August 1679, the newsletter *Domestic Intelligencer* reported her ignoble death: 'We hear that madam Ellen Gwyn's mother, sitting lately by the waterside at her house by the Neat House, near Chelsea, fell accidentally into the water and was drowned.' The 'Neat Houses' were on the site of Millbank today. Narcissus Luttrell in his *A Brief Historical Relation of State Affairs from September 1678 to April 1714* records that

'Mrs Gwyn, mother to Miss Ellen Gwyn, being in drink, was drowned in a ditch near Westminster.' The lampoon *A True Account of the late, most doleful and lamentable tragedy of Old Maddam Gwinn* also mentioned her weight: 'So corpulent a mass of flesh would have outvied Neptune's strength to have delivered her straight on shore.'

However, it is not clear whether Nell's mother drowned in the river, a ditch or, as also suggested, a fish pond (another satire is called *An Elergy upon that never to be forgotten Matron, Old Madamm Gwinn, who was unfortunately drown'd in her own fishpond, on the 19th of July 1679*). What is clear is that despite her drinking problems and Nell's new-found status, the daughter did not desert the mother. Her household accounts show charges for 'plaisters', 'glysters' and 'cordials' for 'Old Mrs Gwyn'. Nell buried her mother in St Martin-in-the-Fields and erected a monument in the south aisle for her. It read:

> Here lies interred the body of Helena Gwynn, born in this parish, who departed this life ye 20th of July, MDCLXXIX, in the LXI yeare of her age.

This casts doubt on Wood's suggestion that Nell's mother was born in Oxford. Another, less reserved epitaph was suggested in a contemporary satire. The alternative ran:

> Here lies the Victim of a cruel Fate,
> Whom too much Element did Ruminate;
> 'Tis something strange, but yet most wondrous true,
> That what we live by, should our Lives undo.
> She that so oft had powerful Waters try'd,
> At last with silence, in a Fish-pond dy'd.
> Fate was unjust, for had he prov'd but kind,
> To make it Brandy, he pleas'd her Mind.

Nell seemingly gave her mother a good send off. Once again *A Panegyric* is our source:

> Nor was her mother's funeral less her care,
> No cost, no velvet did the daughter spare;
> Fine gilded 'scutcheons did the hearse enrich
> To celebrate this martyr of the ditch.
> Burnt brandy did in flaming brimmers flow

Drunk at her funeral; while her well pleas'd shade
Rejoic'd, in the sober fields below,
At all the drunkenness her death had made.

Just over eight years later Nell would join her mother, but there would be no monument to Nell. Her mother's monument only survived 50 years, demolished as it was during the rebuilding of the church in 1721.

Given Nell's apparent illiteracy and the lack of accepted spellings at the time, it is not surprising that we are not even sure how she spelt her last name. The ledgers of Nell's bankers Child & Co show that receipts include the names Ellen Gwyn, Ellin Gwyn, Ellen Gwynne, Ellen Gwin, Eleanor Gwyn, and Eleanor Gwynne.[2] A print in the Crofton Croker collection is labelled, perhaps appropriately, Madame Ellen Groinn. Royal warrants, bills and receipts record her name in the way the writer assumed. So we get Madame Gwynne, Madam Gwin, Madam Guin, Maddam Gwine. The fact that 'madam' has different spellings only heightens the difficulty of determining Nell's last name. Nell herself never wrote any of the letters that have survived. These were all dictated. Receipts and warrants were signed not with her name but with 'her mark': a very scratchy 'EG' – as were all her receipts.

Her will begins, 'I Ellen Gwynne'. Although this was written for her by her solicitor, surely this is one document that should assume accuracy. A letter written in the first person, but actually on Nell's behalf, is signed Ellen Gwynne. However, her sister, who could write, is referred to in government papers as Rose Gwynn. Nell's son wrote on 5 December 1687 shortly after her death 'I doe consent that this paper of request be made a codicil to Mrs Gwinn's will.' Nell's biographers have mainly preferred Gwyn, with a couple opting for Gwynne, and only one for Gwynn (which is surprising given that two family members opted at least once for that spelling). As with the 1640s birthdate and Hereford being her home town, there's no authentic evidence, but 'Gwynne' seems right.

Nell's older sister, Rose, has always been considered her full sister. However, records from the Prerogative Court in Canterbury, suggest that she was Nell's sister 'by her mother'. Rose first makes her mark on history while in Newgate prison accused of robbery. The domestic papers of Charles II list a letter received on 26 December 1663 from:

Rose Gwynn to Mr Browne, cup-bearer to the Duke of York. Thanks for his and Mr Killigrew's civil visit. Begs them to obtain her release on bail from this woeful place of torment, till a pardon is pleaded. Her father lost all he had in the service of the late King, and it is hard she should perish in a gaol. Was never a thief, and was pardoned before judgment, but none know when the pardon will be pleaded.

Rose's plea obviously worked because four days later a royal warrant was issued for her release. It read:

Whereas we are given that Rose Gwynne, having been convicted of — at the late sessions held at the Old Bailey, was yet reprieved by ye bench before judgment, and reserved as an object of our princely compassion and mercy, upon humble suite made to us in favour of ye said Rose, we have thought good hereby to signify our Royal pleasure unto you, that you forthwth grant her liberty and grant discharge upon good bail first taken in order to ye sueing out her pardon, and rendering our gracious mercy and compassion to be effectual. For which, &c, dated 30 Dec^r, 1663

By His Ma^{tys} Command

That such a poor, common woman would be visited in prison by a high ranking official and the king's friend Henry 'Harry' Killigrew (son of Thomas Killigrew, patent holder for the King's Theatre) is intriguing. It is plausible that Rose was known to them either as a regular sexual client or as the daughter of the woman running or working at a brothel frequented by them. However, it is just as likely that Rose was known to them because she worked at the theatre run by Killigrew's father. It is entirely possible that Rose was an orange-seller. And that it was through Rose that Nell was able to take that all-important first step towards the stage.

Although reprieved, Rose's life was not to be free from robbery. She married a John Cassells, who would become a captain in the duke of Monmouth's guards. A bill for carrying Nell ('careing you') by sedan to 'Mrs Knight's and to Mrs Cassells' survives today. As does a receipt written by Rose 'Caslas' to her sister who employed her to help make dresses. John Cassells also appeared to have tried to eke out a living as a highwayman. However, he could not have been too successful as he left Rose penniless on his death in 1675 (he is thought to have been killed at the Battle of Enzheim). None the less, no doubt through his sister-in-law's influence, he secured a pension of £100 a year (which was granted to 'Capt John Cassells and Rose, his wife'). In 1667, the undistinguished Cassells was arrested as a disorderly person but contrived a pardon. Arrested again in 1671, following his wife's example, he petitioned the king for his release, claiming he had been 'reduced to aid in the robbing of Sir Henry Littleton's house' because his father 'lost a plentiful estate in Ireland for his loyalty' and Cassells himself 'having served under his Majesty as ensign till the Restoration'. It worked.

Rose's second husband, Guy Forster, appears to have been more respectable. Nell would leave him £40 (around £3,000 today) in her will to buy himself a mourning ring. Rose would be left £400 in total. Nell looked after her sister: her household accounts show that she bought her clothes. However, Rose was astute enough to make a living out of being a sister. Nell also managed to persuade Charles to increase Rose's pension to £200 a year – payments which were finally stopped by William and Mary in 1688. In 1694, an alone and clearly suffering Rose petitioned the dual monarchs for her pension to be re-instated: she called herself 'Rose Forster, widow, sister to Ellen Gwyn...' It didn't work. The magic was dead.

— 3 —

Oranges and Lemons

But first the basket her fair arm did suit
Laden with pippins and Hesperian fruit.
This first step rais'd, to the wond'ring pit she sold
The lovely fruit, smiling with streaks of gold.

'A Panegyric', anonymous, 1681

Growing up in the divided country that became Cromwell's England was tough for most, but particularly for the poor and dispossessed. Slum-induced sickness and disease plundered the capital's poor. Life was a risky business in seventeenth-century London. It was, as Thomas Hobbes described, 'nasty, brutish and short'. Life wasn't for living: it was for surviving. People scratched about for money in any number of ways. Human litter, helpless and directionless, blew down the dank alleys of the metropolis: out-of-work and unpaid common seamen and soldiers, labourers, out-servants, paupers, vagabonds, rogues, vagrants, gypsies (an underclass then as now), thieves and the idle, all begged, stole and took what they could. The streets were stuffed with the starving.

In reality, crime – most commonly pick-pocketing and burglary – was the only passable road to a prosperity of sorts. But that was a treacherous route, none the less, for ever travelled in the shadow of the gibbet. Following the Restoration of Charles II things seemingly got even worse.

An anonymous letter to the king recorded in the Calendar of State Papers (Domestic) on 30 June 1660 ran: 'The people are in a desperate condition...[they] curse the king, wish for Cromwell, and say come Dutch come Devil they cannot be worse.'[1]

People could ill afford choice, they just did what they could to get by. Children had to earn their keep. With no schools, their classrooms were the dark and dangerous streets. And they needed to learn quickly. It has been suggested that Nell's elusive father sold fruit and vegetables at Covent Garden. As a contemporary satire has it:

> You that have seen in me my youthful age,
> Preferred from stall of turnips to the stage.

However, this is unlikely. Covent Garden Market began life in 1656 as a stall or two either inside or alongside the duke of Bedford's garden on the south side of the piazza. However, it was not until 1670 that a royal charter granted to the fifth earl of Bedford and his heirs the right to hold a market for fruit, flowers, herbs and roots and to collect rent from vendors. Nell's father almost certainly died when she was very young. So, even if Nell was born in 1650, her father would have died before the first fruit and vegetables were sold at the famous old market. The suggestion that he did has survived only as a result of fanciful Victorian romanticism.

However, we do have some clues as to Nell's early career. Children would be employed by traders to market their wares around the streets. *A Satyr*, dated 1677 and possibly by the actor John Lacy, who knew Nell well, tells us that she sold fish in this way:

> Whose first employment was with open throat
> To cry fresh herrings, even at ten a groat.

Another satire refers to Nell as 'an oyster wench'. A number of others refer to Nell as a 'cinder-wench', collecting cinders or burnt coal and wood to resell as fuel. One satire was entitled 'To Mrs Nelly Grown from Cinder Nell'. A line from *A Panegyric* runs 'Ev'n while the cinders rak'd her swelling breast'. Betterton's *History* notes, 'When no better than a cinder-wench, she sold oranges.'

Basing his assertion on some satires of the day, Betterton (or rather Oldys) writes:

[when] first taken care of, it is generally agreed on; and then one Mr Duncan [also known variously as Duggan and Dungan], a merchant, taking a fancy to her smart wit, fine shape and foot, the least of any woman's in England, kept her about two years and then recommended her into the king's Playhouse, where she became an actress in great vogue.

This merchant was apparently something in the city and had been enraptured by young Nell. *The Lady of Pleasure*, relates:

> He that had seen her muddling in the street,
> With face of potlid black, unshoo'd her feet,
> And in her cloudy dust her cinders shaking
> Cou'd he have thought her fit for a monarch's taking.
> Eve'n then she had the charms of brisk and witty
> Which first enslav'd a cully of the city
> He had her arse wash'd clean and smock'd her white
> That she might be his darling and his delight.

Her suitor, after two years, we are told, 'grew Nelly-sick' and could no longer afford to keep her – financially or sexually. She would prosper without him because he

> . . . knew that she had wit and sense,
> Beauty, and such a stock of impudence.
> As to the Play-house well might recommend her
> And thither therefore he resolv'd to send her;
> Where soon she grew, being in her proper sphere
> The pride and envy of the theatre.

However, another aspect of Nell's early career more reliably comes from Nell herself. Samuel Pepys, a keen theatregoer and regular visitor backstage, records a conversation with his friend Mrs Pierce on 26 October 1667, by which time Nell was an actress at the King's Theatre. Mrs Pierce told Pepys that 'Nelly and Beck Marshall [another actress] falling out the other day, the latter called the other my Lord Buckhurst's mistress. Nell answered her, "I was but one man's mistress, though I was brought up in a brothel to fill strong waters to the gentlemen; and you are a mistress to three or four, though a Presbyter's praying daughter."'

Pepys thought Nell's turn of phrase to be 'very pretty'. By her own admission (albeit third hand) Nell worked in a brothel, serving alcohol to the punters.

It is easy to conjecture, given her status and the times, that she served herself as well as the drinks. However, this is unlikely. The scurrilous satires of the day would surely have made great play if one of the king's main mistresses had been a prostitute in a former life. None of them suggested this, and this was not out of fear or respect for Charles II either, as any study of the contemporary scandal sheets will show.

It seems likely that the brothel Nell worked in was run by the notorious Madam Ross in the even more notorious Lewkenor Lane (named after Sir Louis Lewkenor, the meanest courtier and master of ceremonies at the court of James I):

> Then was by Madam Rose, expos'd to th' town
> I mean to those who would give half a crown.

The bawdy house madam would scour the area for lively, likely lasses and the sight of small, pretty Nell with her big smile and voice, and shock of red hair, hawking her fish, must have enchanted the wizened old Ross. Lewkenor Lane – which is today's Macklin Street (named after the actor Charles Macklin – was a well-known centre of prostitution, along with Dog and Bitch Yard, Saffron Hill and Moorfields. It lay (so to speak) at the north end of Drury Lane. We can imagine the young Nell daydreaming as she took a short walk to where the new theatre was being built.

The theatre opened in 1663. Equally significantly for Nell, on 10 February that year, an exclusive licence was granted to the widow Mary Meggs 'to vend, utter and sell oranges, lemons, fruit, sweetmeats and all manner of fruiterer's and confectioner's wares.' The licence was for 39 years and in return for her exclusive contract Meggs was required to pay 6s. 8d. each day the theatre was open. However, despite her monopoly, Meggs ran into financial problems. On 13 June 1670, she was petitioned to appear in court to hear a claim by Grant, vicar of Isleworth, 'for tithe for three years last past for eight acres of fruit trees'.[2]

Unsurprisingly, Meggs, an interminable gossip and mother hen, became known as 'Orange Moll'. More surprising is the popularity of an orange as theatre refreshment. Oranges were a luxury item and cost sixpence each (equivalent of over a pound today), a price that remained amazingly stable. In Aphra Behn's *Young King* produced in 1698, a character says: 'Half crown the play, sixpence my orange, cost.'

Although messy to eat, they were fresh, refreshing and, importantly, were useful weapons to articulate a crowd's displeasure with a play. They could, however, also be hazardous to eat. Pepys records:

> a gentleman of good habit, sitting just before us, eating of some fruit in the midst of the play, did drop down as dead, being choked; but with much ado Orange Moll did thrust her finger down his throat, and brought him to life again.[3]

None the less, oranges were popular. The bitter European oranges were replaced with sweeter ones when Portuguese ships brought back orange trees from India and China. From 1654 oranges were also being imported from South Africa where the Dutch had established a plantation. The English also tried their hands at growing oranges. Sir Francis Carew planted orange trees in 1652 in Surrey which survived until the cold winter of 1740. Sir William Temple, who became a neighbour of Nell's, claimed his oranges were better than any others 'save the best sets of Sevil and Portugal'. Following in the very fashionable footsteps of Louis XIV and his grand orangerie at Versailles, many English noblemen built their own: Robert Spencer, earl of Sunderland at Althorp, Northamptonshire; Henry Bennet, earl of Arlington at Euston; and John Maitland, duke of Lauderdale at Ham.[4]

At times doubt has been cast on whether Nell ever really was a so-called orange girl. But the evidence is strong that she was. Contemporary satires routinely refer to that stage of her career. Other compelling evidence comes from a remark made by her great rival mistress, Louise de Keroualle. Orange girls were renowned for their confidence, repartee and language, which was somewhat less sweet than their wares. In an attempt to put Nell down the pompous Louise remarked: 'Anybody might have known she had been an orange wench by her swearing.' Also in the portrait of Diana de Vere, who would marry Nell's eldest son, she is posing holding an orange blossom, which may well have been a tribute to her mother-in-law, although the blossom is also thought to signify an engagement .

Successful orange girls often resorted to hard-sell tactics. Pepys records being accused by one confident seller of owing for some oranges.

Although declaring his innocence he paid up to save embarrassment. The best girls gave as good as they got. This meant indulging in banter to make sales, flirting, promising to carry messages from admirers to the players, embarrassing people into purchases or charming them to do so. You needed confidence, impudence, wit and looks. It was a person-specification created for Nell. And, indeed, those qualities would give her a sound foundation for the dreamed-about but precarious step up to acting. Nell may have started with oranges, but she was soon to show her true colours.

It's easy to imagine Nell, with her back to the stage and in between the banter with the punters, stealing a peep over her shoulder at the stage and snatching a glimpse of a future. A future that she was not only to be part of, but which, for a while, would belong to her.

— 4 —

Building Brydges, or Harmless Delights

Fate now for her did its whole force engage
And from the pit, she mounted the stage.

'A Panegyric', anonymous, 1681

As the Civil War opened in 1642, so the theatres closed. The puritans had always believed the theatre profane but Parliament's resolution was rooted in far more practical considerations. Anywhere that attracted crowds was ripe for seditious activity and the theatre particularly so as actors were seen as chroniclers of the times and, as such, were feared. So, on Friday 2 September 1642, a newssheet reported that it 'was voted that there shall be no common play-houses for the exercising of stage plays, and no common interludes within this kingdom...'[1] More harshly, a further ordination in 1647 decreed that all actors 'shall be publicly whipped and all spectators of plays for every offence shall pay five shillings'.

Although the theatres were officially closed until the Restoration of Charles II, the parliamentary ordination was not entirely successful as occasional performances were staged (usually one-act drolls derived from known plays) and no doubt many took place in private.[2] None the less, the soldiers were vigilant and theatrical suppression was rigorously pursued. In 1660, even with the scent of Restoration in the air, Thomas

Lilleston was charged at the Middlesex Sessions with acting in a play at the Cock-Pitt on Saturday 4 February.

On his return, Charles II lifted the ban on theatres and so began the reign of one of theatre's greatest royal patrons. However, theatrical freedom was to be controlled. Charles issued a patent giving exclusive rights to produce plays to two theatre companies. Charles was aware of the 'divers[e] companies' who were and had been performing without authority, and declared his 'dislike' of them and ordered 'all other company and companies... to be suppressed and silenced'.[3]

Charles granted what became known as the Drury Lane patent to 'our well trusted and well beloved Thomas Killigrew, Esquire, one of the grooms of the bedchamber', whom Charles had also appointed Master of the Revels. This title meant that he was also, in effect, the court jester with an allowance to buy cap and bells and permission to 'revile or jeer anybody, the greatest person, without offence'.[4] Killigrew was born on 7 February 1612. He was page of honour to Charles I and often referred to himself as the 'illiterate courtier' because he had not gone to university. Killigrew had joined Charles in exile although the family links with Charles did not end there. Elizabeth Killigrew, Thomas's sister, was another of Charles's mistresses for a while, and who, around 1650, gave him a daughter – Charlotte Jemima Henrietta and who, by way of royal acknowledgement, took the name Fitzroy.

Killigrew's patent granted him:

> his heirs and assigns full power license and authority that ... they may lawfully quietly and peaceably frame erect new-build and set up in any place within our cities of London and Westminster or the suburbs thereof where he shall find best accommodation for that purpose... one theatre or play house with necessary tireing and retiring room ... wherein tragedies, comedies, plays, operas and other performances of the stage within the House.[5]

However, it wasn't plain sailing for Killigrew. Under Charles I, a certain Sir Henry Herbert had been granted for life the title of Master of the Revels, part of which gave *him* the right to manage theatres. He fought the validity of Killigrew's patent. Deciding at first to do battle with Herbert, Killigrew soon realised it required too much effort on his part and agreed a compromise. Herbert was to receive £2 (equivalent of about £138 today) for each new play performed and £1 for revivals. He also picked up £50 in damages.

The other company 'to be erected and set up by Sir William Davenant' was to be 'styled the Duke of York's Company'. Davenant (or d'Avenant) was born in Oxford in February 1606, the son of a wine merchant and publican of the Crown Inn. He became, essentially, the poet laureate to Charles I in 1637 on a pension of £100 a year.[6] His father's house was frequented by William Shakespeare. As, indeed, was his mother's bedchamber if the rumours are to be believed. Davenant's mother, according to the diarist Anthony à Wood, was 'a very beautiful woman of good wit and conversation'. He adds that 'Sir William would sometimes, when he was pleasant over a glass of wine with his most intimate friends... say that it seemed to him that he wrote with the very spirit that Shakespeare [did], and seemed contented enough to be thought his son.' If not his actual father, Shakespeare certainly was his godfather.

Despite being named after the king and his brother there would be no fraternal love lost between the two companies. Indeed the rivalry would be intense.

Although opening on 8 November 1660 with *Henry IV, Part 1*, 'in Gibbon's Tennis Court in Clare-Market' (which had originally been built in 1634) in Vere Street, Killigrew quickly turned his energies into seeking a suitable site to purpose-build his new theatre. He was attracted to the Drury Lane area. An ancient and narrow road, once known as Via de Aldwych, Drury Lane ran between St Giles and the modern day Aldwych (derived from *aldwic* meaning 'old settlement'). It was named after Sir Thomas Drury who had had a large house at the Strand end of the lane. It was an upmarket, fashionable place. Stow in his *Survey of London* (first published in 1598 and updated in the eighteenth century by John Strype) described 'diverse fair buildings, hostelries, and houses for gentlemen and men of honour'. For a while in 1646 it even counted Oliver Cromwell among its residents. An article in *The European Magazine* in July 1807 described Drury Lane in Charles II's time as 'the centre of gayety and dissipation, and consequently of attraction to the looser and more juvenile parts of his majesty's subjects'. It seemed a perfect place for a young Nell.

Nell took lodgings either in or certainly near the Cock and Pie tavern by Wych Street (which disappeared during the construction of the Aldwych which opened in 1905). A bookseller in the early nineteenth century whose shop was 'over against' the site of the Cock and Pie claimed that a room was known as the Nell Gwynne parlour.[7] The tavern itself was known as far back as the reign of Henry Vll 'as a place of relaxation for the citizens of London'. One story of the origin of the tavern's name runs thus:

> In the days of chivalry it was the fashion to make vows for the performance of doughty deeds. The knight often took his vow at a feast, swearing by the peacock, which noble bird was brought in to be roasted...Long after this, peacock-pie was still a favourite dish, and it is easy to suppose that the recollection of the peacock vows gave birth to the jesting oath 'by cock and pie'.[8]

On 1 May 1667 Pepys tells us that on his way to Westminster he came across many milkmaids celebrating Mayday 'with their garlands upon their pails, dancing with a fiddler before them, and saw pretty Nelly standing at her lodgings door in Drury-lane in her smock sleeves and bodice, looking upon one – she seemed a mighty pretty creature.' Mayday was a huge public holiday and Drury Lane was one of the better places to be. On the green of St Mary-le-Strand, which was once off Maypole Lane (later Drury Court, later still demolished), a new 134-foot-high maypole was with royal consent erected after the coronation of Charles II. The original sixteenth-century maypole had been demolished during the Civil War in 1644. This new maypole lasted until 1713 and its replacement just five years later. It was bought by Sir Isaac Newton to support a telescope (then the largest in Europe) at Wanstead Park. As *The Dunciad* records:

> Amid that area wide they took their stand,
> When the tall Maypole once o'erlooked the Strand,
> But now (so Anne and piety ordain)
> A church collects the saints of Drury Lane.

However, as the eighteenth century sauntered in, Drury Lane took a decidedly downward turn. The poet and satirist Alexander Pope (1688–1744) described the place as being full of 'drabs' (variously translated as whores, strumpets and sluts). In 1708 he wrote that in 'the town it is ten to one but a young fellow may find his strayed heart again with some wild streeter Drury Lane damsel'. This showed that while he may have had a keen social eye, Pope hadn't a basic grasp of gambling: the odds of ten to one are not the dead cert odds he thinks they are.

Drury Lane is also the setting for Plate 3 of William Hogarth's *The Harlot's Progress*. And the poet and dramatist John Gay (1685–1732) wrote:

> O may thy virtue guard thee through the roads
> Of Drury's mazy courts and dark abodes!

So it was here, just off Drury Lane in Brydges Street, that Thomas Killigrew decided to build his theatre. He bought a lease from the fourth earl of Bedford who had married into the Brydges family – the original owners of the land. Brydges Street was built in the 1630s to join Russell Street and Exeter Street. In 1673, an extension took the street south to the Strand and was named Catherine Street after Charles II's queen. In 1872, Brydges Street also became part of Catherine Street – the street we have today.

On 20 December 1661, Killigrew and his partner Sir Robert Howard signed the lease on condition that by Christmas 1662 a new theatre would be built at a cost of £1,500 (the equivalent today of £114,210). In addition, ten actors signed the lease: Hart, Mohun, Burt, Lacy, Shatterell, Clun, Cartwright, Wintershall, Hewett and Clayton. After the last two named sold out their interest in January 1662, the property was divided into 36 parts or shares: nine each to Killigrew and Howard, four to Lacy and two to the rest. All the actors contracted to work exclusively for the theatre.

Exclusivity became the name of the game and set the tone for the intense rivalry between the two companies. Playwrights also had to write for one company or the other. As they fought for new plays, they fought over the old ones as well. Killigrew grabbed *Othello*, *Julius Caesar*, *A Midsummer Night's Dream*, *The Merry Wives of Windsor* and *Henry IV*. He also managed to get four Ben Jonson plays, including *The Alchemist* and *Catiline his Conspiracy*, and all the best plays by the enormously popular Beaumont and Fletcher. Davenant, with the powerful Thomas Betterton in his company, made sure he had the pick of Shakespeare's big acting roles and scored with *Hamlet*, *Macbeth*, *King Lear*, and *Henry the Eighth*, along with *Romeo and Juliet*, *The Tempest* and *Twelfth Night*. Of the new blood, Killigrew (who wrote plays himself) would retain, among others, John Dryden, Charles Sedley, Nathaniel Lee and Sir Robert Howard. Davenant's playwrights included himself, George

Etherege and Lord Orrery. Shakespeare was beginning to make something of a comeback. More recently playgoers had preferred Ben Jonson; indeed, James I thought Shakespeare to be greedy and over-rated. Shakespeare was wont to say that he never crossed out a line in his life: Jonson said that he wished the bard had crossed out a thousand.

Killigrew's theatre, formally known as Theatre Royal, Brydges Street, or more popularly as the King's House, opened on 'Thursday in Easter week, being the 8th day of April, 1663'.[9] It staged John Fletcher's tragicomedy *The Humorous Lieutenant*, which ran for 12 successive days and was, understandably, a huge hit. A playbill, which has been condemned as fake, but interesting none the less, for the opening day read:

By his Majesty's Company of Comedians,
At the new theatre in Drury Lane,
This day being Thursday April 8, 1663, will be acted a comedy called
The Humorous Lieutenant

The King	Mr Wintershall
Demetrius	Mr Hart
Selevas	Mr Burt
Leonatus	Major Mohun
Lieutenant	Mr Clun
Celia	Mrs Marshall

The play will begin at three o'clock precisely. Boxes 4s.; pit 2s. 6d.;
middle gallery 1s .6d.; upper gallery 1s.

Playbills like this would be put up on all public posts (thus becoming 'posters') to advertise productions in town.

The theatre itself was 100 feet long and 60 feet wide. The apron-shaped stage jutted out into the audience, bringing them closer to the action and making them feel more involved. Audience involvement and appreciation was all-important. A play could only be counted a success if it got through its first performances (usually three) and made it into repertory. The audience had the power to kill plays dead. Pepys saw a play called *The Ladies à la Mode* (probably Richard Flecknoe's *Damoyselles à la Mode*) on the second of its opening three days. Neither he nor the audience were impressed: 'so mean a thing as, when they came to say it would be acted again tomorrow, both he that said it, Beeson, [probably Beeston who once managed the Cock-Pitt theatre] and the pit fell a-laughing, there being this day not a quarter of the pit full.'[10]

Women who attended the theatre would wear vizards (a form of mask); the purpose of which ostensibly was to hide their blushes at the racier comments and dialogue that the theatre became noted for. It also allowed them to check out potential or flirting partners. For their part, it became great sport among the men to work out who was behind each mask.

The King's House had a pit, side gallery and upper tier. The king himself would regularly attend the theatre and watch from the royal box. Charles was the first British monarch to go the theatre regularly; in the past theatre would travel to a monarch's residence. Charles would also indulge in having private performances at Whitehall, but he preferred going to the theatre. Apart from being a very enjoyable diversion for the king, which took him away physically as well as mentally from political offices, this policy was part of Charles's very public monarchy. People would come to watch the king and his reactions to a play as much as to watch the plays themselves. Pepys was always more enthralled at the theatre if the king was present, seeing who he was with and how he reacted to a play.

While the new theatre was being built for the King's Company, they made use of a theatre set up on the site of Gibbon's tennis court (which had originally been built in 1634) in Vere Street at the Clare Market. It opened on 8 November 1660 with *Henry IV, Part 1*. On 26 November 1660 Pepys saw *The Beggar's Bush*, a comedy by Beaumont and Fletcher, and was most impressed with Killigrew's temporary accommodation: '...to the new playhouse near Lincoln's Inn...It was well acted: and here I saw one Moone, who is said to be the best actor in the world, lately come over with the king, and it is indeed the finest playhouse, I believe, that ever was in England.'[11]

The duke's company during this time had moved from Salisbury Court into their new house, also formerly a tennis court (Lisle's), in Lincoln's Inn Fields and close to Killigrew's makeshift theatre. Davenant's theatre was on the site now occupied by the Royal College of Surgeons in Portugal Street. The duke's company would remain there until their move to Dorset Gardens in 1671.

Theatres in Restoration times opened for business at about midday, with the performance starting at 3 to 3.30 pm. In Shakespeare's time plays began at 1 pm but, by the end of the century, as artificial lighting techniques improved, plays started at 4 pm. The stage was lit with newly developed wax candles, which previously had been made of tallow (animal fat), and these were set around the stage and mounted on censers or cressets.[12]

Theatre, as today, was not a cheap pastime: the prices on the forged playbill are accurate. There is a generally held misconception that the pit was noisy and unruly if not riotous. Undoubtedly, it had its moments, but it was far from the seething pit of rowdiness of popular imagination. It was filled with relatively well-off people: the young well-to-do, the wits and the dandy beaux of the day who would gather near the stage in the so-called 'Fops Corner'. Pepys preferred the pit. The upper gallery was more a cause of concern – being the cheapest area it was more accessible to ordinary citizens. Also people were usually permitted free entrance after the fifth and final act had begun. Oranges and other fruit were not sold in the upper gallery because, quite simply, in the hands of the drunk, the disgruntled, the outraged, the bored or the mischievous, they could be lethal weapons from that height and distance.

Another novelty for playgoers was the introduction and development of scenery. In past times plays were acted in front of one painted backdrop. The duke's company under Sir William Davenant led the way with more innovative scenery. Most notable was a production of Shakespeare's *Henry the Eighth*. One contemporary noted that 'Every part by the great care of Sir William, being exactly performed; it being all new cloathed and new scenes; it continued acting 15 days together with general applause.' Pepys had heard all about this production and on New Year's Day 1664 went to see what all the fuss was about. He enjoyed the stage production but was disappointed with the play itself. He writes:

> To the Duke's House, the first play that I have been at these past six months, according to my last vow, and here saw the much cried-up play of 'Henry the Eighth', which though I went with resolution to like it, is so simple a thing, made up of a great many patches that, besides the shows and processions in it, there is nothing in the world good or well done.

As well as restoring theatre to English life, Killigrew's patent had one other major impact on the theatre in general and on Nell's life in particular: women were permitted for the first time to act on the stage. Although an alien and, to some, profane concept, it was not so to Charles II, who had spent his exile on the Continent. Italian and French drama had long included actresses. Indeed, a touring French troupe used women during a performance at Blackfriars Theatre in 1629. The austere audience was scandalised, however, and translated their horror into missiles and jeers. No tour de force, this: the ensemble exited en bloc.

Looking to restore the audience's bonhomie, the patent stated: 'And we do likewise permit and give leave that all the women's parts to be acted in either of the said two Companies for the time to come may be performed by women.' Women could act provided their parts 'be esteemed not only harmless delight, but useful and instructive representations of human life.' Women had been kept off the stage because plays had included 'several profane, obscene and scurrilous passages' which were considered too indecent for women to speak, hear or be part of. Despite the royal blessing to appear on stage it was stiil considered by some that the 'the stage was not a proper place for proper young gentlewomen'. Indeed, many believed that theatre was profane enough without adding sinful women to the whole devilish brew. John Evelyn, a spiritually austere man who recorded religiously in his diary each Sunday's sermon, was wholly opposed to the theatre: '... very seldom at any time, going to the public theatres, for many reasons, now as they were abused, to an atheistical liberty, foul and indecent.'[13]

In the past all female parts had been played by men or, more usually, boys or pretty-faced younger-looking men. However, women weren't ready in sufficient numbers to act immediately, naturally needing time to be recruited and learn their profession. This meant that for a while men had to continue playing female parts. An anecdote by Colley Cibber is worth the retelling.[14] Towards the end of 1660, the king, he says,

> ...coming a little before his usual time to a tragedy, found the actors not ready to begin, when his Majesty not chusing to have as much patience as his good subjects, sent to know the meaning of it; upon the which the master of the company came to their box, and rightly judging that the best excuse for their default would be the true one, fairly told His Majesty that the Queen was not *shaved* yet. The King, whose humour loved to laugh at a jest as well as to make one, accepted the excuse, which served to divert him until the male Queen could be effeminated.

This would become doubly amusing to Charles as his future queen would receive into her retinue from Portugal her 'barber': the purpose and role of whom caused great speculation and amusement at the court.

For the first time playwrights were free to create as many female characters as they wished. Elizabethan drama, for example, bequeathed very few female roles. The Restoration dramatists saw to remedy this by altering stock plays, including those by Shakespeare. For example, Davenant, in his production of *Macbeth*, wrote larger parts for Lady Macbeth and Lady Macduff and, in collaboration with Dryden, added a couple of female roles to *The Tempest*.

As with actors, the actresses were signed up exclusively to each company. The King's House company were styled 'His Majesty's Company of Comedians in Drury Lane' and had to visit the Lord Chamberlain's office and be sworn in to serve Charles II. They were now his servants. Should they have any disputes with the company's management they could petition the king to intervene – and would frequently do so.

On 3 January 1661, Pepys went, once again, to see *The Beggar's Bush* at the Vere Street theatre, and recorded historically: 'To the theatre, where was acted "Beggar's Bush", it being very well done; and here the first time that ever I saw women come upon the stage.'

But when was the first time that a woman performed on the stage and who was it? Unfortunately we are unable to answer either question with any conviction. Cases for the first actress have been put forward for Anne Marshall (who was certainly the first actress on stage at the new Brydges Street theatre, playing the role of Celia in *The Humorous Lieutenant*), Mrs Norris, and Mrs Saunderson (who later married Thomas Betterton and who L'Abbé du Bos informs us was the first actress on the English stage).[15]

The first role played *professionally* by a woman in England was Desdemona in *Othello*. This is confirmed by Thomas Jordan's 'A prologue to introduce the first woman that came to Act on the Stage in the Tragedy, called *The Moor of Venice*'. This was performed on Saturday 8 December 1660 at the Vere Street theatre. Downes tells us that Margaret 'Peg' Hughes played Desdemona. On this evidence Peg Hughes is most widely thought to have been the first, and perhaps was.

However, the claims for Kathleen Mitchell, who probably married the playwright John Corey, cannot be easily discounted. For example, in listing the actresses at the King's Company, John Downes puts Corey's name at the top of the list.[16] Also, and perhaps most compellingly, during a dispute with the company, following a refusal to re-admit her after a walk-out, she petitioned the courts in 1689. She said that she had served the Killigrew family for 27 years (Thomas Killigrew had in 1677 handed over the Company to his son Henry) and claimed that she was 'the first... and last of all the actresses that were constituted by King Charles the Second at his Restauration.'[17]

Pepys thought Corey a fine actress. He called her Doll Common after the role she made famous in Ben Jonson's *The Alchemist*. On 27 December 1666 he wrote: '... by coach to the King's playhouse, and there saw "The Scornful Lady" well acted, Doll Common doing Abigail most excellently...' However, not all things in Mrs Corey's career went most excellently.

In January 1669, Pepys recorded the events that landed Corey in prison for a short time. The venerable actress decided to act the part of Semphronia in *Catiline his Conspiracy* as an unflattering imitation of Lady Elizabeth Harvey. Her husband, Sir Daniel Harvey, had recently been despatched to Constantinople as ambassador to Turkey. She was also cousin to the earl of Manchester, the lord chamberlain. Barbara Castlemaine, the king's mistress, was particularly enjoying the send-up. At one point when Nicholas Burt, playing Cicero, asks 'But what will I do with Semphronia?' Barbara shouted: 'Send her to Constantinople!' So incensed was Lady Harvey at the outrage of Corey's performance that she 'got my Lord Chamberlain, her kinsman, to imprison Doll'. However, this turned out to be somewhat foolhardy as 'Lady Castlemaine made the King to release her' – proving her influence over Charles – 'and to order her to act it again, worse than ever... where the King himself was; and since it was acted again, and my lady Harvey provided people to hiss her and fling oranges at her.'[18]

The French ambassador in London, Colbert de Croissy, also recorded the incident in a letter dated 11 January 1669: '[Lady Harvey]... furious at having been represented on stage, caused the actress who had impersonated her so effectively to be imprisoned on the authority of the Lord Chamberlain. The King, either because he felt obliged to protect the players, or because he had been earnestly requested to do so by Lady Castlemaine... was able to set her free.' On 21 January, de Croissy added that Charles had reportedly returned to the play and refused all demands that Corey apologise to Lady Harvey or that the actors be prevented from satirising members of court.

Clearly self-righteousness was not a virtue in Restoration England,

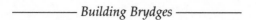

unlike impudence, wit and the ability to laugh at oneself as well as others. These characteristics were not hard to squeeze out of the personality of a certain appealing orange-seller who was, with her tiny, pretty feet, about to tread the boards for the first time.

— 5 —

A Playhouse Degree, or
Her Hart's Content

Then enter Nelly on the public stage.

'The Lady of Pleasure', anonymous, c. 1687

With such a flood of energy and lively natural talent the stage didn't call Nell so much as demand her and she may have joined the company in 1664. Downes notes that 'Mrs Ellin Gwin...came into the Company some few years after' the original women who joined in 1660.[1] She certainly came under the stewardship of two of the company's best actor-managers Charles Hart (who taught her to act) and John Lacy (who taught her to dance). Nell would certainly have been known to them as an orange-seller and, just as likely, socially through the Cock and Pie which all three frequented.

Charles Hart, who is continually but erroneously referred to as the great-nephew of Shakespeare, was undoubtedly one of the best actors of his time. Cibber tells us that he 'was famous for his Othello'. Charles II said that Hart 'might teach any king on Earth how to comport himself'.[2] Hart was a child of the theatre: as a boy he played female roles at the Blackfriars theatre. Having fought for the Royalists during the Civil War, upon Restoration he was set for more commanding roles as the leading man in the King's Company. Thomas Rymer said:

[what] Mr Hart delivers, every one takes upon content; their eyes are prepossessed and charmed by his action, before aught of the poet's can approach their ears; and to the most wretched of characters he gives a lustre and brilliance which so dazzles the sight, that the deformities in the poetry cannot be perceived.[3]

Downes tells us that in 'all comedies and tragedies, he was concerned he performed with that exactness and perfection, that not any of his successors have equalled him.'[4]

Hart was renowned for his ability to become his characters to the exclusion of all else. So involved would he be that he would not hear the banter from the audience or notice anything happening other than that which the play presented the character. For example, during a production of *Catiline his Conspiracy*, Hart clashed with a successful but newly arrived actor called Joseph Haines. Haines 'the incomparable dancer of the King's House'[5] was famed, as Nell would be before him, for the delivery of prologues and epilogues to plays:

There happened to be one night a play acted called Catiline's Conspiracy, wherein there was wanting a great number of senators. Now Mr Hart being chief of the house, would oblige Jo to dress for one of these senators, although Jo's salary, being then 50s a week, freed him from any such obligation. But Mr Hart, as I said, before being sole governor of the playhouse, and at a small variance with Jo, commands it, and the other must obey.

Jo being vexed at the slight Mr Hart had put on him, found out his method of being revenged on him. He gets a Scaramouch dress, a large full ruff, makes himself whiskers from ear to ear, puts on his head a long Merry-Andrew's cap, a short pipe in his mouth, a little three legged stool in his hand; and in this manner follows Mr Hart on stage, sets himself behind him, and begins to smoke his pipe, laugh and point at him. Which comical figure put all the house in an uproar, some laughing, some clapping, and some hollowing. Now Mr Hart, as those who knew him can aver, was a man of that exactness and grandeur on the stage, that, let what would happen, he'd never discompose himself, or mind anything but what he then represented; and had a scene fallen behind him, he would not at that time look back, to have seen what was the matter; which Jo knowing remained still smoking. The audience continued laughing, Mr Hart acting, and wondering at this unusual occasion of their mirth; sometimes thinking it some disturbance in the house, again that it might be something amiss in his dress: at last turning himself towards the scenes, he discovered Jo in the aforesaid posture; whereupon he immediately goes off the stage, swearing he would never set foot on it again, unless Jo was immediately turned out of doors, which was no sooner spoke than in practice.[6]

Haine's career at the King's House might have been over but he was a big name and was snapped up by the Dukes' House straightaway. He remained on the stage until 1701 in which year he contracted an illness and died of a fever shortly afterwards. Ironically, given the story above, he died in his lodgings in Long Acre in a street called Hart Street. As for Charles Hart, he would retire in 1682 to Middlesex to his country house in Stanmore Magna on a half-salary pension of 40s. a week, dying of stone (a painful infection of the bladder or kidney) on 18 August 1683.[7]

Nell's other tutor was John Lacy who was one of the king's favourite actors. So much so that he commissioned a painting of Lacy in three of his most famous roles: Teague in *The Committee*; Mr Scruple in *The Cheats*; and Monsieur Galliard in *The Variety*. Charles kept the painting in his dining-room at Windsor Castle. Evelyn recorded on 3 October 1662 that he visited 'Mr [Michael] Wright, a Scotchman, who had lived long in Rome, and was esteemed a good painter', adding that he thought his best painting was the one of Lacy 'in three dresses, as a gallant, a Presbyterian minister, and a Scotch highlander in his plaid'.

Lacy was born near Doncaster. Ben Jonson adapted his Yorkshire expressions (including 'Gad kettlepins!') for his play *A Tale of a Tub*. Lacy was thought to be 'of elegant shape, and fine complexion.'[8] (Only for 'elegant' read 'large'). His acting talent, however, was prodigious. Gerard Langbaine believed that he 'performed all parts that he undertook to a miracle: insomuch that I am apt to believe, that as this age never had, so the next never will have his equal, at least not his superior.'[9] Lacy was also a satirist, playwright and poet, writing or adapting at least four plays. He also may well have written *A Satyr* (of which more to come) on Nell Gwynne in about 1677 and which, in balance with the times, was extraordinarily unkind to its subject. Although a talented man, Lacy's size – 'a body of rare shape' – helped at times to exaggerate his comic roles.

Lacy, as his writings show, was not a man without opinion. He insulted the playwright the Honourable Edward Howard, son of the earl of Berkshire, by calling him 'more a fool than a poet'. This was unacceptable for a 'man of quality' (as anybody born into the nobility was apt to be called) to take from a mere actor. Howard responded by slapping Lacy. Lacy then took his stick to Howard. Luckily for Lacy the king was not really one of the 'I demand satisfaction, sir' brigade and, anyway, Lacy was one of his servants. So, despite Howard's protestations that Lacy should be run through, the mere actor was only imprisoned for a few days in the porter's lodge at Whitehall (a sort of Restoration cooler or sin bin).

Being nurtured under the wings of Hart and Lacy – two such powerful, respected and admired players – it's not surprising that Nell succumbed to their charms and they to hers. There was every likelihood that she was Lacy's lover early on, but she certainly became Hart's long-term lover, preferring the younger, more agile man:

> Then enter Nelly on the public stage...
> But there what Lacy's fumbling age abused
> Hart's sprightly vigour more robustly used.[10]

Colley Cibber confirms that Charles Hart 'introduced Mrs Gwyn upon the dramatic boards, and has acquired the distinction of being ranked among the lady's first felicitous lovers.' Certainly for Nell's career it was at least fortunate if not out-and-out in-your-face shrewdness to find herself the lover of the company's leading man and one of the theatre's managers. Killigrew, from early on, had delegated the day-to-day management of the theatre to Hart and others, preferring to oversee things from a regal-like distance while counting the money.

Nell didn't have to wait too long to make her debut, probably being blooded with walk-on or bit parts. Thomas Killigrew's largely autobiographical two-parter *Thomaso, or The Wanderer*, written in 1654 and telling the story of the scrapes of cavaliers in exile, was slated to have been produced in Nell's first season around November 1664. The play is huge with over 40 characters. A 'Nelle' was set down to play Paulina, a courtesan.

A manuscript of William (son of Thomas) Killigrew's *Siege of Urbin* for the 1664–5 season had 'Mrs Nell' down to play the role of Pedro (the maidservant Melina dressed as a man). There is an interesting stage direction on a surviving script (at the Bodleian Library) which alludes to the probability that neither Nell nor Anne Marshall (who was to play the 'tall handsome heroine') could handle their swords very well. The direction requires that 'Florio [Anne] and Pedro [Nell] must not fight on the stage through the whole play'.

However, we can be sure that Nell was known around this time. Pepys tells us that on 3 April 1665 he went to see a production of Lord Orrery's *Mustapha* at the Duke's Theatre, which 'not being good, made Betterton's part and Ianthe's[11] but ordinary also. All the pleasure of the play was the King and my Lady Castlemaine were there; and pretty witty Nell, at the King's House, and the younger Marshall[12] sat next to us; which pleased me mightily.'

The sheer casualness of Pepys's description of Nell as pretty and witty serves to suggest that he knew of her quite well. What is strange is that he makes no mention that this pretty, witty creature is only and just 15 years old, if we accept 1650 as her birth date.

Nell's first major part may well have been in April 1665 as Cydaria in *The Indian Emperor, or The Conquest of Mexico by the Spaniards*, although it has been suggested that she was not in the original production but rather a later revived one. The play was the fourth by John Dryden. Born on 9 August 1631, Dryden's name remains interchangeable with the heroic verse epics that provided Restoration drama with such a flamboyant signature. Roger Boyle, earl of Orrery may well lay claim to have written the first play in this style, but Dryden was always up there in the van and was certainly its best driver. He weathered a storm of criticism to lead the way with extravagantly exaggerated characters speaking an extravagantly exaggerated language. Heroic epics where love and honour reigned and the poetry poured, and the rhyming beat down with a subtlety of a hailstone. He felt that this form was 'not so much a new way amongst us, as an old way new revived'.[13]

However, if Dryden craved success, money and recognition – and he did – he would have to write for the times. And he did exactly that. He gave the punters what they wanted. The plays of Francis Beaumont and John Fletcher, who fished the fertile seas of Spanish history for their plots, were incredibly popular. Dryden also cast his lines in similar waters. As the playhouse had largely 'become the rather riotous haunt of the upper classes,' he wrote for a 'cavalier and courtly' audience that found a misty-eyed solace in the nobility of love and honour.[14] Indeed, so much did Dryden pander to the baying pit that out of the 26 plays he wrote, he claimed that he only ever wrote one to satisfy himself (*All for Love* in 1678 in imitation of 'the divine Shakespeare').[15] As the epilogue to his *The Conquest of Granada, Part Two* notes:

> They, who have best succeeded on the stage,
> Have still conformed their genius to their age...
>
> Yet, though you judge (as sure the critics will),
> That some before him writ with greater skill,
> In this one praise he has their fame surpassed,
> To please an age more gallant than the last.

Dryden married Lady Elizabeth Howard, eldest daughter of the earl of Berkshire, making him the brother-in-law of those four playwright-ing Howard boys: Robert, James, Edward and Colonel Henry. Dryden seems, on the whole, to have been a man of honour. Apart from some (largely unfounded) suggestions of an affair between him and the actress Ann Reeves, he seems to have been faithful to his wife which, unlike his drama, was certainly out of kilter with the times. His first play, *The Wild Gallant*, produced in 1663, resembled the London streets: it stank. Pepys called it 'so poor a thing as I never saw in my life.'[16] The second, *The Rival Ladies*, fared a little better in Pepys's eyes ('a very innocent and most pretty witty play').[17] His first hit, however, was with *The Indian Queen* which he co-wrote with his brother-in-law Robert Howard.

Nell was almost certainly part of the company during the year that Dryden was writing *The Indian Emperor* (as a follow up to *The Indian Queen*) and he could well have written her part with her in mind. Pepys did not see the play during this run, so we don't know if or how she performed. However, he would see it on future runs and if Nell's first performances resembled her later work, Pepys at least, would have been critical. He thought Nell unsuited to serious drama, much preferring her in comic roles.

Pepys thought *The Indian Emperor* a very good play but not quite what it was talked up to be but he enjoyed it enough to buy a copy for his own reading. Although Nell's first lines on the stage may never be known for sure, her first lines in *The Indian Emperor* are the first we know to have been hers. Her role was given an additional (and probably deliberate twist) by playing her opposite her lover, Charles Hart. Restoration audiences loved to identify characters with the players themselves and to get the nod and a wink in-jokes or to fall about laughing at the absurdity of a character doing or saying something out-of-character with the real life of the player. Nell's character Cydaria had two suitors, one being Cortez played by Hart. Her opening lines were:

> So strong an hatred does my nature sway,
> That, spite of duty, I must disobey.
> Besides you warned me still of loving two;
> Can I love him, already loving you?

Later we see an allusion to Nell's undoubted good looks:

Cydaria: My father's gone, and yet I cannot go: Sure I have something lost or left behind!

Cortez: Like travellers who wander in the snow I on her beauty gaze until I am blind.

As Nell's new career made its, presumably, rather unspectacular start in a heroic tragedy, a more very real tragedy was about to beset London, and to strike down any immediate dreams of stardom. As the players took their bows, they would soon have to take their leave, for the Plague was about to take its toll.

— 6 —

So Dismal a Calamity

... I went all along the city and suburbs from
Kent Street to St James's, a dismal passage and dangerous,
to see many coffins exposed in the streets and the street thin
of people, the shops shut up and all in mournful silence, as
not knowing whose turn might be next.

Diary, John Evelyn, 7 September 1665

There was great belief in heavenly signs, portents and omens. Before both the Plague and Fire, comets had brightened the sky and had been felt to signify that heavy judgements would befall the city. Daniel Defoe's *Journal of a Plague Year*, although steeped in fact, gives a fictional account of life in the city. His character (only referred to as H.F.) records how the

> ... comet before the pestilence was of a faint, dull, languid colour, and its motion very heavy, solemn and slow; but that the comet before the fire was bright and sparkling... and its motion swift and furious; and that accordingly one foretold a heavy judgement, slow but severe, terrible and frightful, as with the plague; but the other foretold a stroke, sudden, swift and fiery as the conflagaration.

The Great Plague of 1665–6 although London's worst, was by no means its first. Indeed you could say that the capital has been plagued by them.

Bede records a plague in south-east England as early as AD 646. The inhabitants of Barking Abbey had a date with the devil being wiped out in AD 666. Another major plague hit in 1258, followed by the Black Death in 1348–9. A plague in 1407 claimed 30,000 lives, while one in 1499–1500 claimed 20,000. Henry VIII was forced to move his court around (to Greenwich and Southampton) to avoid the pestilence in London throughout most of his reign. Ten thousand were accounted for in the plague of 1592–3.

Mild plagues and plague-free years were shattered in the summer of 1624 when 35,000 people died. In his diary, Evelyn described it as 'the yeare in which the pestilence was so epidemical, that there died in London 5,000 a weeke'. Such was the fear and terror (lawlessness reigned as the magistrates fled the city) that Charles I's coronation – look no further omen-hunters – was delayed until 1625. The last epidemic before the Great Plague was between 1638 and 1643.

On 5 June 1665, the lord chamberlain decreed:

> Whereas it is thought dangerous that soe greate resort of people should be permitted at your theatre in this tyme of infection of the plague these are therefore to require you that you forbeare acting any more playes until you shall receive future Order from me.

As well as the theatres, Bartholomew Fair and Southwark Fair were closed down. One of Nell's biographers noted starkly that many who had seen her 'star at its rising were never to see her again'.[1]

It is unclear where Nell and most other actors and actresses spent the next 18 months, but is likely that they went wherever the court went; they were the king's servants after all, and would surely give impromptu performances wherever they could. Charles took his court to Oxford but also set it up at Hampton Court on 29 June 1665. One month later the court had moved again, this time to Tunbridge Wells.

During the theatre's closure we hear nothing of Nell except that she is mentioned on a royal warrant dated 30 June 1666. The warrant ordered that the usual four yards of bastard scarlet cloth and one quarter of a yard of velvet be delivered to 'Ellen Gwyn' and each of the other 11 'women comedians in His Majesty's theatre'.

Some may have gone to stay with relatives and friends away from the plague, just as some may have stayed in London not wishing (or not having anywhere) to go. During the plague, for example, Pepys met up with his close friend the actress Mary Knepp (whose name he always spelt 'Knipp') over twenty times. He also met with [Joseph] 'Harris the player' and the actress Mrs Norton. The two great diarists of the time stayed in London but did send their families away. Pepys sent his wife to Woolwich; Evelyn sent his wife and family to his brother's at Wooton, choosing to stay himself 'trusting in the providence and goodness of God'.[2]

The fear of infection was profound, not least because nobody was sure how the plague spread (although now we know that it was caused by fleas from rats). Naturally this ignorance forced people into taking few or no chances. People would not meet in groups or touch one another. Shopkeepers would not take money from people's hands – customers had to place their coins into bowls of vinegar. Infection and fear was so pervasive that people took to lighting bonfires to purify the air, dreading that just to inhale the London air could be fatal. The lord mayor even ordered the killing of all dogs and cats, believing the plague related to them. So, on a desperate whim 40,000 dogs and about 200,000 cats were killed, which simply meant that the rat population increased and with it so did the intensity of the pestilence.

More often than not popular images of history are misplaced, exaggerated or plain wrong. But with the plague the images of popular imagination: red crosses painted on doors of infected houses alongside the words 'Lord have mercy upon us'; men with carts ringing a bell and calling out 'Bring out your dead' and the dead being brought out and thrown on to open carts; and bodies piling up on the streets and outside churchyards; all these images were as real as death itself. If one member of the household was infected the house was closed up with all household members locked inside, even those uninfected.

Guards, known as 'the watch', were placed on duty outside infected houses, making sure that nobody left or entered the house. Vincent's *God's Terrible Voice in the City* describes the '... watchmen standing before them with halberts,[3] and such a solicitude about those places, and people passing by them so gingerly and with such fearful looks, as if they had been lined with enemies in ambush that waited to destroy them.'[4]

However, it was not uncommon for the uninfected and infected members of the family or house to escape. The watch had to run errands and fetch food and drink for those locked up in their houses. While carrying out these tasks, people would break down doors or leap from windows. Jumping from windows may have been more immediately hazardous but it did have the benefit of disguising the fact that an escape had occurred, thereby giving the escapees valuable time to get away. The watch would sometimes spend days guarding empty houses.

The popular children's rhyme 'Ring-a-ring of roses' is based on the plague:

Ring-a-ring of roses:	a red or rosy rash was the first sign that the plague had struck (Rev. John Allin who saw the plague victims described them having 'a particular symptom...they are generally circled about with red or blue circles').[5]
A pocketful of posies:	small bunches (posies) of herbs were carried as a protection against the plague.
A-tishoo, a-tishoo:	sneezing was a common indicator of approaching death.
We all fall down:	the approaching death arrives.

Records of death were unreliable and the 'official' death rate of 68,756 is almost certainly short of the real mark, which could be over 100,000. Special hospitals (called pest-houses) were built or set up, each with their own roads. The sheer numbers meant that churchyards and grave-diggers were under great pressure. Bodies simply could not be buried within 24 hours – they lay stacked up for days at a time. Mass graves or plague pits were dug and lined with quicklime, but bodies lay so close to the surface that the stink of death choked the air.

Pepys records events of 'this plague time' with a very troubled and very human heart: 'I this day [26 June 1665] seeing a house, at a bit-maker's, over against St Clement's Church, in the open street, shut up: which is a sad sight.'; 'Lord! to see how the plague spreads, it being now all over King's Street, at the Axe, and next door to it, and in other places.'; 'Sad news of the death of so many in the parish of the plague, forty last night, the bell always going'. Everyday activities become potentially treacherous as 'the sickness increases mightily'. On 23 June 1665, Pepys travels home 'by hackney coach, which is a very dangerous passage nowadays'.

This enormous human tragedy is perhaps most poignantly described in another contemporary account, in Dr Hodges's *Loimologia*: 'Who would not burst with grief to see the stock for a future generation hang on the breasts of a dead mother?' Who indeed?

The images are of a bustling city brought to its knees. The throng of the crowds, the busy-ness of the streets were but memories. Pepys records 'But, Lord! what a sad time it is to see no boats upon the river; and grass grows all up and down White Hall court, and nobody but poor wretches in the street.'[6] The streets 'thin of people' was an eerie experience: Evelyn says 'but now how few people I see, and those looking like people that had taken leave of the world.' And let's not forget that a war with the Dutch was being fought at this time. *The Intelligencer*, on 18 September 1665, commented that the Dutch 'were so pleasant as to say, the English nation is now brought so low with the plague, that a man may run them down with his finger.' Evelyn also sought the use of a 'pest-ship' for the use of infected sailors. Lives were being lost in great numbers at home and abroad.

On 30 January 1666, the city kept solemnly the seventeenth anniversary of the execution of Charles I, or as Pepys called it, good Royalist as he was, 'the King's murder'. Pepys went to church for his first visit since the plague took hold and records how 'it frighted me indeed to go through the church more than I thought it could have done, to see so many graves lie so high upon the church-yards, where people have been buried of the plague.'

As the numbers on the mortality bills increased, so Pepys' matter-of-factly recorded them: 'Above seven hundred died of the plague this week.' Uninfected people, in that naturally morbid way, were fascinated by the plague's progress. Pepys, while journeying to Dagenham on 3 August 1665, recorded that 'all the way people, citizens, walking to and fro, enquire how the plague is in the City this week by the Bill; which, by chance, at Greenwich, I had heard was 2,020 of the plague, and 3,000 and odd of all diseases; but methought it was a sad question to be so often asked me.' With increasing numbers of dying people in August 1665 'they are fain to carry the dead to be buried by daylight, the nights not sufficing to do it in.' By the end of August – in which 17,036 died of the plague – Pepys records:

> Great sadness upon the public, through the greatness of the plague...Every day sadder and sadder news of its increase. In the City died this week 7,496

and of them 6,102 of the plague [the following week it was 6,978]. But it is feared that that the true number of the dead this week is near 10,000: partly from the poor that cannot be taken notice of, through the greatness of their number, and partly from the Quakers and others that will not have any bell ring for them.

London was not the place to be unless you were conducting official business (like Pepys) or intending to make some money. Desperate times need desperate measures and you can charge well for desperate measures. Quack doctors and part-time apothecaries or chemists would declare that they had the cure or antidote for the plague. People were willing to try anything. But people mostly remained because they had nowhere else to go. This meant, of course, that while London's business seemed to be death, it was open for daily living also: people still needed to eat, drink and survive. And despite the appalling and humbling death count, survive it was what most people did. Many people must have had or built up a natural immunity to it, and a great number who contracted the plague survived it. As the contemporary Boghurst's *Loimographia* recorded: 'The plague is a most acute disease, for though some died eight, ten, twelve or twenty days after they had been sick, yet the greatest part died before five or six days, and in the summer about half that were sick died, but towards winter three parts in four lived.'[7]

Many doctors and physicians being mostly well-to-do had deserted, but many stayed and won the respect of the citizens. However, for some, like Pepys's own doctor, respect was no defence against the plague: 'This day [26 August 1665] I am told that Dr Burnett, my physician, is this morning dead of the plague; which is strange, his man dying so long ago, and his house this month open again. Now himself dead. Poor unfortunate man!' Defoe's character believes that in August such was the move to leave that he 'began to think there would be really none but magistrates and servants left in the city'.

However, those who stayed were received gratefully about both the city and court. Both Evelyn ('he told me he was much obliged to me...in a time of great danger, when everybody fled their employments'[8]) and Pepys (he 'came to me of himself, and told me "Mr Pepys," says he, "I do give you thanks for your good service all this year, and I assure you I am very sensible of it"'[9]) record that they were thanked personally by the king for staying at their stations. Pepys was the only member of the naval board to do so.

Those who fled had to come up with reasons and not excuses for their flight. Pepys tells us that at the Crown tavern on 22 January 1666 he listened to Dr Goddard talk 'in defence of his and his fellow physicians going out of town in the plague-time; saying that their particular patients were most gone out of town, and they left at liberty.'

While London took the brunt of the plague, it was by no means confined there. As the plague began its slow decline, Pepys saved a thought for the victims outside of London. He notes that 'in the country, in several places, it rages mightily, and particularly in Colchester, where it hath long been, and is believed will quite depopulate the place.'

London was slowly picking itself up from its knees. The return of the king was seen as a sign of a return to normality and that the worst was over. More pleasingly for Pepys he heard good news about his beloved theatre. On 29 August 1666, he went looking for Sir William Penn, and found him 'talking to Orange Moll, of the King's House, who to our great comfort, told us that they begun to act on the 18th of this month'. A notorious gossip, Orange Moll may have been misinformed or perhaps it was just wishful thinking because so long as the theatres were closed so was her business. The theatres were not open yet. But perhaps the players were rehearsing and probably performing at Whitehall for the king and court. Yes, it seemed that the worst was over and better times were simply awaiting their cue.

As the plague skulked away as slowly as it first arrived, the cheer in the heart of London was undoubtedly battered, torn and subdued. The one-time vices that had become everyday diversions – drinking, gambling and play-going – were treated as vices once again. Society was press-ganged by guilt as it struggled to have fun in the wake of such devastating sorrow. The pestilence had been a physical onslaught – it seemed now amusement was the victim of a new plague: a plague of conscience.

Only time would heal the hurt of the nation's capital. But time wasn't about to be given a chance. London must have thought that the curtain had fallen on its misfortune, but it was about to stage an infernal encore. The slow-quick-slow infectious assault by the plague on the city was to be followed by a most devastating fire. In short of four violent days one third of the city would exist no more.

— 7 —

A Most Malicious, Horrid, Bloody Flame

...Light seen for above 40 miles round-a-bout. The noise
and cracking and thunder of the impetuous flames, the
shrieking of women and children, the hurry of people, the
fall of towers, houses and churches, was like a hideous storm,
and the air all about was so hot and inflamed that at the last
one was not able to approach it.

Diary, John Evelyn, 3 September 1666

Thomas Farriner, the king's baker – he had a contract to bake biscuits for
the navy – had his bakehouse at Pudding Lane.[1] Having finished for the
day he, as ever, carefully put out the flames in his ovens. Or so he thought
and certainly would so defend himself later.

Just before two o'clock on Sunday morning, 2 September 1666,
Farriner was awoken by his man who had been awoken by smoke and
the noise of fire. Farriner evacuated his house, but his maidservant being
too scared did not follow. She soon became the first human casualty of
what was to become known as the Great Fire. The closely built dry
timber houses became sweet snacks for the fire to feast on as it devoured
its hungry way down Fish Street Hill: a hunger that was not to be
appeased for four days. Farriner would later defend himself vigorously

when questioned by the committee researching the cause of the fire, saying that the fire did not start from his ovens. Such defence is understandable as he would not relish carrying the blame for starting such a disaster.

The lord mayor at the time was the 56-year-old Sir Thomas Bludworth. He had only become a councilman in 1658 but within seven short but very successful years had become lord mayor – a position of great importance and power. However, he was about to experience the four longest days of his life. His political inexperience coupled with Pepys's assessment of him just over a month before the fire as 'a silly man' have been used to malign him, although he was probably just very unlucky. His involvement with the fire certainly began somewhat infamously. Called from his bed to inspect the fire, he rode out from the other side of the city, but was decidedly unimpressed with what he saw: 'Pish,' he said, 'a woman could piss it out!' And back home he rode. Fires were not unusual. Bludworth also apparently replied to the suggestion that four or five houses be pulled down to contain the fire, by asking who would have to pay to rebuild them. The final rebuilding would cost a tad more. An expensive error for London and his reputation.

Although slow to begin (Farriner's neighbours had time to move their goods out from their homes), the momentum soon built up. Evelyn watched from Southwark 'where we beheld that dismal spectacle, the whole city in dreadful flames', which burnt with such ferocity that the heat 'ignited the air'.[2]

Understandably the chaos was great. Pepys records the streets being 'full of nothing but people; and horses and carts loaden with goods, ready to run over one another, and removing goods from one burned house to another.' Evelyn saw 'the Thames covered with goods floating, all the barges and boats laden with what some had time and courage to save, as on the other, the carts &c carrying out to the fields, which for many miles were strewed with moveables of all sorts, and tents erecting to shelter both people and what goods they could get away'. People fled to open fields. London was then a shadow of its modern self with places like Greenwich and Islington being considered distant from the city. Evelyn visited the refugee camps: 'I then went towards Islington and High-gate, where one might have seen two hundred thousand people of all ranks and degrees, dispersed, and laying along their heaps of what they could save from the *Incendium*.'

The fire reached its infernal height on the Tuesday. Pepys, from safety across the river, watched how the fire grew noting how much stronger it appeared as the day darkened. He saw the fire 'in corners and upon steeples, and between churches and houses, as far as we could see up the hill of the City, in a most horrid, malicious, bloody flame, not like the fine flame of an ordinary fire.' This surely was hell on earth. Coming after such a long drought, everything seemed combustible, 'even the very stones of churches'. Evelyn agreed: St Paul's was smothered in flames, its stones exploding 'like granados', its lead roof melted and rolled down the streets like lava: 'the lead melting down the streets in a stream, and the very pavements of them glowing with fiery redness, so as nor horse nor man was able to tread on them . . .'

Houses that stood helpless in the path of the wind-directed fire were pulled down by gangs of men, under the direction of the exhausted, help-less and defeated Bludworth, in the hope of containing the fire. But as soon as houses had been pulled down or, later in desperation, blown up to create a safety gap, the marauding flames skipped contemptuously over the empty spaces and continued on their relentless and aggressive jour-ney. The wind proved a heartless accomplice. However, by Wednesday, the wind had dropped and the containment policy began to take effect.

At the end one-third of the city was ash and embers. When the smouldering reckoning took place, the capital had lost its cathedral, its guildhall, its exchange, 13,200 houses, 84 churches, but amazingly only nine people. The fire had burnt nearly 400 acres within the city walls and some 63 acres outside. For some time after the flames had died, the ground, in some places, remained too hot to walk on. The king remained in London and even went out to talk to refugees to assure them that in the long term the city would be rebuilt and more immediately that they would at least get bread. He was genuinely distraught at the plight of his subjects and they loved him all the more for it. Dryden said that Charles had 'out-wept a hermit and out-prayed a saint'.[3]

While some feared divine retribution for the immorality of the age, others smelt a plot in the retreating smoke. Rumours that the fire had been started by Papists, by the French, by the Dutch, cracked through the city as hot, unstoppable and destructive as the fire itself. Take away the fear and despair from Londoners and all they had left was rank paranoia. Even Pepys began to believe that 'there is some kind of plot in this' and records the great talk about 'the French having a hand in it'.[4]

The duke of Buckingham, who as lord lieutenant of Yorkshire, wrote to his deputies on 6 September 1666, saying that he had received information from London claiming it 'being impossible that a thing of this nature could be effected without a farther design,' adding that '...about three score French and Dutch are taken, that were firing of houses'.[5]

Such intensity, misplaced as it was, demanded revenge – which it duly received in October 1666. Robert Hubert, a Frenchman, was convicted of starting the fire and hanged. That Hubert wasn't even in the country when the fire started counted for nought as the mob bayed. The sickeningly inaccurate bill tells its own shameful story:

> ...not having the fear of God before his eyes, but moved and led away by the instigation of the Devil... voluntarily, maliciously and feloniously...did throw fireball into the mansion house of one Thomas Farrier the Elder, Baker set and being in Pudding lane... devilishly... his malice aforethought.

The Monument, at the junction of today's Monument Street and Fish Hill Street, was erected as a memorial of the fire. Designed by Sir Christopher Wren with assistance from Robert Hooke, it cost £13,450 11s. 6d. (over £1,000,000 today). This stand-alone stone column is the world's largest. It stands 202 feet high – that being the distance from the site of the Monument to the spot where the fire started. The balcony is reached by climbing the spiral staircase of 311 steps. In 1681, an inscription, which was added to the Monument, read:

> This pillar was set up in perpetual remembrance of that most dreadful burning of this protestant city, begun and carried out by ye treachery and malice of ye popish faction in ye year of Our Lord, 166[6], in order for carrying on their horrid plot for expirtating the Protestant and old English liberty, and introducing popery and slavery.

Although removed on the accession of the Catholic James II, it was restored in the following joint reign of William III and Mary II and remained in place until 1830. In similar bigoted vein, a plaque was erected on the site of Farriner's shop. This read: 'Here by ye permission of Heaven Hell broke loose upon this Protestant City from the malicious hearts of barbarous Papists.'

— 8 —

Those Darlings of the Stage, or Come, You're Handsome, There's No Denying It!

...she being of a gay, frolicksome and humorous disposition.

History of the English Stage, Thomas Betterton, 1741

And once Nell Gwynne, a frail young sprite,
Looked kindly when I met her;
I shook my head, perhaps – but quite
Forgot to quite forget her.

Frederick Locker-Lampson

Despite the tragic circumstances that caused the closure of the theatres, the players must have been longing to get back to work. They must have struggled during the closure. Many actresses may have found some well-to-do fop with a heart, bed and inheritance to share, but it would be more difficult for an actor to find a benefactor. Killigrew wasn't sitting as idle as his theatre: he decided to use the time for a spot of refurbishment. On 19 March 1666, Pepys informally inspected the progress:

After dinner walked to the king's playhouse, all in dirt, they being altering of the stage to make it wider. But God knows when they will begin to act again; but my business here was to see the inside of the stage and the tiring-rooms and machines; and, indeed, it was a sight worth seeing. But to see their clothes, and the various sorts, and what a mixture of things there was, (here a wooden leg, there a ruff, here a hobby-horse, there a crown), would make a man split himself to see with laughing: and particularly Lacy's wardrobe, and Shotrell's. But then again to think how fine they show on the stage by candlelight, and how poor things they are too near hand, is not pleasant at all. The machines are fine, and the paintings very pretty.

As a shadow of normality began to cast itself over the bruised and battered city, the players petitioned the king, offering to donate one day's earnings per week to help with the relief of those who had suffered plague or fire. It was an act that won great sympathy and respect. A newsletter dated 29 November 1666 records that 'the players have upon great proffers of disposing a large share to charitable uses prevailed to have liberty to act in both Houses which they began this day.'[1]

The King's House re-opened with the safe bet of *The Maid's Tragedy*, one of the company's stock Beaumont and Fletcher plays and one of the era's most popular. The Duke's House re-opened the following day with another sure-fire hit revival of 'Gentle' George Etherege's *The Comical Revenge, or Love in a Tub*. This piece had been first produced in March 1664, when, says Downes it '... got the Company more reputation and profit than in any preceding comedy' taking £1,000 in a month: a blockbuster, no less. However, in the aftermath of plague and fire, blockbusters would be few and far in between. Killigrew bemoaned the situation to Pepys saying that nearly six months on, 'the audience at his house was not above half so much as it used to be before the late fire.'[2]

On 24 November 1666, a warrant was issued to pay Thomas Killigrew £1,050 (equivalent to nearly £80,000 today) for plays seen by the king and acted by the King's Company between 31 March 1663 and 20 November 1666. Clearly one of the benefits of having your own servants as actors in your own playhouse is that you can, at your leisure, run up an impressive tab.

However, Nell had to wait until 8 December 1666 to make her mark. And that she did in James Howard's *The English Monsieur*, playing Lady Wealthy 'a rich widow in love with Mr Wellbred, a wild gentleman'. Pepys was there. He thought it a 'mighty pretty play, very witty and pleasant. And the women do very well; but, above all, little Nelly, that I am mightily pleased with the play, and much with the house, more than I ever expected, the women doing better than I ever expected, and very fine women.' Although obviously a man with a soft spot for a pretty female face, it also seems that women were by now becoming very accomplished at acting in what, it must be remembered, was still a new profession for them. But, for Pepys at least, it was Nell's star that shone the brightest. For, indeed, a star she was about to become. She had found her niche in comic roles and would reign supreme for the best part of the next four years.

However, Nell did not originate the role of Lady Wealthy. The play was first staged by July 1663. It was revived regularly with Pepys watching it again on 7 April 1668 commenting that it 'had much mirth in it'. Once again Nell played opposite Charles Hart playing Wellbred – a role which he would have originated. The audience loved the cut and thrust of lovers (on stage and off) duelling with words:

Lady Wealthy: Go, hang yourself
Mr Wellbred: Thank you for the advice.
Lady Wealthy: Well, then, shall I see you again?
Mr Wellbred: When I have a mind to it. Come, I'll lead you to your coach for once.
Lady Wealthy: And I'll let you for once.

Another piece of dialogue spoken by Nell is uncannily reflective of her own life:

Lady Wealthy: This life of mine can last no longer than my beauty; and though 'tis pleasant now – I want nothing while I am Mr Wellbred's mistress – yet, if his mind should change, I might even sell oranges for my living; and he not buy one off me to relieve me.

Nell's next appearance, in December 1666, was as Celia in one of the company's stock plays *The Humorous Lieutenant* by John Fletcher. Pepys had seen this first on 20 April 1661 but thought it 'not very well done' even with the king in the audience. He saw it again on 8 May 1663 but he still felt that the play 'hath little good in it', despite John Lacy replacing Walter Clun in the cast at the king's request. It was in this production that scenery was used at the King's House for the first time and it ran, Downes tells us, 'for twelve days successively', thus marking it down, despite Pepys's ambivalence, as a big hit. The 1667 revival still did not do it for Pepys who saw it on 23 January: 'a silly play, I think', he mused, although he admired Nell's performance. However, as he was about to leave the theatre he saw his old friend Mrs Pierce, after which Mary Knepp 'took us all in, and brought us to Nelly, a most pretty woman, who acted the part of Celia today very fine, and did it pretty well: I kissed her, and so did my wife; and a mighty pretty soul she is.' Knepp then made them 'stay in a box and see the dancing preparatory to tomorrow for *The Goblins*, a play of [Sir John] Suckling's, not acted these twenty-five years; which was pretty. And so away thence, pleased with this sight also, and specially kissing of Nell.'

Dancing rehearsals were not uncommon. Quite often dancing or singing would be used between acts to keep the crowd entertained, as well as being served up as light relief during a play or, indeed, as an integral part of it. Music was also used. On his travels through England, Cosmo III of Tuscany enjoyed the English approach to theatre, especially the pre-show entertainment. He wrote home on 15 April 1669: 'Before the comedy begins, that the audience may not be tired with the waiting, the most delightful symphonies are played; on which account many persons come early to enjoy this agreeable amusement.'[3]

Restoration audiences delighted in a good jig. And Nell was without question one of the best stage dancers. Her comical jigs would have the audience cheering and laughing uproariously. Sometimes if a play was not going well, there would be a temptation to put in a dance to help win the crowd back. Indeed, this very practice would be commented upon in Nell's next play, another John Fletcher revival, this time of *The Chances*. However, this had been adapted by the duke of Buckingham who significantly added new fourth and fifth acts. Buckingham was a man of the age with a sharp and satirical eye. In *The Chances* he lampoons those dramatists who hear the loud applause, presuming it to be a fulsome appreciation of their art, when in fact it was won by a dancing Nell:

> Besides, the author dreads the strut and mien
> Of new praised poets, having often seen
> Some of his fellows, who have writ before,
> When Nell danced her jig, steal to that door,

Hear the pit clap, and with conceit of that,
Swell, and believe themselves the Lord knows what.

Play adaptation or alteration was a fairly common, if usually
unsatisfactory, practice. For example, Davenant amalgamated (somewhat
unsuccessfully) *Measure for Measure* and *Much Ado About Nothing*.
However, Buckingham's alteration of *The Chances* was generally thought
to have improved it. Even Dryden agreed on that. In his *History of the
English Stage*, Jean Genest went so far as to describe it as 'the happiest
material alteration of any old play ever made.' Pepys saw the original
version on 27 April 1661, which must have been a forgettable production
as he passes no verdict other than that he saw it. He was more buoyed by
the Buckingham version he saw on 5 February 1667: 'a good play I find
it, and the actors were most good in it.' However, his appreciation is
enhanced because Mary Knepp sang, and sang well: 'and pretty to hear
Knipp sing in the play very properly, "All Night I Weep"; and sung it
admirably.' Curiously, little is known about this song as it has not
appeared in either of the published versions (Fletcher's or Buckingham's). But the marriage of a pretty woman and a pretty song was a
pretty perfect match for Pepys.

Players' lives were far from glamorous and often not without danger.
Once off the stage they fell firmly back into a reality that offered little
immunity to the violence of the day. In February 1667, Beck Marshall
charged that Sir Hugh Middleton had paid a 'ruffian' who 'clapped a
turd on her face and hair' after she left the theatre on Tuesday 5 February
and asks 'protection and justice...for the future.'[4] On 1 February
(clearly not a good month to be an actor) 1669, Edward Kynaston from
the Duke's House was also waylaid by ruffians. Kynaston was well known
for his female roles in the theatre's pre-actress days. He was considered
'the compleat female stage beauty'. Pepys thought him 'the loveliest lady
for a boy' and 'the handsomest man' on the stage. Downes said that 'it
has been disputable among the judicious, whether any woman that
succeeded him so sensibly touched the audience as he'. However, the
pretty-faced, notoriously bisexual actor had the audacity to impersonate
Sir Charles Sedley. He was beaten 'with sticks by two or three that
assaulted him...so he is mightily bruised, and forced to keep his bed.'
Seemingly, Restoration actors never had understudies, as Kynaston's
part the next day was read by Beeston: literally read by him – he 'read it

out of a book all the while, and thereby spoils the part.'[5]

As 1667 progressed with London still trying to get back on its feet, Nell had moved to centre stage. She established herself as a leading actress. In her next play, which opened on 14 February, she took the title role in Richard Rhodes's *Flora's Vagaries*. It had previously been acted by students at Christ Church, Oxford 'in their common refectory on the 8th January 1663'[6] and came to London around November of that year. Pepys saw it on 8 August 1664 and thanks to a 'most ingenuous performance of the young jade Flora, it seemed as pretty a pleasant play as ever I saw in my life.' He saw it again on 5 October 1667, and after sitting with Knepp in the scene room, eating fruit and helping her with her lines: he once again found it a 'pretty good' play. However, with his mind distracted by the illness of his wife and he not wanting to be seen at the playhouse, Pepys's enjoyment of the play when he saw it again on 18 February 1668 was minimal: 'a very silly play' he broods. It was not recorded who played the jade Flora in the 1664 production, but it most likely wasn't Nell. It was her performance, however, that was mainly responsible for the sustained popularity of *Flora's Vagaries*.

Pepys's enjoyment of the October 1667 performance was undoubtedly heightened by his experience of going behind the scenes before the play started. 'To the King's House,' he writes, 'and there, going in, met with Knipp, and she took us up to the tiring-rooms and to the women's shift,[7] where Nell was dressing herself, and was all unready, and is very pretty, prettier than I thought.' This little bonus was offset for Pepys by Nell and Knepp's make-up: 'But, Lord!', he exclaims, 'to see how they were both painted would make a man mad, and did make me loathe them.' As if that wasn't bad enough for this master of public outrage over what he quite enjoys privately, he had to suffer the coarse and colourful banter: 'and what base company of men comes among them, and how lewdly they talk!' But despite the crudity of language, Pepys was quite taken with seeing 'how Nell cursed, for having so few people in the pit' thinking it 'pretty'. He was also impressed with how 'poor the men are in clothes, and yet what a show they make on the stage by candle-light, is very observable.'

Nell's next role was written specially for her by Dryden and was her first chance to originate a part. She was to play the character Florimel, opposite Hart's Celadin, in *Secret-Love, or The Maiden Queen*. Florimel and Celadin are madcap, sparring lovers of the type mastered by

Dryden. The play was a huge hit – and Nell succeeded in defining a comic role. Pepys, who saw it on 2 March 1667, was beside himself:

> After dinner with my wife, to the King's House to see *The Maiden Queen*, a new play of Dryden's, mightily commended for the regularity of it, and the strain and wit; and, the truth is, there is a comical part done by Nell, which is Florimel, that I never can hope ever to see the like done again, by man or woman. The King and the Duke of York were at the play. But so great performance of a comical part was never, I believe, in the world before as Nell do this, both as a mad girl, then most and best of all when she comes in like a young gallant; and hath the motions and carriage of a spark the most that I ever saw any man have. It makes me, I confess, admire her.

Dryden exploited exquisitely Nell's powers of mimicry neatly combining it with the irony of a woman playing a man on stage. Such was the impact of Nell's impersonation of a man that not only did it bring crowds to the play, but also started a fashion. So stylish did she look in men's clothing that it took the town by storm: men's clothing, thanks to Nell, became fashionable for women in London. Indeed, it would be just the start of Nell's trend-setting ways. Later, when much more famous, it would be her hairstyles – most notably when worn short with spiralling ringlets – that would be much copied.

Pepys saw the play again 'in the pit' on 25 March 1667 with his friend Sir William Penn: 'which indeed the more I see, the more I like, and is an excellent play, and so done by Nell, her merry part, as cannot be better done in nature.' And again on 24 May: 'which, though I have often seen, yet pleases me infinitely, it being impossible, I think, ever to have the Queen's part, which is very good and passionate, and Florimel's part, which is the most comical that ever was made for woman, ever done better than they are by young Marshall and Nelly.' He enjoyed the play so much that, as soon as it was printed, he bought himself a copy of the play, 'which I like' on 18 January 1668. He went again on 23 August 1667 ('which pleased us mightily') and on 24 January 1668 –'which the more I see, the more I love, and think one of the best plays that I ever saw, and is certainly the best acted of anything ever the House did, and particularly Beck Marshall, to admiration'). As Pepys's prosperity increased, his next visit to see *Secret-Love, or The Maiden Queen* on New Year's Day 1669 was occasioned by travelling there in his own coach and viewing it from a box. He saw it one last time (as covered by his diary) 15 days later.

The king was a big fan of the play also. Not least since he claimed he had suggested the plot to Dryden, who based it partly on the life of Queen Christina of Sweden. None the less, Dryden tells us that Charles 'graced it with the title of *his* play.'[8]

Towards the end of the play Florimel and Celadon discuss marriage – 'a bugbear' to them – and try to negotiate with each other a more flexible arrangement, which was no doubt aimed to both shock and mirror society:

Celadon: As for the first year, according to the laudable custom of new married people, we shall follow one another up into chambers, and down into gardens, and think we shall never have enough of one another – So far 'tis pleasant enough, I hope.

Florimel: But after that, when we begin to live like husband and wife, and never come near one another – what then, sir?

Celadon: When I have been at play, you shall never ask me what money I have lost.

Florimel: When I have been abroad you shall never inquire who treated me.

Celadon: Item, I will have the liberty to sleep all night, without you interrupting my repose for any evil design whatsoever.

Florimel: Item, then you shall bid me good night before you sleep.

Celadon: Provided always, that whatever liberties we take with other people, we continue to be honest to one another.

Florimel: As far as will consist with a pleasant life.

Celadon: Lastly, whereas the names of husband and wife hold forth nothing, but clashing and cloying, and dullness and faintness in their signification; they shall be abolished for ever betwixt us.

Florimel: And instead of those, we will be married by the more agreeable names of mistress and gallant.

More dialogue also gives us two teasingly tasty morsels: a clue to her looks and a hint to her age. Given that Dryden wrote the part for Nell, it is tempting to swallow Celadon's description of Florimel as one of Nell herself (sadly, the fashion for flattering portraiture has meant that paintings – on the face of it – cannot be trusted to give us the full picture). The tempted Celadon, who has yet to lay eyes on Florimel, describes what he is sure lies beneath her mask:

A turned-up nose, that gives an air to your face: oh, I find I am more and more in love with you! – a full nether lip, an out-mouth, that makes mine water at it, the bottom of your cheeks a little blub and two dimples when you smile: for your stature 'tis well, and for your wit 'twas given you by one that knew it had been thrown away upon an ill face. Come, you're handsome, there's no denying it!

Celadon also anticipates his lover-to-be to have 'such an oval face, clear skin, hazel eyes, thick brown eyebrows, and hair as you have for all the world'. Although another character, Flavia, assures Celadon that Florimel 'has nothing of all this' it does seem to fit in with the picture we have of Nell. *The Manager's Note-book* also has a description of Nell: 'She was low in stature, and what the French call *mignonne* and *piquante*, well formed, handsome, but red-haired and rather *embonpoint* . . . she had remarkably lively eyes, but so small they were invisible when she laughed; and a foot, the least of any women in England'.[9] Clearly the anonymous manager did not think red hair an asset of beauty, but it most certainly helped Nell to stand out. Popular imagination suggests that Nell was buxom, although there is little evidence that she had large breasts. Certainly her portraits do not suggest this, although with small breasts being considered more beautiful, or rather, more fashionable, they may have been painted as fashion rather than as like. The only clue is the anonymous theatre manager's phrase of 'well formed', but this could be interpreted in many ways. It would seem that, although small, she was well proportioned.

A hint, admittedly circumstantial, to her age comes in the following dialogue:

Celadon: But dost thou know what it is to be an old maid?

Florimel: No, nor do I hope I shan't see these twenty years.

Celadon: But when that time comes, in the first place thou wilt be condemned to tell stories how many men thou might'st have had: and none believe thee: then thou growest forward, and impudently weariest all thy friends to solicit men for thee.

Florimel: Away with your old common-place wit: I am resolved to grow fat, and look young till forty, and then slip out of the world with the first wrinkle, and the reputation of five and twenty.

Nell's clear white skin seemingly kept her youthful-looking in a time when people aged quickly. Intriguingly, if we were to accept 1642 as Nell's birth date, she would, while first delivering these lines specially written for her, be 25 years old. However, this is probably best judged as coincidental as clearly Florimel is saying that she simply desires to be considered as 25 when she is 40. It has also been argued that the above exchange illustrates that Florimel believes 40 to be the age of 'an old maid' and that she has 20 years to go, thus making her character 20.[10] If we accept the 1650 birthdate, Nell would have been 17 while uttering these words for the first time. Nell's other biographers have used this sample of dialogue to illustrate a sad prophecy – in their view their Nell, born in 1650, *would* 'slip out of this world' three years shy of her fortieth birthday. The arguments put forward for this passage are all feasible, but sadly inconclusive.

While both houses would take great delight in lampooning each other, this didn't preclude them from indulging in a little self-satire either. In the 1669–70 season, the King's House would revive the popular Beaumont and Fletcher's *The Knight of the Burning Pestle*. In a new epilogue, which Nell would speak, Dryden's *Secret Love, or The Maiden Queen* was sent up:

> The prologue durst not tell, before 'twas seen;
> The plot we had to swinge *The Maiden Queen*;
> For had we then discovered our intent,
> The fop who had writ it had not given consent,
> Or the new peaching trick at least had shown,
> And brought in others' faults to hide his own.
> Thus our poor poet would have 'scaped today,
> But from the herd I single out his play.
> Then heigh along with me –
> Both great and small, you poets of the town,
> And Nell will love you – for to run him down.

Florimel was a big part for Nell. As the play centred around her character, she was barely off stage throughout: exhausting but triumphant. Dryden knew she would be good, but she was great. She was now a star. She was also known as 'Nelly' from this point on. It defined her: she, or anybody else come to that, would hardly need to use her last name again. Even in the official government exchequer records payments were made to 'Mistress Nelly' or 'Maddam Nelly'. Betterton called her 'Nelly, for by that name she was universally known'. Just as in recent years, Diana sufficed for the Princess of Wales, so 'Nelly' did for Nell Gwynne. The automatic familiarity was at odds with a formal society: but somehow with Nelly that was just the point. She might not know who they were, but they felt they knew her. And in an age without electronic media, to win the hearts of the people in that way was a truly impressive achievement. If those that loved her called her Nelly, then it seems right that, from now on, we do the same.

Her next role was to bring her into direct competition, and not for the last time, with another actress: Mary 'Moll' Davies (or Davis) of the Duke's House. The conflict was also to act as a catalyst in both their love lives.

In the spring of 1664, the rival Duke's Company first produced *The Rivals*, an alteration by William Davenant of Fletcher and (probably) Shakespeare's *The Two Noble Kinsmen*. It was revived in 1667 at the Lincoln's Inn Fields theatre and, despite being a mediocre version (Pepys thought it 'not good', although Downes was enthusiastic), it was to make the name of Moll Davies, who took the role of Celania. Earlier that year, on 7 March, Pepys had seen her in a 'pretty good...but not eminent' tragedy by John Caryl (Baron Caryl of Dunford). Pepys wrote:

> 'Only little Miss Davis did dance a jig after the end of the play, and there telling the next day's play; so that it came in by force only to please the company to see her dance in boy's clothes; and, the truth is, there is no comparison between Nell's dancing the other day at the King's House in boy's clothes and this, this being infinitely beyond the other.'

Indeed, Moll must have been an excellent dancer to have out-jigged Nelly. Pepys also later thought her dancing in 'a silly play' *Love's Tricks, or the School of Compliments*, a comedy by James Shirley, was the only thing of note, pleasing him 'mightily'. Pepys was not the only admirer of the dancing Moll. A contemporary tribute called 'To Mis Davies, on her excellent dancing' was published on the subject.

However, it was in *The Rivals* that Moll caught a prince's eye, but not through her acting or even her dancing, but through her rendition of a song: *My Lodging it is on the Cold Ground*. Moll sang:

My lodging it is on the cold ground,
And very hard is my fare,
But that which troubles me most is
The unkindness of my dear.
Yet still I cry, O turn love,
And I pr'ythee, love, turn to me,
For thou art the man that I long for,
And alack what remedy!

I'll crown thee with a garland of straw, then,
And I'll marry thee with a rush ring,
My frozen hopes shall thaw then,
And merrily we will sing.
O turn to me, my dear love,
And pr'ythee love, turn to me,
For thou art the man that alone canst
Procure my liberty.

But if thou wilt harden thy heart still,
And be deaf to my pitiful moan,
Then I must endure the smart still,
And tumble in straw alone.
Yet still, I cry, O turn love,
And I pr'ythee, love turn to me,
For thou art the man that alone art
The cause of my misery.

At the end of the song, the stage direction requires her to lie down and fall asleep. King Charles, who had already proven his weakness for actresses, and who fell in love with an alarming regularity, watched young Moll curl up and fall asleep, and felt his heart awaken. The monarch was in love. Again. Downes comments, rather sweetly, that all 'the women's parts were admirably acted, but what pleased most was the part of Celania, a shepherdess, mad for love, and her song of 'My lodging is on the cold ground', which she performed so charmingly that not long after it raised her from her bed on the cold ground to a bed royal.'[12]

Some time later, in January 1668, Pepys records the gossip surrounding Moll. Knepp tells him that 'Miss Davis is for certain going away from the Duke's House, the King being in love with her; and a house is taken for her, and furnishing; and she hath a ring given her already worth £600.' Three days later, on 14 January, he hears more about Moll, who is reckoned 'a most impertinent slut' and to be the king's mistress. The value of the ring given her by the king had risen to £700 and her house most 'richly furnished' was in Suffolk Street. His source added that she was 'the most homely jade as ever she saw', although adding, no doubt to Pepys's agreement, that 'she dances beyond anything in the world'.

Moll left the stage, preferring, as Clifford Bax puts it, the fringe of the court to the centre of the stage.[13] However, Moll did not figure much in court beyond giving birth to a daughter – Mary Tudor. Charles acknowledged paternity but Moll never figured as an official mistress. She might have sung her way into his heart but she soon danced back out again. Charles became particularly bored with her manner and affectations: she would act as a lady of quality with all the airs and graces irritatingly imaginable

Although it was a characteristic of the king to tire quickly of most of his women who made it past the one night, he was hardly guilty of harshness or vindictiveness towards them. He would feel obliged to help them out, at least financially, particularly the mothers of his children. Moll secured herself another new home, moving into what would be 22 St James's Square (off Pall Mall), being part of the land where today the Army & Navy Club stands. She also received an annual pension of £1,000 a year and very little was heard of her again. Her daughter married Francis, the second earl of Derwentwater. Moll's grandson, James, the third earl, was beheaded for treason during the Jacobite rebellion.

Pepys also puts forward the opinion that Moll was the natural daughter (actually Pepys calls her 'a bastard') of Thomas Howard, the first lord Berkshire.[14] This would have made her a half-sister to the playwright-ing Howards. Which, if true (although there is a suggested alternative that she was the daughter of a blacksmith from Charlton in Wiltshire), provides a neat link between Moll's successful rendition of her song in *The Rivals* and Nelly. For while Moll was causing a monarch's heart to beat faster, the King's House was plotting something to rival the duke's success. And it was to come from the pen of Moll's supposed half-brother, James Howard. Nelly had already shone in another of Howard's plays *The English Monsieur*, and was about to do so again in his third play for the King's House *All Mistaken, or The Mad Couple*.

Nell took the role of Mirida who was the 'mad mistress' of the leading male character Philidor, played, as usual, by Charles Hart. Pepys saw the play on 20 September 1667 but passed no comment. However, he is more open about it on his second visit three months later on 28 December: '. . . to the King's House, and there saw *The Mad Couple*, which is but an ordinary play; but only Nell's and Hart's mad parts are excellently done, but especially hers.' On this occasion Pepys treats us to an episode during the play, not in the script, and one that he enjoyed. 'It pleased us mightily,' he says relishing the story, 'to see the natural affection of a poor woman, the mother of one of the children brought onto the stage: the child crying, she by force got upon the stage, and took the up her child and carried it away off of the stage from Hart.'

This 'mean' play, although another successful vehicle for the dream team of Hart and Nelly, was most worthy of note for an inserted parody of *The Rivals*. Nelly's character Mirida is pursued by 'two ridiculous lovers' Pinguister (a very fat man, played by the rotund John Lacy) and Lean-man (an unhealthily thin man). Mirida pledges to marry Lean-man when he should put on ample weight, and Pinguister when he presents himself slim and elegant. The final act between little Nelly and the fat Lacy sets up the parody to bring the house down:

Mirida: Dear love, come sit thee in my lap, and let me know if I can enclose thy world of fat and love within these arms. See, I cannot nigh compass my desires by a mile.

Pinguister: How is my fat a rival to my joys! Sure I shall weep it all away. (*Cries*)

Mirida: Lie still, my babe, lie still and sleep,
It grieves me sore to see thee weep,
Wert thou but leaner I would be glad
Thy fatness makes thy dear love sad.

Pinguister: Nay, if I had not taken all these courses to dissolve myself into thy embraces, one would think my looking on thee were enough; for I never see thee but I am like a fat piece of beef roasting at the fire, continually drop, drop, drop. There's ne'er a feature in thy face or part about thee but has cost me many a pint of fat with thinking on thee. And yet not to be lean enough for thy husband – O fate! O fate! O fate! O fat!

Mirida: What a lump of love have I in my arms!

(she lets him fall)

O Lord sir, I have let you fall, how shall I do to get you up again?

Pinguister: Nay, that is more than all the world can tell.

Mirida: I'll e'en lie down by thee then.

(she lies down out of his reach)

Pinguister: Nay, but pr'ythee lie near me; thou hadst as good lie a league off as at that distance.

Mirida: Were I thy wife, fat love, I would.

(she sings)

My lodging is on the cold boards,
And wonderful hard is my fare,
But that which troubles me most is
The fatness of my dear.
Yet still I cry, Oh melt, love,
And I pr'ythee now melt apace,
For thou art the man I should long for
If 'twere not for thy grease.

Pinguister:

Then pr'ythee don't harden thy heart still,
And be deaf to my pitiful moan,
Since I do endure the smart still,
And for my fat do groan;
Then pr'ythee now turn, my dear love,
And I pr'ythee now turn to me,
For, alas! I am too fat still
To roll so far to thee.

At this point Lacy rolls towards Nelly who herself rolls away at speed. The sight of the fat man rolling after Nelly might have caused riotous laughter in the house, but the ample showing of her undergarments caught the eye of a member of the audience. Not for Nelly, just yet at least, the eye of a prince, but a glint in the right direction. A look of love was about to break her Hart and break down her defences: the poet, wit and nobleman, Charles Sackville, Lord Buckhurst, had Nelly full square in his sights.

Yet Hart more manners had, than not to tender,
When noble Buckhurst begged him to surrender.

He saw her roll the stage from side to side
And, through her drawers the powerful charm descried.
'Take her my Lord,' quoth Hart, 'since you're so mean
To take a player's leavings for your queen.'[15]

A Merry House of Retirement, or Sparring Partners

None had so strange an art,
His passion to convey
Into a listening virgin's heart
And steal her soul away.

The Man of Mode, George Etherege, 1676

'Twas once indeed with her, as 'tis with ore
Uncoyned, she was no public store,
Only Buckhurst's private whore.

'An Essay of Scandal', Anonymous, 1681

On 13 July 1667, James Pierce the surgeon to the duke of York and husband of his friend, had troubling news for Pepys. He is told that 'my Lord Buckhurst hath got Nell away from the King's House, and gives her £100 a year, so she hath sent her parts to the house, and will act no more.' That she had sent her scripts ('parts') back is intriguing, because there is an assumption that Nelly was illiterate. She almost certainly couldn't write – or chose not to because it was too much of a struggle. Very few letters thought to have been sent by Nelly have survived – and all of these were either dictated to someone else or letters sent by trustees on her behalf. In one such letter written in November 1679 by Sir Robert Howard to the duke of Ormonde, concerning Nelly's Irish pension, he comments that 'Mrs Nelly...presents you with her real acknowledge-ment for all your favours, and protests she would write in her own hand but her wild characters she says would distract you.'[1]

All existing examples of Nelly's signature show that her forte was verbal rather than literary: all she could manage was a scratchy and somewhat forced 'EG'. Despite writing being a problem, she still had scripts to send back to the playhouse. Perhaps reading was less of a problem. Or, perhaps and more likely, she still needed the scripts for others to read the parts to her, so she could practise her lines and cues. If this was the case, we can add an excellent ear and memory to her list of personal qualities.

Finding yourself a rich, noble man to keep you – as Nelly had with Buckhurst – so you could give up the stage was pretty much the deal for actresses. And it happened rather a lot. Evelyn despaired at how many men of quality would settle for such playthings:

> Women now (& never 'til now) permitted to appear & act, which inflaming several young noble-men & gallants, became their whores, & to some their wives, witness the Earl of Oxford, Sir Robert Howard, Prince Rupert, the Earl of Dorset, & another greater person than any of these, who fell into their snares, to the reproach of their noble families, & ruin both of body & soul.[2]

The top male actors would also occasionally attract the attentions and favours of women of quality. Although Killigrew, just to make sure that the other men in the company kept their minds on the job required on the stage, took the precaution of retaining a woman on 20s. a week to service them.[3] None the less, the wits, gallants and the titled revelled in trophy wives or (more usually) mistresses. There's no reason why Nelly shouldn't have conformed to this. In fact she had done rather well. The poor, deprived, disadvantaged, illiterate young woman had bagged herself a lord. And not just any old lord either.

Charles Sackville (1643–1706), Lord Buckhurst (as we shall call him), was later to become the sixth earl of Dorset and the fourth earl of Middlesex. By the time of his death, he was a man of great achievement and stature. Horace Walpole would refer to him as 'the finest gentleman in the voluptuous court of Charles II'. Buckhurst's contemporary, the righteous Bishop Burnet, the historian would say of him that 'never was so much ill-nature in a pen as his, joined with so much good-nature as in himself'. The earl of Rochester would write that:

> For pointed satyrs, I would Buckhurst choose:
> The best good man with the worst-natured muse.

However, the capture of Buckhurst meant the release of Charles Hart. It would not be surprising if an echo of Nelly's very first lines in *The Indian Emperor* began ringing in her ears. At the time of his wooing of Nelly Buckhurst was mainly a man of pleasure but was also known as a poet. However, he was chiefly famous for his ballad *To all you ladies now at land*, which he wrote, probably between 30 November and 3 December 1664, while serving on a ship in the Dutch war. It begins:

> To all you ladies now at land
> We men at sea indite;
> But first would have you understand
> How hard it is to write:
> The Muses now, and Neptune too,
> We must implore to write to you
> With a fa, la, la, la, la.
>
> For though the Muses should prove kind
> And fill our empty brain,
> Yet if rough Neptune rouse the wind
> To wave the azure main,
> Our paper, pen, and ink, and we,
> Roll up and down our ships at sea –
> With a fa, la, la, la, la.

It made a huge splash back home becoming one of the most popular ballads of the time. Buckhurst had also just embarked on what would be a remarkably successful career as a patron of the arts. George Etherege's *The Comical Revenge, or Love in a Tub* had been dedicated to Buckhurst in 1664. In total he would have 35 books dedicated to him by writers such as John Dryden, Thomas Shadwell, Thomas Otway, Nathaniel Lee,

Thomas Rymer and William Congreve – a thundering roll call of Restoration literary icons.

His antics, however, befitting the licensed debauchery expected of the restored nobility, had afforded him a clinking chunk of notoriety. On 16 June 1663, during one infamous drunken afternoon, Buckhurst and his partners-in-wine, Sir Charles Sedley and Sir Thomas Ogle, met for dinner at the Cock Tavern (an unfortunately apt name for what was to happen) in Bow Street, Covent Garden. Their meal ('six dishes of meat') was brought in by 'six naked women'.[4] After dinner and many bottles of wine they adjourned to the balcony.

Unsurprisingly, any calming ballasts of diplomacy or restraint were sunk with the last bottle of wine. Among their high-spirited jests and men-ofquality pranks were mock church sermons, the blasphemy of which outraged the passing crowd. Indeed the outraged crowd was soon rooted to the spot to witness the offending spectacle. By the end near a thousand people had gathered. That's a lot of outrage for anybody's money. It ended with (at least) Sedley naked, and the men indulging in a light spot of mock buggery, and throwing bottles 'pist in' into the crowd. Ogle and Sedley, who were members of Parliament, ended the session by declaring 'Come now, let us go in and make laws for the nation.' Sedley, as the ringleader, was arrested, fined 2,000 marks, imprisoned for a week and bound over to keep the peace for three years.[5] It appears that Buckhurst along with Ogle escaped unpunished.

It was the second time that Buckhurst had got off scot-free. Over a year previously, in February 1662, Buckhurst and his brother, Edward, were two of five men who had attacked and killed a suspected robber around Stoke Newington.

At the time of the Restoration highwaymen were such a scourge that the king placed a £10 bounty on each one captured. In fact the suspected highwayman, John Hoppy, was no such thing: he was a tanner. It was thought that these 'five persons of quality' may have been hanged within a week had the king not intervened. In the end, on 10 April 1662, they were convicted of manslaughter, only to be pardoned by the king one week later.

This, then, was the man that was to take Nelly from her adoring public and settle her down in the spa town of Epsom. It was a happy and pleasant proposition. But whether he was Lord Right would be a different matter.

The regularity with which the court delighted in taking the waters meant that spa towns sparkled. Bath, Tunbridge Wells and Epsom were great favourites. Water had many uses in London, but drinking was never one of them. Epsom enjoyed a surge of popularity that had, until the court's patronage, otherwise evaded it. Thomas Shadwell in his comedy *The Virtuoso* would later write that 'Your glass coach will to Hyde Park for air; the suburb fools trudge to Lambs Conduit or Tottenham; your sprucer sort of citizens gallop to Epsom.' The resort was also the inspiration for Shadwell's *Epsom Wells*.

It was by no coincidence (we may somewhat safely surmise) that on being told on 13 July 1667 of Nelly's retirement to Epsom that Pepys visited the town with his wife the very next day. Leaving at just past five o'clock in the morning (a little annoyed that his wife had taken so long to get ready) and armed with 'wine and beer and cold fowl', Pepys arrived in Epsom about three hours later thanks to his coach and four horses. After drinking four pints of water at the well, he went to the King's Head in the town to 'hear that my Lord Buckhurst and Nelly are lodged at the next house, and Sir Charles Sedley is with them: and they keep a merry house. Poor girl! I pity her; but more the loss of her at the King's House.' The 'merry house' had two little bay-windowed rooms overlooking the street, and came complete with a secret exit door (a structural extra that has become almost a traditional requirement of any house, inn or tavern claiming little Nelly ever lived, stayed or supped there).

Given the reputation that Buckhurst and, in particular, Sedley had for scrapes and debauchery, Pepys's pity for Nelly is hugely understandable. Apart from the incidents already related, in October 1668, Buckhurst and Sedley would be arrested for running up and down the streets almost naked and beating up the watch.

The hats-off reputation of Sir Charles Sedley (1639–1701) was magnificently inglorious. During his stay with Buckhurst and Nell, he left them on 5 August 1667 to attend dinner at Durdans, the big country house nearby. Among the guests was the pious and therefore very anxious countess of Warwick, Mary Rich. She notes in her diary that she went 'with Lady Robartes and her Lord to Durdans to see my Lord who was there. At dinner that day dined Sedley, which was much trouble to see him for fear he should be profane.' But the countess's anxiety was misplaced. 'But it pleased God,' she notes with gales of relief, 'to restrain him: yet the knowledge I had how profane he was troubled me to be in his company.'

Not all those in his company were so troubled by Sedley. The playwright Thomas Shadwell said that Sedley spoke 'more wit at a supper than all my adversaries with their heads joined together can write in a year'. Another contemporary, the critic Gerard Langbaine wrote that Sedley's wit 'is so well known to this age.' Even Charles II said of him that 'Nature had given him a patent to be Apollo's viceroy'. Profanity, debauchery and drunkenness (he was a thoroughly able drinker) aside, Sedley, who could run people through with his wit, was to play an historic role in the politics of the nation. He voted for the accession of Prince William of Orange and Mary Stuart, daughter of the then King James II, to assume the throne in 1688. Sedley's daughter, Catherine, was a mistress to James when he was duke of York. On his accession James created Catherine countess of Dorchester. Sedley commented: 'James made my daughter a countess, and I now make his daughter a queen.' Catherine's mother and Sedley's first wife, Katherine, was a stranger to reality at times, believing herself to be queen and insisting on being called 'your majesty'.

Sedley was also a poet and playwright. During a performance of his aptly-named-for-the-times *The Mistress*, the theatre roof collapsed on him. His friend Fleetwood Shepherd suggested to the distraught Sedley that the play had so much fire that it had blown up the theatre, the poet himself and the audience. 'Nonsense,' countered Sedley, 'it was so heavy it brought down the house and buried the poet in his own rubbish.'

On 1 August 1667, Pepys records that Mary Knepp told him 'the story how Nell is gone from the King's House, and is kept by Lord Buckhurst.' This was evidently the gossip of the town. *The Lady of Pleasure* suggests, in isolation, that Buckhurst during this time permitted Nelly to service other men:

> To Buckhurst thus resigned in friendly wise,
> He takes her swinge and sometimes lends her thighs
> To bestial Buckingham's transcendent prick
> And sometimes, witty Wilmot had a lick.
> And thus she traded in on noble ware,
> Serving the rest with what her Lord could spare;
> For Buckhurst was Lord of the Hairy Manor,
> The rest were only tenants to his honour.

These accusations can be dismissed as mischief-making. One of the remarkable things about Nelly is that she appears to have always been faithful to the man she was with: a sort of serial monogamist. This *is* remarkable, given the times, her upbringing and her availability. The story related earlier of Nelly's reply to Beck Marshall, who accused her of being Buckhurst's whore, that 'I was but one man's mistress...and you are a mistress to three or four' illustrates the point. She was loyal. Being such a public figure it would be unthinkable to imagine that Nelly could keep any lovers secret. The lampoons and vicious satires of the day would have exploited any of Nelly's relationships (particularly with such notorious noblemen as George Villiers, duke of Buckingham and John Wilmot, earl of Rochester), but only one or two make any such comment. It must be concluded that the writers chose not to attack this part of her character because it was not a legitimate target. Satires had to have some footing in reality or in the popular understanding (no matter how misplaced) to have any effect. Otherwise the writing would be exposed as merely vindictive and, as such, worthless.

The removal to Epsom for a merry retirement for life turned out to be nothing more than a summer sojourn. Within six weeks, Nelly was back in London, embarrassingly asking for her old job back. Buckhurst was not a man of bottomless funds. Nelly had been simply too expensive for his not yet rich blood. The merry house lost its mistress. She now looked to regain her place once more, grabbing the candlelight at Drury Lane. The cupboard in her old lodgings looked anything but bare with all that humble pie to chew on and all that pride to swallow. Being a kept woman might not yet have agreed with her but with a relentless supply of spirit and constant mischief in her eyes, nothing was going to keep this woman down.

Nelly's return was inevitably awkward. She had walked out on the company and her lover who, let's not forget, also managed the company. Despite her box office appeal, it's hard to imagine any arms opening up to welcome back the prodigal daughter of the stage. This wasn't going to be easy.

Not one to miss out on the gossip, Pepys 'had a great deal of discourse' with Orange Moll, who was not one to withhold any. She told him:

[Nelly] is already left by my Lord Buckhurst, and that he makes sport of her, and swears that she hath had all she could get of him; and Hart, her great admirer, now hates her; and that she is very poor, and hath lost my Lady Castlemaine, who was her great friend also: but she is come to the House, but is neglected by them all.

The segments of Moll's comments are certainly juicy, but we need to peel them with care. It is certainly not clear that Buckhurst and Nelly split up – indeed the Epsom adventure may have been a deliberately short break. It is hard to imagine either of these two characters forsaking London for long. There is good evidence that Buckhurst and Nelly were together right up until Nelly was 'sent for' by the king which was a few months away yet.

That Buckhurst made 'sport of her' is likely. However, he was just as likely to get it back. She certainly cost him a lot and that would surely not pass without comment. That she left him for the king may well have left him bitter. A poem called *Lord Buckhurst Rodomandado upon-his-Mistress* (most likely not by Buckhurst himself) may well have captured the hurt he was feeling at around this time:

> Seek not to know a woman, for she's worse
> Than all ingredients framed into a curse:
> Were she but ugly, peevish, proud a whore
> Perjured and painted, so she were no more,
> I could forgive her and connive at this
> Adjudging still she but a woman is:
> But she is worse and may in time forestall
> The devil, and be the damning of us all.

Buckhurst and Nelly would remain friends for the rest of her life, however. He would be a regular visitor to her house, part of her 'merry gang', and would even be a trustee for her.

The irony of Barbara Castlemaine, the king's chief mistress, being a friend of Nelly's, is often overlooked. Barbara was a patron of drama and clearly she befriended actresses. She was on good terms with Beck Marshall whose help she would enlist in April of 1668 to gain an introduction to Charles Hart who then became her lover. As Pepys records: 'Mrs Knipp tells me that my Lady Castlemaine is mightily in love with Hart, of their house: and he is much with her in private, and she goes to him and do give him many presents.'[6] Knepp adds that the scheming Barbara 'by this means is even with the king's love to Mrs Davis'. And Hart revenged on Nelly, no doubt: as by this time she would also be the king's mistress.

Orange Moll's comment that Charles Hart now hates Nelly is perhaps understandable. However, he had a business to run and despite his personal feelings towards Nelly, she was good for business. By 22 August 1667 she was back on the stage. Pepys records on that day 'with my Lord Brounckner and his mistress to the King's playhouse and there saw *The Indian Emperor*; where I find Nell come again, which I am glad of, but was most infinitely displeased with her being put to act the Emperor's daughter; which is a great and serious part, which she doth most basely.' Pepys's review of Nell's performance pulls no punches – and remember he's a fan – and points clearly for the first time that tragedy was not her calling. With oodles of charm, spark and motion coupled with natural wit and mimicry, Nelly was built for comedy. It might be suggested that she could not have been all that bad in 'serious parts' or else they wouldn't have persevered with her; or that Dryden,who championed the heroic drama form would not have written parts specifically for an actress who couldn't act. But she was the *star* act, was contracted to play and was popular. Perhaps her audience could forgive her easily. It might also be suggested that casting Nelly in serious parts was Hart's way of taking revenge on her for quitting the company and him. But he also revived the roles in which she was triumphant, so that makes little sense; as does the fact that as actor-manager he would take a share of the profits – so why drive the audience or his star attraction away?

Four days later on 26 August, Pepys went to see the revival of Sir Robert Howard's first play (originally produced on 23 April 1662), *The Surprisal*. Nell played the role of Samira, another serious role: the Hart conspiracy theory gains ground. However, Pepys only commented that it was 'a very mean play' and that there 'was not very much company in the house'. Genest only thought it 'on the whole a moderate piece'.[7] Pepys did not like the play, once recording that *Polichinello*, a puppet show he saw the same day as *The Surprisal* on 8 April 1667, was three times more entertaining than the play. In spite of his dislike Pepys managed to see it several times. Perhaps he hoped it would get better (it didn't). More likely is the reason that theatre-going was a habit with him; a place to see and be seen (he could always ogle the women if nothing else) and, anyway, there was little daily entertainment other than taverns and coffee houses.

He saw it again on Boxing Day of the same year. Unsurprisingly, he was once again irritated by *The Surprisal*: '. . . the actors not pleasing me; and especially Nell's acting of a serious part, which she spoils'. Just for the record, he saw it one more time (17 April 1668) and was dispirited by the 'base singing' – except Knepp's naturally (who played Emilia). He did, however, spend two shillings on oranges – so maybe Orange Moll had a good day.

Downes tells us that Nelly played Panthea in Beaumont and Fletcher's *A King and No King*, and it was in a revival of this in September 1667 that she had her next assignment. It was a popular play and was later accorded the respect of the time by being duly parodied by Nahum Tate's *A Duke and No Duke* in 1684. Although there is nothing left us about Nelly's performance, her next part brought her back to top form – speaking the epilogue in *The Great Favourite, or The Duke of Lerma*. But by the time the company presented this play, Nelly's circumstances had changed, and would soon change further: for the better and for ever.

As the pages closed on another year, Nelly was opening up a new chapter on her love life. Coincidentally, as she learnt her lines for *The Great Favourite*, a play that Pepys would think, perhaps reading too rnuch into it, was an indictment of the king's fondness of mistresses, Nelly was about to be added to his list: but unlike all but a few, she *would* become a great favourite. Her career in the public eye had started in the King's Company. And, indeed, it would be in the company of the king that she would continue it for pretty much the rest of her life.

— 10 —

The Acting Mistress

If I'll keep a passion, I'll never starve it in my service.

An Evening's Love, or The Mock Astrologer

(spoken by Nelly's character Jacintha), Dryden, 1671

She's now the darling strumpet of the crowd.

'A Panegyric', anonymous, 1681

A remarkable thing about Restoration England is that very little seems to have happened naturally. Everything required layers of plotting, intrigue, fashioning and complication. The duke of Buckingham was right on the money when he coined the phrase 'the plot thickens upon us'. The getting of Mrs Nelly for the king was no different. Nothing so natural or obvious as having a king with a rampant partiality towards actresses, taking a fancy to the leading actress of the day, arranging a rendezvous, indulging in some pleasurable business, falling in love and sleeping together happily ever after. No chance.

Having fallen out with Barbara Castlemaine, Buckingham set about plotting her downfall or at least engineering a decrease in her influence over Charles. It was well known that the easy-going king could be and was manipulated by his mistresses or by what Clarendon referred to contemptuously as 'petticoat influence'. Pepys recognised this also, fearing that the king was 'only governed by his lust, and women and rogues

Charles II and Nell Gwynne.

Victoria & Albert Museum, London, UK. Ward, Edward Matthew (1816-79). Bridgeman Art Library

Left: **Charles II, 1630-1685.**

Studio of (?) John Michael Wright, c. 1660-1665. © National Portrait Gallery.

Left: **Studio of Peter Lely. Portrait of a Lady, called 'Nell Gwyn'.**

Formerly in the collection of The Sarah Campbell Blaffer Foundation, Houston, Texas.

Left: Barbara Villiers, who married Roger Palmer, Earl of Castlemaine, but who became Duchess of Cleveland as a reward for being Charles II's main mistress in the 1660's. Charles acknowledged paternity of her five children.

From an engraving after a miniature by Samuel Cooper.
© Foto Nationalmuseum

Right: Louise de Kerouaille, Duchess of Portsmouth, 1649-1734.
Pierre Mignard, 1682. © National Portrait Gallery.

Left: Black chalk drawing of Charles II's youngest sister Henriette-Anne ('Minette') as a young girl by Claude Mellan (1598-1688). Minette was possibly the woman that Charles loved the best.

Above: The Theatre Royal (Drury Lane Theatre), London. Designed by Henry Holland, it opened in 1794 and was destroyed by fire in 1809.

Engraving by Matthew C. Wyatt, 1810.

Below: Drury Lane Theatre.

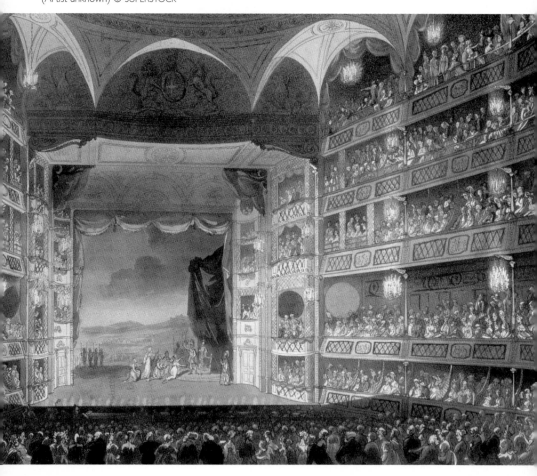

Left: Nell Gwynne's House, 1820, (Pall Mall).
© Mander and Mitchenson Theatre Collection.

Below: Reputed birthplace of Nell Gwynne at Hereford. From a photograph taken in 1858.
© Mander and Mitchenson Theatre

Left: Right profile of Nelly's youngest son, Lord James Beauclerk, by Abraham Blooteling (Bloteling) (1640-1690). James died in Paris, aged 8.

(From The Crofton Croker Collection by kind permission of His Grace the Duke of St Albans.)

Below: Large line engraving by Henri Gascar of Nelly and her sons.

(From The Crofton Croker Collection by kind permission of His Grace the Duke of St Albans.)

Right: Eleanor Gwynne. Mezzotint by Richard Earlom (1742 or 1822), after Samuel Cooper (1609-72). The original portrait dated about 1670 is now thought lost.

(From The Crofton Croker Collection by kind permission of His Grace the Duke of St Albans.)

Below: Nelly and her two sons. This portrait by Henri Gascar has been engraved by Masson, Annan and Swan, E Stodart and anonymously. Charles II can be seen in the background. This mezzotint is by Gascar himself.

(From The Crofton Croker Collection by kind permission of His Grace the Duke of St Albans.)

Nelly as Cupid. This drawing by the miniaturist Peter Cross (c1630-c1716) is surely a copy of the one kept by Samuel Pepys. It is to Cross that Nelly paid £34 for two drawings of her (after Cooper) and one of the king in April 1675. He was also paid £31 out of Nelly's estate following her death.

(From The Crofton Croker Collection by kind permission of His Grace the Duke of St Albans.)

around him'.[1] So, if you want the mind of the king, first command the ear of a mistress. And the best way Buckingham could see to reduce the influence of Barbara was to introduce a rival. He saw Nelly as that rival.

Mistresses needed installing. He would have to persuade the king that he needed another woman (not too difficult a task one imagines) and if it was to be Nelly, compensation for her current noble lover would be needed. As *The Lady of Pleasure* graphically describes:

> Damn me, quoth Buckingham, in duty bound,
> Am I to give your kingship counsel sound:
> I wonder you should dote so, like a fop
> On Cleveland's cunt which all her footmen grope:[2]
> D'you think you don't your parliament offend
> That all they give, you on a baggage spend;
> Permit me, Sir, to help you to a whore,
> Fuck her but once, you'll ne'er fuck Cleveland more;
> She'll fit you to a hair, all wit, all fire,
> And impudence to your own heart's desire;
> And more than this, Sir, you'll save money by her.
> She's Buckhurst's whore at present, but you know
> When Sovereigns want a whore, that subjects must let go.

There is good evidence, although not conclusive, that Buckhurst was compensated for giving up Nelly to the king. Indeed around this time Buckhurst was sent on royal business to France. He visited three times between July 1669 and July 1670 – once to express Charles's regrets to Louis XIV over the illness of his son, the Dauphin, and twice to take messages to Ralph Montagu, the English ambassador in Paris. Each visit was, in all truth, trivial business ('a sleeveless errand' Dryden called one trip) but prestigious to be the king's envoy none the less. Buckhurst was also appointed a Gentleman of the Bedchamber – not only a prestigious position but one with a lucrative thousand pounds a year to boot. The king also promised him the earldom of Middlesex at the death of Buckhurst's childless uncle. The contemporary *Flagellum Parliamentarian* said that he 'with a good will parted with his play wench, and in gratitude is made one of the Bedchamber'. It also said that he was granted land and was awarded £6,000 'at three several times'.

It might be argued that these appointments, favours and grants were coincidental. But the public clearly thought not. A manuscript held at Oxford University's Bodleian Library lists fee farms that have been granted or sold between 1670 and 1679. Listed for 1672 is Bradbury Manor with directions that the annual rent of £550 be paid to Lord Buckhurst. Interestingly at the bottom of this account sheet is a note written in the same hand as the accounts: 'This rent of 550 pounds I have heard say was granted to the late Earl of Dorset in exchange for the person of Nell Gwinn whom the king had a fancy for and was then kept by his Lordship.'[3]

In June 1671, Buckhurst was granted the land (for 99 years) in Blackfriars where the King's Wardrobe had stood before it was burnt down in the Great Fire (its site is marked today by Wardrobe Place). Originally a fourteenth-century private house it was acquired by Edward III who removed there his ceremonial gowns from the Tower. It held all the clothing needed by all the royal family for all ceremonies: births, weddings, coronations and deaths. Not only was this valuable land for rent but it also had special privileges. For example, it was free from the jurisdiction of the lord mayor and aldermen, and tenants were exempt from taxes and duties. This was but further proof (not that it was needed) to convince the public that Charles was paying Buckhurst off. *The Lady of Pleasure* alleges that Buckhurst himself had demanded the compensation rather than allowing Charles to assuage his guilt:

> This put old Rowley's codpiece in a heat:
> Go, Mrs Knight, (quoth he) and fetch me her straight.
> Soft, quoth Lord Buckhurst, then first pay my score,
> (She's cost me many a pound) then take the whore.
> Old Rowley knew his meaning, and to lay his itch
> Gave him an earldom to resign the bitch.
> For such was his indulgence to his tarse
> To please his pintle, he would give his arse.[4]

If, indeed, Charles did pay Buckhurst off, it certainly cost him a penny as pretty as Nelly herself. Clearly he felt she was worth it.

Unlike Buckhurst, however, once Nelly became his mistress the king did not take her off the stage straightaway. Indeed, she needed her job to pay her way: the only thing Charles paid her was attention. And in any case only established mistresses were permitted to untie the purse strings. This would set a pattern for their lives together. True to

Buckingham's alleged prediction that he would save money by her, Nelly would never cost him as much as any of his other main mistresses. They learnt that Charles would almost always give in to demands and, although unquestionably generous, he would rarely do anything of his own choosing. So they demanded and he gave. Nelly asked for little (early on) and got exactly that.

There are no reliable records detailing salaries paid to actors and actresses. However, with the possible exception of those actor-managers who also took a share of profits, it was a poorly paid job, particularly so for those on the fringes of the Company. The records of the lord chamberlain throw up many examples of petitions for recovery of debts being made against not only actors and actresses, but also other theatre staff – carpenters, scenekeepers and casual staff. Debts being petitioned for were from as little as £3. The lord chamberlain, in a sensible attempt to prevent people being thrown into debtors' prison, would order the repayment of debts by paying a few shillings a week. Two actors, who would be leading men of the stage, Jo Haines and Cardell Goodman, were frequently petitioned for debt.

Goodman's poverty was such that not only was he forced to share a bed with another actor 'for reasons of economy', but that they only had one shirt between them' and had to plan their assignations with the fairer sex on alternate nights.[5] Goodman was even arrested for highway robbery, although was pardoned. Thomas Clarke, another actor from the King's Company, was, in July 1667, named as being party to the holding up of the York coach.

In February 1667, Thomas Killigrew, playing gloriously to his eager audience, told Pepys that his friend Mary Knepp 'is like to make the best actor that ever came upon the stage' and that he is to give her an extra £30 a year. We don't know what percentage an increase this amounted to, but it would probably have been substantial. That Nelly would have deserted the stage for £100 a year suggests that they would be fortunate to make half that a year. Cibber tells us of his own experience, which we can safely assume to be the norm. The first three to six months at the theatre were spent serving an apprenticeship for which no payment was received. After nine months pay would begin at 10s. a week. In 1695, Cibber, who at that time was 24, was on 30s. a week. He was no leading actor and thus received £78 a year (equivalent today of about £6,000 a year). So we can assume that 30 years earlier, people were earning even less. Haines at his height was on 50s. a week (£10,000 a year today). Even Charles Hart, one of the theatre's legendary leading men, on his retirement was only awarded a half-pay pension of 40s. a week (£152 a week today).[6]

However, some undoubtedly did make good money from the stage. Certainly those with profit-sharing status would have been more comfortable. The comedian James Nokes seems to have made a substantial living, but may have had the additional income from owning a toy shop. *The Protestant Mercury*, dated 9 September 1696, reported that 'Last night dyed Mr Noaks, the famous comedian, some miles out of town, and 'tis said has left a considerable estate, tho' he has not frequented the playhouse constantly for some years.' He estate was thought to be about £1,500 (about £108,000 today). Also, Thomas Betterton, in his *History of the English Stage*, commented that Edward Kynaston, one of the last boy-players of female roles, 'acquired a handsome fortune by the stage'. He no doubt supplemented his actor's salary early on when it became fashionable for the well-to-do ladies about town to take the young Kynaston in his petticoats and drive about the park showing him off after the play. However, despite the occasional success story, the stage was not, in itself, the best place to make your fortune.

An amusing (although, as with many of them, probably apocryphal) anecdote recounted in the historically unsafe *Fairburn's Edition of the Life, Amours & Exploits of Nell Gwin, the Fortunate Orange Girl* has Charles and Nell on their first date. He has taken a fancy to her at a play and has organised to meet her in a tavern for dinner afterwards. Unfortunately, she has a male companion, Charles Villiers, so the king brings along his brother James, duke of York, to distract Villiers while he concentrates on Nelly. The king and the duke are disguised. By the end of the evening, the barkeeper has come over to the party to seek settlement of the bill, not recognising the well disguised six-foot-plus royal brothers. Nelly naturally looks to the king to pay the bill, as he had invited her out. Charles, who carries no money then looks to James, who is carrying some money but not enough. They both then look to the hapless Villiers who has to pay the bill. 'Oddsfish!' cries Nelly, 'sure this is the poorest company that I ever kept in a tavern!'

On 11 January 1668, Pepys is informed by Mary Knepp that 'the king did send several times for Nelly, and she was with him'. But Pepys worries that he 'can hope no good for the state from having a prince so devoted to his pleasure'.

And devoted to pleasure he was. Without taking into account his main, long-term mistresses or even the hundreds of liaisons that began and ended at the backstairs courtesy of the Chiffinch procurement services, Charles built up an impressive list of minor mistresses, many of whom were actresses. These included Moll Davies, Elizabeth Farley, Elizabeth Weaver, Beck Marshall and the singer Anna Maria Knight (soon to be out of tune with Charles). Away from the stage a fertile seam was mined in the queen's household appointments. This included a maid of honour to the queen, Winifred Wells, who walked like a goddess but had sheepish looks that 'gave but a bad opinion of her wit: and her wit had the ill-luck to make good that opinion'.[7] No such problems for Nelly. Indeed, although very attractive, it was her sharp mind and wit that set her apart from the crowd (for that is what they were) of minor mistresses. Charles knew who to send for if he was feeling down in the dumps.

A good example of the wit that would cause a royal chuckle was the name she gave him. Because her two previous lovers were called Charles (Hart and Sackville) she called the king 'my Charles III'. The French ambassador at Charles's court, Colbert de Croissy, so enjoyed the sparkle of Nelly's 'buffooneries' that he wrote to the secretary of state Lionne saying how the king's spirits would rise when he was with Nelly compared with his yawning in the presence of Lady Castlemaine.[8] Although Nelly's destiny would see her as a main mistress, she still had some work to do: both off the stage and on.

In *The Great Favourite, or The Duke of Lerma*, she played Donna Maria, the script directions required that the prologue and epilogue be 'spoken by Mrs Ellen'. In fact she spoke the prologue with Mary Knepp, but did the epilogue alone. She turned their delivery into an art form and succeeded in making them entertainments in their own right. Prologues and epilogues were sweet to the taste of the times and provoked much animated expectation. If the play was not up to much at least you could look forward to the epilogue.

The epilogue to *The Great Favourite, or Duke of Lerma* confirms her and her audience's preference for comedy:

> I know you in your hearts
> Hate serious plays – as I hate serious parts –
> To trouble us with thoughts and state designs,
> A melancholy plot tied with strong lines!

I had not the least part today, you see;
Troth, he has neither writ for you nor me.

Although licensed to their theatres, the companies would also regularly perform at Whitehall for the court. On 4 February 1668, Evelyn records that he saw a production of the tragedy *Horace*, as adapted by 'the virtuous' Kathleen Phillips. However, it was the women in the select audience that grabbed the attention with all their finery.

Such riches bestowed on the king's mistresses must have seemed the stuff of fairy tales for the down-to-earth Nelly. Although sent for with increasing regularity, she still had to work outside the king's bedchamber for her money. On 7 May 1668, Pepys called at the King's House to collect Mary Knepp after the play (he had actually watched *The Man's the Master* at the Duke's House that day). He, as ever, enjoyed himself backstage:

> I did see Beck Marshall come dressed, off of the stage, and looking mighty fine, and pretty, and noble; and also, Nell, in her boy's clothes, mighty pretty. But, Lord! their confidence! and how many men do hover about them as soon as they come off the stage, and how confident they are in their talk.

Confidence was not something lacking in Nelly's character. Around this time the king's mistress actress Moll Davies was showing off the ring the king had given her, valued at £600–£700. Nelly, realising that the ring signified that Moll was more in favour than her, sought her stage rival's downfall with a devious plan. Nell invited Moll to her lodgings to inspect the ring, knowing that Moll was to be with the king that night. She prepared some sweetmeats (sugared cakes) which she had carefully laced with jalap – a potent laxative that has been used to purge elephants. Needless to say, Moll's evening assignation with the king did not go how either of them had planned. From that night on Moll's ascendancy crashed down the pan.

Back on stage, Nelly's next assignment was in *The Mulberry Garden* (originally named *The Wandering Ladies*), the first play by Sir Charles Sedley. Sedley's mistress at that time was probably the actress Peg Fryer who had just moved from the duke's to the King's House. It may well be that this link secured Sedley's 'long expected' play for that house. Pepys saw its opening performance on 18 May 1668. The house was 'infinitely full' and expectation high because Sedley was 'so reputed a wit, all the world do expect great matters'. However, Pepys was most disappointed, noting that the house hardly laughed and the king not once, 'insomuch that I have not been less pleased at a new play in my life, I think'. Pepys went to see it again two days later but still couldn't 'reconcile' himself to it. However, it did induce him to visit the actual Mulberry Garden but he found that as disappointing as Sedley's work – 'a very silly place' he concludes, although he does revisit the place at least twice. We have no notice of Nelly nor are we sure which role she played. Some biographers have suggested the character Victoria, but this was played by Mary Knepp. This we know from Pepys who watched her practise a song which was sung by Victoria in the play.

Next up for Nelly-was the role of Bellario opposite her ex-lover Charles Hart's title role in Beaumont and Fletcher's popular *Philaster, or Love Lies a Bleeding*. Langbaine comments that it 'has always been acted with success: and has been the diversion of the stage, even in these days [1691].' Pepys had seen the November 1661 production of this stock romantic tragi-comedy, but he 'found it far short of my expectations'. He saw the revival on 30 May 1668, but only commented how pleased he was that he could remember all the lines of the character Arethusa (played by one of the Marshall sisters) which he was to have played as a boy 'but more to think what a ridiculous thing it would have been for me to have acted as a beautiful woman'. The play would be later adapted by the duke of Buckingham, who had successfully adapted another of Fletcher's plays – *The Chances*.

Nelly and Hart were, once again, triumphant together – no doubt all the more explosive given their past and present liaisons. The play was revived in 1695 having been adapted by Elkanah Settle. The prologue, written by Hildebrand Horden, refers to the 1668 production:

> That good old play, Philaster, ne're can fail,
> But we young actors, how shall we prevail?
> Philaster and Bellario, let me tell ye,
> For those bold parts we have no Hart, no Nelly,
> Those darlings of the stage that charmed you there.

Dryden provided Nelly with her next role in his *An Evening's Love, or The Mock Astrologer* which opened in June 1668. Pepys's wife, Elizabeth, saw the play on 19 June, and again, this time with her husband, the next day. Although 'the world commends' the play, Elizabeth didn't like it, and Samuel agreed, finding it 'very smutty'. He compares it unfavourably to those other works 'of Dryden's making' *The Maiden Queen* and *The Indian Emperor*. He was to see the play often, but would still consider it 'ordinary'. If Pepys found it smutty, it's little wonder that the righteous Evelyn, who was not a real fan of the theatre at the best of times and who also saw it on 19 June, thought it irreverant: 'a foolish plot,' he writes, 'and very profane, so as it afflicted me to see how the stage was degenerated and polluted by the licentious times.'

This play provides a very racy piece of dialogue between Nelly's character Jacintha and Wildblood, played by Hart, the pertinence of which would not be lost between the protagonists or the audience.

> *Wildblood:* Then what is a gentleman to hope from you?
>
> *Jacintha:* To be admitted to pass my time with him while a better comes; to be the lowest step in my staircase, for a knight to mount upon him, and a lord upon him, and a marquis upon him, and a duke upon him, till I get as high as I can climb.

Richard Flecknoe provided Nelly with her next role. He wrote the character of Lysette in *Damoyselles à la Mode* which, as we've already seen, sank quicker than a Dutch ship in the North Sea. Flecknoe, though, was a keen admirer of Nell. Not content with writing a truly awful part for her, he wrote her a truly awful poem also. He lovingly entitled it 'On a Pretty Little Person' and gushed:

> She is pretty, and she knows it;
> She is witty, and she shows it;
> And besides that she's so witty,
> And so little and so pretty,
> She has a hundred other parts
> For to take and conquer hearts.
> 'Mongst the rest her air's so sprightful,
> And so pleasant and delightful,
> With such charms and such attractions
> In her words and in her actions,
> As whoe'er do hear and see,

Say there's none to do but she.
But who have her in their arms,
Say sh'has hundred other charms,
And as many more attractions
In her words and in her actions.
But for that, suffice to tell ye,
'Tis the little pretty Nelly.

The next new production involving Nelly would not open until 18 December 1668 in the revival of Ben Jonson's *Catiline his Conspiracy*. Hart took the lead (in which he was to be 'universally applauded'), but there was no part for Nelly. She may well have been dropped from the cast because it was a tragedy. She would, however, delight the audience with what was becoming her trademark speciality: as an appetiser for the audience the play began with a prologue 'Merrily spoken by Mrs Nell in an Amazonian habit', which consisted of 'a crested helmet, a belted tunic, cut short above her bare knees, buskins, and a bow and quiver full of arrows slung over one shoulder.'[9] Nelly was to have the last word for she delivered the epilogue also.

The prologue sends up the play and the playwright's snobbery (Jonson generally thought all his contemporaries, except Shakespeare, were uneducated hacks). It hopes that the play will appeal to all and, while recognising that the educated will appreciate the inspiring poetry, it's bums on seats that matters for the House:

Which, if they prove the greatest number, then
The House hath cause to thank Nell more than Ben;
Our author might prefer your praise perhaps,
We'd rather have your money than your claps.

There had been talk about putting the play on a year or so previously, but the company needed costumes which the king had promised but had failed to provide. Even though he adored the theatre, the players suffered quietly and equally with everyone else from the king's tendency to promise to attend to something in a due course that simply didn't exist. His promises were often as empty as his treasury.

Pepys saw *Catiline his Conspiracy* on the second day of its opening run. As usual, on these occasions, the theatre was full (and one reason why the management charge double for the opening three days). Pepys, unable to get to his usual seat – 'the pit being full' – has to pay extra for a box. This extravagance is offset by having the actress Betty Hall, the playwright Sir Robert Howard's mistress, sit next to him. This pleases him: 'a mighty pretty wench,' he thinks. But decides, shrewdly for once, not to commend Hall's looks to his wife. The players finally got their costumes (£500 was granted by the king, which was partly spent on 16 scarlet robes) and Pepys comments positively on their fine clothes.

There is a view that this tragedy was encouraged upon the company by people like Buckingham and Buckhurst who had declared themselves the enemy of the heroic drama (as championed by Dryden). They felt that if people saw 'proper' tragedy it would act as the catalyst to drive the pomposity and extravagance of rhyming heroism from the stage for ever. Buckingham would bring his campaign to a glorious finale in December 1671 in the shape of his satirical play *The Rehearsal*. Some years in the writing, the play satirises the heroic drama. The playwright, Bayes, is based on Dryden, who had become poet laureate (who wears the bays – hence the name). Buckingham himself coached John Lacy to move and speak like Dryden who had a notoriously poor, stilted and nervous reading voice. Bayes was even dressed in all black – just like Dryden. Although *The Rehearsal* and *Catiline* were hugely successful, if the ultimate aim was to rid the theatres of the heroic drama then it failed miserably. Dryden would also exact revenge on Buckingham. In his epic poem 'Absalom and Achitophel', he cast his grace as Zimri:

> Some of their chiefs were princes of the land;
> In the first rank of these Zimri did stand:
> A man so various, he seemed to be
> Not one, but all mankind's epitome.
> Stiff in opinions, always in the wrong;
> Was everything by starts, and nothing long:
> But, in the course of one revolving moon,
> Was chemist, fiddler, statesman and buffoon.

We know that Nelly also appeared in a revival of *The Sisters*, a comedy by James Shirley (1596–1666). Shirley, who died of exposure during the Great Fire, was popular with Restoration audiences. We can be no more precise about the dates of performance other than that they occurred between 1668 and 1671. A prompt book from the time has survived, complete with some interesting stage directions. We know that Nelly was in the cast, because the prompter, Charles Booth, noted in the margins 'Ellen', 'Mrs Ellen' or 'Mrs Nelle' when she was required on stage. Again showing for Nelly that her first name – in whatever format – was enough.

After a glut of roles in the summer of 1668, Nelly's new roles were decreasing. Perhaps the management feared she would soon be departing to become a full-time mistress to the king and did not want the hassle of replacing her in new roles once she had left. It is noticeable that her last two original roles were written specially for her by Dryden.

Nelly might well have been spending less time on the boards, but she was still never far from the theatre. Pepys saw her at the King's House watching John Fletcher's tragi-comedy *The Island Princess* on 7 January 1669. Interestingly, his tone towards her is cool, reflecting his unease at her exalted status of mistress (thereby being one of the pleasures keeping the king from his duty'. 'We sat in an upper box,' he wrote, 'and the jade Nell came and sat in the next box: a bold, merry slut, who lay laughing there upon people, and with a comrade of hers of the Duke's House, that came to see the play.'

By this time, Nelly's year-long status as mistress was rewarded with a move to lodgings in the more fashionable Lincoln's Inn Fields, the largest square in London. Lincoln's Inn is one of the four inns of court (the others being Middle Temple, Inner Temple and Gray's). William Newton, with the permission of Charles I, had built 32 houses by 1641. The Society of Lincoln's Inn objected but managed with Newton's agreement to secure that most of the fields should 'forever and hereafter be open and unbuilt'.[10] However, for all its modish qualities it retained a reputation for duelling and robberies.

The square was also used as an occasional place of execution, as William, Lord Russell, would find out in 1683, losing his head for his part in the Rye House Plot (a plaque today marks the spot where he was executed). None the less, as well as Nelly, Lincoln's Inn Fields was home to among others the second and third lords Coventry, and Edward Montagu, first earl of Sandwich who had 'a fine house but deadly dear'[11] whose rent in 1664 was £250 a year (about £19,000 a year today).

By the time Nelly's next new role appeared on stage she had been the king's mistress for about 18 months. She took the part of Valeria in Dryden's *Tyrannick Love, or the Royal Martyr*. She has sometimes been accorded the role of Saint Catherine, but this was played originally by Peg Hughes and later by Mrs Boutell. Despite some delays caused by a legal dispute between the company and Isaac Fuller 'painter and one who sometimes did apply himself for painting of scenes',[12] concerning the date for delivery of the scenery, the play made it to the King's House about 23 June 1669. It was a huge success, running for 14 days consecutively in its opening run. It was to remain in the company's repertory until 1702.

Dryden dedicated the play to James Crofts, the duke of Monmouth, Charles II's eldest acknowledged natural son.[13] He had also dedicated his earlier play *The Indian Emperor* to Monmouth's wife. Little was Dryden, the king's playwright, to know that within a couple of months or so, his favourite actress would be carrying another natural son of the king.

The end of the play caused a sensation. Nelly's Valeria, a Roman princess who, in doing the tragically decent thing, stabs herself to death in the final act. To a hushed house she was picked up and carried off. However, before she was taken off stage, she suddenly, and to tumultuous acclaim, leapt up and berated the person carrying her off:

> Hold! Are you mad, you damn'd confounded dog!
> I am to rise to speak the epilogue!

And that was what she proceeded to do. The audience were in the palm of her hand, as she continued:

> I come, kind gentleman, strange news to tell ye,
> I am the ghost of the poor, departed Nelly.
> Sweet ladies, be not frightened, I'll be civil,
> I'm what I was, a harmless little devil.
> For, after death, we sprites have just such natures,
> We had for all the world, when human creatures;
> And therefore I that was an actress here,
> Play all my tricks in hell, a goblin there.
> Gallants look to it, you say there are no sprites,
> But I'll come dance about your beds at nights.

Once again the epilogue then gives her a chance to reflect on her playing of serious parts:

And faith you'll be in a sweet kind of taking,
When I surprise you between sleep and waking.
To tell you true, I walk because I die
Out of my calling in a tragedy.
O poet! damned dull poet, who could prove
So senseless, to make Nelly die for love,
Nay, what's yet worse, to kill me in the prime
Of Easter-term, in tart and cheesecake time!

The last two lines given above provide evidence that the play was meant to open earlier in April. However, the deceased Nelly knocks the audience dead with the epilogue's end lines:

As for my epitaph when I am gone,
I will trust no poet, but will write my own:
Here Nelly lies, who, though lived a slattern
Yet died a princess acting in St Cathar'n.

The play seemingly changed its name late on with Dryden preferring *Tyrannick Love* to *St Catherine*. The legal dispute with Fuller, the scenery painter, refers to the play as 'a new play or tragedy called *The Royal Martyr, or St Catherine.*' William Oldys, in Curll's *History of the Stage*, asserts that the king was so pleased with Nelly's delivery of this epilogue that he went backstage and whisked her off to supper before whisking her off to his bedchamber for the first time. Apart from there being entirely too much whisking in one night, Nelly, as we know, had long been the king's mistress by this time.

Bringing back Nelly from the dead proved so inspirational that it was used in other plays. A contemporary epilogue ran:

It is a trick of late grown much in vogue
When all are killed, to raise an epilogue.
This some pert rhymer wittily contrived
For a surprise, whilst the arch wag believed
'Twould please you to see Pretty Miss revived.[14]

Valeria would be Nell's last original role for 18 months. By the time she originated her next, and last, role for the stage she would no longer simply be the king's mistress: she would also be the mother of his son.

— 11 —

Pregnant Pause

The sculpter's part is done, the features hitt,
Of Madam Gwin, no arte can shew her witt.

Inscription beneath an engraving of Nell Gwynne by G Vlack

On 8 May 1670, Nelly gave birth to her first son. The diarist Anthony à
Wood writing in Oxford errs by a week when he records that '[a]bout the
14 or 15 [of May], Elianor Quin, one that belongs to the King's play
hous, was brought to bed of a boy in her house in Lyncoln's Inns feilds,
next to Whetstones Park – the King's bastard.'[1] Charles acknowledged
the child straightaway. The boy was called Charles, the third of the king's
natural sons to be so called: Charles Fitzcharles (*c*. 1650–80), was his son
by Catherine Pegge; while Charles Fitzroy, was Barbara Castlemaine's
first son.

We can imagine that it would have been the last thing on her mind,
being tearfully happy and deliriously in love, but Nelly's status was now
secure: financially, at least. As mother of the king's child neither she nor
her son, as long as the king lived, would starve. The king doted on his
children and he always looked after them. Poverty would now be
something that happened to other people.

However, at this time, although being kept up to date with the
developments of mother and baby, it was another woman that Charles
had on his mind: a woman, perhaps, whom he loved best of all. He was

to travel to Dover to meet his youngest sister, Henriette-Anne: his Minette.

Born in 1644, she was 14 years younger than Charles. Charles was the second son; the first son, also called Charles, was born and died in 1629. The family's other siblings included Mary (1631–60); James (1633–1701); Elizabeth (1635–50); Anne (1637–40); Catherine (born and died 1639); Henry (1640–60). The year 1660 was clearly one of mixed emotions for the royal family: they reclaimed the throne but the year claimed two of their lives.

Minette had not returned to England immediately on Charles's Restoration; staying on in France with her mother, but did cross the Channel six months later. The dowager queen, Henrietta Maria, had no stomach for London – the city in which her husband was executed. In exile and poor, Minette had not been able to find a husband. However, the events of 1660 changed all that. Suddenly this sweet, charming and attractive (if a little thin) young woman was a most fine prospect for a suitor. Madam Lafayette said that Minette had 'a pair of black eyes that burned with a flame so hot that no man could look into them without taking fire.'[2] Her mother had hoped she would marry Louis XIV, but this was denied, despite their undoubted affection. However, Louis's brother, Phillipe, duc d'Orleans, known at court as 'Monsieur', was a more politically agreeable match – although a sexually disagreeable one. They married in the spring of 1661, but Monsieur did not love his wife, preferring as he did the company of other monsieurs, most notably the Chevalier de Lorraine.

With her daughter's match completed, the queen dowager, despite her feelings for London, compelled herself to visit on hearing reports from England that her eldest son was cavorting openly with Barbara Villiers, and that her second son had married in private the heavily pregnant Anne Hyde. 'I go tomorrow for England,' she growled, 'to marry my son the king and try to unmarry the other.' Despite the low-key visit, for fear that the arrival of Charles I's French queen would incite riots, Pepys tried to watch the landing at the Thames. He hired a sculler for 6d. but 'could not get a look at the queen'. When he managed to see her three weeks later he was not impressed: 'a very little, very plain old woman'. He was more taken with Minette though, but not greatly: 'The Princess Henrietta is very pretty,' he concedes, but adds cautiously, 'but much below expectation; and her dressing of herself with her hair frizzed short up to her ears did make her seem so much the less to me.' He thought his own wife was 'much more handsomer than she.'[3]

Ten years later, Minette was still very thin – perhaps unhealthily so. Louis XIV once called her 'the bones of the Holy Innocents'.[4] But Charles was happy just to see her, just to hold her. And she would be home for his fortieth birthday. Everything seemed perfect.

Minette sailed over from Dunkirk with the vice-admiral of England who tells us that on arrival the king 'came on board us and carried Madam ashore to Dover'.[5] The 237-strong French entourage included one person who was to play a major role in Nelly's life. This openly royal visit had nothing discreet attached to it: save for its real purpose. The small business of a big family reunion, although genuine, was also a cover for a secret treaty. So secret that Charles did not even trust his prime minister, Buckingham, with the details. Indeed, Charles even sent him into France to negotiate a bogus treaty to keep him away from the real discussions.[6]

Charles clearly trusted his four co-signatories: Henry Bennet (earl of Arlington), Sir Thomas Clifford, Henry Arundel and Sir Richard Bellings. The treaty was a dangerous undertaking. Charles was to receive two million livres a year from Louis XIV, which he believed to be about £200,000. However, he miscalculated the exchange rates as it was nearer £180,000 (or about £13.7 million in today's money). In reality, he would receive annually about two-thirds of that amount. In return, Charles agreed to remain neutral while France annexed lands to its empire and fought Spain and the United Provinces (Holland); to convert himself to Catholicism; and to convert England back to the faith also.

Charles was desperate to be financially independent of Parliament. The trustworthy and dependable William Chiffinch would be treasurer of the French money. His accounts show that between 18 February 1671 and 13 November 1677 he had administered £689,750 (some £52.5 million today). However, Charles's annual deficit was some £400,000, so an average yearly payment of just under £124,000 would clearly not make him wholly independent of Parliament. Of that total money less than five per cent (£33,591.10s.) was accounted 'for his Majesty's own hands and to sundry persons for gratuities and other secret services'.[7]

The conditions attached to the treaty regarding Catholicism would not have caused much loss of sleep in the royal bedchamber. Charles was very easy and tolerant towards religion. However, as defender of the faith his attitude contrasted starkly with the intolerance of the faithful who saw nothing venial in the mortal enemy Catholicism. And yet Charles had an understandable soft spot for Catholics: after all, it was English Catholics who had helped him escape after the Battle of Worcester. He may well have had Catholic sympathies (evidenced, perhaps, by his deathbed conversion) but he was too wily and streetwise to do anything but play the games that needed playing. Charles was, after all, not a man of his word: he would say whatever he had to say to get to the next business and say whatever he had to say again. That was the man. He didn't want to offend or upset people: he wanted to be liked. He might well have been sincere about meeting all the conditions for his money, but he wouldn't worry too much if none of them actually happened.

Delighted at seeing his sister again, he persuaded her to stay longer than originally intended. He organised plenty of entertainment – much of it at sea, and trips to Canterbury, where plays were performed. A contemporary newsletter reported on 28 May 1670 that 'the court... continues at dover till wensday next... There is the greatest gallantry and mirth imaginable. The Duke's players have been there all the time past came up yesterday and the Kings goe downe this day.' Downes confirms that the Duke's 'Company were commanded to Dover, May 1670. The King with all his court, meeting his sister, the Dutchess of *Orleans* there. This comedy [*The Sullen Lovers*] and *Sir Solomon Single* pleased Madam Dutchess and the whole court extremely.'[8]

The duke's players included James Nokes, the top-notch comedian, who had that timeless ability to bring the house down by just walking on to the stage or fixing the audience with one of his looks. Cibber described his 'silent perplexity (which would sometimes hold him several minutes) gave your imagination as full content as the most absurd thing he could say.' Nokes was, continued Cibber, 'an actor of quite different genius from any I have ever read, heard of, or seen, since or before his time'. On his arrival at Dover he was confronted with Minette's entourage and their, well, frankly, French fashions. Always, as ever, the French being more adventurous in their dress, Nokes was deeply amused at the men's short jackets and wide belts, and the female penchant for wide-brimmed hats. It gave him an idea. He sent up their fashions wearing a large brimmed hat, short jacket and huge waist belt. The duke of Monmouth so enjoyed the prospect of the send-up that he gave 'Nokes his sword and belt from his side, and buckled it on himself, on purpose to ape the

French... which on first entrance on the stage put the King and court to an excessive laughter: at which the French looked very shaggrin, to see themselves aped by such a buffoon...' Nokes, we're told, kept Monmouth's sword until his dying day.

With the visit over and the treaty complete, Charles and Minette said their emotional goodbyes. Charles gave Minette a number of personal presents. Minette, returning the compliment, asked if out of her collection would Charles care to select a jewel? Typically, Charles asked if he could have just the one jewel: a young, baby-faced maid of honour who had taken his ever-roving eye. Minette refused her brother saying that she had responsibility for her and had promised the young woman's parents that she would bring her home safely. However, thwarted as he was at this time, his disappointment was to be but temporary. Louise Renée de Penancoet de Keroualle would soon seize a sizeable chunk of his ever-softening heart and mould it in her hands for the rest of his life.

Charles was truly distraught at Minette's leaving. He boarded her ship and three times a tearful Charles said goodbye only to come back again and hug her. Colbert de Croissy wrote how touched he was that the easy-going monarch was capable of such affection:

> It has appeared during her stay at Dover that she has much more power over the King her brother than any other person in the world, not only by the eagerness the other ministers have shown to implore her favour and support with the king and by the favours he has accorded simply at her request... but also by the king's own confession and the tears he shed on bidding her farewell.[9]

Little could Charles have suspected that his goodbye to Minette would be so permanent. For, on 30 June 1670, the king received the devastating news that his beloved sister was dead. She was 26 years old. Suspicions circulated very quickly that she had been poisoned – with her husband's gay lover, Chevalier de Lorraine, the prime suspect. Charles also carried similar suspicions at first. However, Minette had been ill for some time and studies of her post-mortem suggest strongly that she died of acute peritonitis caused by the perforation of a duodenal ulcer.

Charles was overwhelmed with grief. The earl of Rochester wrote to his wife that 'the king endures the highest affliction imaginable'. Colbert de Croissy wrote on 2 July 1670 that 'the grief of the king of England is deeper than can be imagined'. The whole country went into mourning.

The theatres closed. An entry in the Bulstrode papers reads that 'the playes are silenced dureing this tyme of sadness'.

The French feared that the death of 'Madame' – as Minette was known to them – would also be the death of the secret treaty (which became known as 'Traite de Madame'). However, the Sun King rose to the challenge and arranged for Louise de Keroualle to be sent to England to help ease Charles's grief and strengthen his resolve to the treaty. It was an inspired move. At Minette's funeral sermon (Charles did not attend), Boussuet said: 'The worthy link which bound the two greatest monarchs of the earth was broken, but now is soldered up again.'[10] However, if Louise thought she could solder herself to Charles at the expense of everyone else, she hadn't reckoned on his touring libido or his affection for others. She came to solder, but she would soon be playing with fire as red as the hair of a certain actress.

— 12 —

The Final Call

But there's no mercy for a guilty muse:
For, like a mistress she must stand or fall
And please you to a height or not at all.

Epilogue to *An Evening's Love, or The Mock Astrologer*
(the last words spoken by Nelly on the stage), Dryden, 1671

Nelly was not the only actress to have fallen for royal blood. Margaret 'Peg' Hughes had met and become mistress of the king's cousin Prince Rupert of the Rhine at Tunbridge Wells in 1668. Born in Prague in 1619, the impetuous and good-looking Rupert was riddled with panache. At just 23 he arrived in England to fight for his uncle, Charles I, in the Civil War. He was, as Sir Philip Warwick wrote of him at the time, 'a brave prince and a hopeful soldier'.[1] Even approaching 50 he was still a commanding presence. Rupert bought a house for Peg (Brandenburgh House, Hammersmith) in 1673, the year that their daughter, Ruperta, was born. He also had his own town house in Spring Gardens, near St James's Park. But following his appointment by Charles II, in 1668, as governor and constable of Windsor Castle, he made the castle his permanent home. Thus Nelly would invariably meet up with Peg when the court moved to Windsor – as, of course, it did often.

The summer of 1670 was one such time but the Windsor laughter soon gave way to tragedy. A duel was fought which left Peg's brother (who worked for Rupert) dead. The dispute was over the two actresses.

A letter dated 20 June 1670 from Lady Chalworth to her brother Lord Roos at Belvoir Castle comments on the incident. She writes that 'One of the k[ing's] servants hath killed Mr Hues, Peg Hues' brother, servant to P[rince] Robert [Rupert] upon a dispute whether Mistress Nelly or she was the handsomer now at Windsor.'[2]

This wasn't to affect their friendship adversely. Indeed Rupert would harbour hopes that his daughter might one day marry Nelly's son. The *Verney MSS* reveal that 'some say he sent his garter to the king, desiring that [Nelly's son] might have it with his daughter by Peg Hughes…'

Rupert also gave Peg a necklace of 'fifty pearls evenly matched', which had probably been a family heirloom. Rupert died on 29 November 1681; he was 62 years old. He left his estate equally to 'Margaret Hewes and…Ruperta, my naturall daughter begotten on the bodie of said Margaret Hewes…' However, mainly because of his generosity towards Peg he left many debts. Peg gambled away what was left of the estate and had to sell her jewellery – including the necklace – to clear his (and her) debts. She sold the necklace to Nelly in 1682. In accounts published in the appendix to Warburton's *Prince Rupert and the Cavaliers*, it is recorded that £4,520 was 'Received of Mrs Ellen Gwynne for the great pearl necklace'. That is the equivalent today of about £344,000. Their stage poverty was clearly behind them, although Peg had continued to act through the 1670s.

There are at least two portraits of Nelly posing with this necklace. Identifying genuine portraits of Nelly, as we will see later, is a hazardous game. However, one thought to have been painted in 1670 by Simon Verelst (1644–1710) hangs in the National Portrait Gallery. Nelly, a pretty, rounded face, sensual eyes seemingly a fraction closed, a very kissable full bottom lip, and lots of reddish hair worn up, is wearing a loose smock that teasingly exposes the top of her left nipple. She is also wearing the necklace: it being identical to the one worn by Peg Hughes in her portrait. However, as Nelly did not own the necklace until 12 years after the supposed date of this portrait, this presents one of two possibilities: the date of the portrait is wrong (which may not be the case given Nelly's youthful looking face); or that Nelly simply borrowed the necklace to pose in. It would suggest that she fell in love with it, and thus, when it became available, who else would her friend Peg turn to? It must have been hard enough to sell it (as there's every reason to believe that Peg genuinely loved Rupert), but selling it to a friend must have softened the anguish – as, indeed, must have the price it fetched.

Another of Nelly's supposed portraits is dated about 1670 – this time by Sir Peter Lely. However, the long-held belief that this was indeed Nelly has been seriously questioned. Another portrait of Nelly by Verelst (also dated *c*. 1670) shows her in seductive, reclining pose with her top opened down to her waist exposing her breasts. As with the other Verelst, this shows a similar pretty, slight chubby face, full bottom lip, and lots of hair (this time worn down). Both pictures depict the sitter at about the same age – so could both well have painted the same year. What is more clear, the actress was firmly establishing herself in the affections of the king. Not only did he still spend a lot of time with her, but he wanted to see her face even when she wasn't there. She was now by his side, in his bed and on his wall.

However, she was still an actress and she still had work to do. Dryden had written an epic ten-act two-parter *Almanzor and Almahide or, The Conquest of Granada by the Spaniards* and he wanted no others but Hart and Nelly to play the leading and title roles. It finally made it to the stage in December 1670, with Part Two debuting in January 1671. Indeed, the production had to be delayed while Nelly debuted on the stage maternal. This is referred to in the epilogue of Part One when the usual apology is made for the playwright's inadequacies:

> Think him not duller for this year's delay;
> He was prepared, the women were away;
> And men, without their parts, can hardly play.
> If they, through sickness, seldom did appear,
> Pity the virgins of each theatre:
> For, at both houses 'twas a sickly year!
> And pity us, your servants, to whose cost,
> In one such sickness, nine whole months are lost.

On her first day back at work, Nelly's adoring fans were treated immediately as she delivered her now customary prologue. The effect of Nokes's send-up of French fashions was clearly still tickling the playgoing public. The prologue was to be 'spoken by Mrs Ellen in a broad brim'd hat, and wast belt'. Whereas Nokes gently exaggerated the fashion, Nelly took it to its fullest extent, wearing a hat the size of a cartwheel. Waldon, in his 1789 edition of Downes's *Roscius Anglicanus*, comments that the 'whole theatre was in a convulsion of applause, nay, the very actors giggled, a circumstance none had observed before. Judge, therefore, what a condition the merriest prince alive was at such a conjuncture! 'Twas beyond *odso* or *odsfish*, for he wanted little of being suffocated' with laughter.

This was especially sweet for Nelly as Charles's latest mistress 'the Frenchie' Louise was in for the first performance. And wearing the very fashion being exploited for laughs. She was suitably offended. Nelly was suitably contented. Indeed for a while it gave Louise a new name. The English, caring little for Louise (well, she was French and Catholic, after all) and finding 'Keroualle' difficult to pronounce, decided to anglicise the pronunciation calling her 'Carwell'. Thanks to Nelly's hat Louise also became known as 'Cartwheel'. Nelly would have a few more choice names for her also.

It was with the subject of that costume that Nelly began the prologue:

> This jest was first of the other house's making,
> And, five times tried, has never failed of taking;
> For 'twere a shame a poet should be killed
> Under the shelter of so broad a shield.
> This is the hat, whose very sight did win ye
> To laugh and clap as though the devil were in ye.
> As then, for Nokes, so now I hope you'll be
> So dull, to laugh once more for love of me.
> I'll write a play, says one, for I have got
> A broad-brimmed hat, and waist-belt, towards a plot.
> Says the other, I have one more large than that.
> Thus they out-write each other with a hat!
> The brims still grew with every play they writ;
> And grew so large, they covered all the wit...
> Thus, two the best comedians of the age
> Must be worn out, with being blocks o' the stage.

Sadly, Pepys who thought he was going blind – he wasn't and didn't – discontinued his diary on 31 May 1669 and therefore we have no review of the performance. Pepys went on to have a successful career as secretary of the Admiralty and also became an MP. He still came into contact with Nelly, organising a yacht for her use on several occasions.[3] His admiration for her wavered little it seems as he kept an engraving of a portrait of her wearing only a pair of angel wings.[4] Pepys died of the stone in 1703 and was buried next to his wife (who had died in 1669) in St Olave's, Hart Street.

The Conquest of Granada was an expensive but successful production. It was still being performed in 1709, after which it dropped out of the theatre's repertory. Although Pepys's diary finished before this play made the stage, Evelyn (whose diary still had 35 years to go) saw the play performed at the Whitehall. The old theatre sceptic notes that he saw 'the famous play, called *The Siege of Granada* two days acted successively: there were indeed very glorious scenes and perspectives, the work of Mr [Robert] Streeter [His Majesty's Sergeant Painter], who well understands it.'[5]

As the part of Almahide, queen of Granada, was written for Nelly, Dryden is able to portray his heroine as a beauty to die for and someone who usually embodies happiness. Almahide's slave, Esperanza, appeals to her queen in the play's first scene:

> Madam, you must not to despair give place;
> Heaven never meant misfortune to that face.

But it was another face, or rather part of one, that scandalised the town around this time. Nelly, an innocent bystander, was implicated in the incident of Coventry's Nose. Sir John Coventry, MP for Weymouth, in a debate in the House of Commons on raising moneys, suggested that a tax should be levied on the playhouses. Opposing the motion, Sir John Birkenhead said that the playhouses had brought great pleasure to the king. Coventry knew, as did everybody, about Charles's relationship with Nelly and other actresses. He replied by questioning whether the king's pleasure lay with the men or the women that acted there. Angered by this remark, supporters of the king exacted the cowardly revenge that was all too common a feature of Restoration London: they (for they were always a few to the target's one) lay in wait and set upon their detractor. Overpowering the MP, they slit his nose.

Furious that their privilege of open speaking had been assaulted in this violent way, Parliament passed what was known as the Coventry Act, or the Coventry Maiming Act. Poet, satirist and civil servant Andrew Marvell in a letter explained:

[whoever] 'after the 16th of February next shall put out the eye, cut the lip, nose or tongue of any of His Majesty's liege people, upon malice aforethought, or in short provocation, shall be guilty of felony without benefit of clergy. And whoever shall in any manner wound or maim any Parliament man, or any of the House of Lords, during their attendance, or their coming or returning from Parliament, shall be imprisoned for a year, pay treble damages, to be assessed by jury, and be deprived and made incapable of all offices whatsoever.

The incident was captured in a ballad ('The Haymarket Hectors'), which has also been attributed to Andrew Marvell, but is too poorly written to have come from his pen. This asserts, somewhat absurdly, that the assault was carried out at the request of 'the comediant' Nelly:

> Our good King Charles the Second, too flippant of treasure and moisture,
> Stooped from the Queen infecund to a wench of orange and oyster;
> Consulting his Catzo, he found it expedient
> To waste his time in revels with *Nell* the comediant.

> Oye Hay-Market Hector, how cam you thus charmed,
> To be dissectors of one poor Nose unarmed?
> Unfit to wear sword, or follow a trumpet,
> That would brandish your knives at the word of a strumpet?

> If the sister of Rose be a whore so anointed
> That the Parliament's Nose for her be disjointed,
> Then should you but name the prerogative whore,
> How the bullets would whistle, the cannons would roar.

However, Nelly was about to retire from the stage and be a *comediant* no more. The acting mistress was about to accept a permanent position. No doubt recalling the outcome of her Epsom adventure nearly four years ago, and the experiences other actresses that had peformed in his majesty's bedchamber, she told the theatre's management that she would be back as soon as the king tired of her. She need not have worried (and probably didn't, to be fair), but even this most lazy of princes would never tire of his Nelly. Nor she of him.

— *13* —

The Road to Pall Mall

Oh bear me to the paths of fair Pell Mell!
Safe are thy pavements, grateful is thy smell.
At distance rolls along the gilded coach,
Nor sturdy Carmen on thy walks encroach.
No louts would bar thy ways were chairs denied
The soft supports of laziness and pride.
Shops breathe perfumes, thro' sashes ribbons glow
The mutual arms of ladies and the beaux.

Trivia, John Gay, 1716

So having taken her final bow, how should we analyse her stage career? Nelly's inability to impress in serious parts has meant that, rather meanly, theatrical posterity pays her few compliments. *The Penguin Dictionary of the Theatre* labels her an 'actress of no particular talent but great charm and vivacity'. The *Oxford Companion to the Theatre* acknowledges that 'during her short stage career, she was one of the best loved of the day', but notes sourly that she 'was not a good actress'. They treat her with the stuffy disdain of a TV soap star treading the boards: attracts the punters, darling, but that's all.

Theatre historian W J MacQueen-Pope, who admittedly had a soft spot for Nelly, got it about right, I think. He recognised that she was the theatre's most famous actress (although her fame had not actually come from her acting). She was talented, but her talent for comedy only highlighted her struggle with tragedy. She was a great comedy actress and that surely cannot be doubted. The trouble is that the snobbery that pumps the blood of professionalism through the veins of the theatre can never reconcile comedy with greatness. To over-extend the medical metaphor (already in need of surgery), those that excel at serious drama are ranked as consultants, while those that make you laugh are just the junior doctors: they have potential, but as yet have proved nothing.

It is unfair to disregard her ability as an actress in this way. She was clearly superior in some parts and less than convincing in others. In times when audiences participated in plays (but certainly not to the extent of popular imagination), Nelly's voice, which was as strong as her spirit, was a great asset. Dryden said that only Thomas Betterton and Nelly could be heard at all times. Betterton's voice 'enforced universal attention, even from the fops and the orange girls'.[1]

One critic thought that 'she acted the most spirited and fantastic parts, and spoke a prologue or epilogue with admirable address. Indeed, it was sometimes carried to extravagance: but even her highest flights were so natural, that they rather provoked laughter than excited disgust.' Cibber refers sincerely to Nelly as a 'sister of the stage'.

But what might be most remarkable of all was her age: if we accept 1650 as Nell's birth year, she would have been in the company at 14 and making her debut at the ripe old age of 15. At the height of her stardom she would still not be 20. Unfortunately, history has not left us any of the Restoration actresses' birthdates, so we are unable to make comparisons. Their real ages are modestly and gallantly lost in the swirls of time. Highfill's biographical directory estimates that Kathleen Corey was born around 1635. This would make her 15 years older than Nell (or seven if we accept a possible 1642 birthdate). Corey would have been around 26 by the time she started acting and into her thirties by the time Nell arrived.

However, we do have a hint about how age was perceived. It hinges on a comment made by Downes about the exceptional actor Betterton – 'the greatest figure of the Restoration stage'.[2] Cibber says that 'Betterton was as an actor, as Shakespeare was as author, both without competitors.' Interestingly, Downes tells us that 'Mr Betterton, being then but 22 years old, was highly applauded for his acting...' Probably the finest Restoration actor was considered an exceptional talent at *only* 22. We can gauge from this that Downes considered 22 years of age young for the theatre. That Nelly was a star is incontestable; what is patently unclear is her age. So what would Downes really have made of a 17- or 18-year-old being the female star of the King's House, taking all before her? Even if technically she wasn't in the same acting league as Betterton (which clearly she wasn't), surely Downes would have commented on the age of this youthful star. But he didn't. Perhaps, quite simply, she was much the same age as the other actresses.

Women in the late seventeenth and early eighteenth centuries would have grown up with actresses being the norm and, arguably therefore, more likely to enter the profession at an earlier age. The top two actresses of the era were probably Anne Bracegirdle (?1663–1748) and Anne 'Nance' Oldfield (1683–1730). Bracegirdle was at least 17 before she was first noticed and Oldfield was 20 before she made her mark. Nelly would have been 14 when Dryden wrote a significant lead part for her in *The Indian Emperor*. As much as I wish to believe it, as it would only make her all the more remarkable, I have to think that she must have been older. Without any alternatives, the bells of an earlier birthdate are beginning to peal irresistibly.

In a short career that lasted only six years, however, of which over two were interrupted by plague, fire or pregnancy, she made a huge impact. She surely was, as she herself said in the prologue to *The Conquest of Granada*, one of the two best comedians of the age. The top playwright of the day wrote parts for her, and would rather delay productions than see them put on without her. One of his characters, Florimel, must rank as her greatest part. She was great box office and that's all that mattered.

Academics and serious students of theatre may turn their noses up at the little actress with the 'turn'd up nose', but for her and for those that loved her, the smell of success was sweet enough.

In the winter of 1670–1, as Sir John Coventry nursed his 'cut-up nose', another Coventry enters the outskirts of our story. In 1667, Sir William Coventry (uncle of Sir John), who was secretary to the duke of York, a commissioner of the navy and privy councillor, was looking for a new house. He moved into the developing Pall Mall, which took its name from the croquet-like game (Pell-Mell) that was enormously popular in France but which had been invented in Italy as *pallo a maglio* (ball to mallet). Sir William was said by Henry Savile to have paid £1,400 for the house (about £105,000 today).

Originally, Charles II had a pall mall alley in St James's Park, but the dust that flew up from passing carriages made it impossible at times to see the balls. So, in 1661 a new pall mall alley was laid out on the site of today's Pall Mall. It was officially called Catherine Street, in honour of the queen, but every one knew it as Pall Mall: the name stuck and remained. In 1665, Henry Jermyn, earl of St Albans (who many thought had secretly married Charles's mother), was granted a lease to develop some of the crown lands in St James's Fields just north of St James's Park and Pall Mall. He built large aristocratic houses creating St James's Square and the area quickly became ultra fashionable. Sir William Coventry's house was one of just six big houses on the south side of Pall Mall (there were smaller houses, too) and enjoyed excellent views out on to St James's Park. In 1670, Sir William sold the lease to Nicholas Leake, earl of Scarsdale. But his tenancy was to be very short-lived.

In her fashionable Lincoln's Inn Fields lodgings, Nelly was isolated from the court at Whitehall and longed to be closer to her royal lover. Fast becoming established as a main mistress, she started, understandably, feeling poorly treated by comparison. Charles arranged for her to move to Pall Mall – an entirely agreeable geographical arrangement. Nelly moved in to a smallish house (the rates were just 16s. a year) at the eastern end of the road. It is almost certain that this house was on the south side (the park side) of Pall Mall: it is listed in the rate books as being on the south side in 1669 and 1671, but on the north side in 1670. Unless prefabricated homes were invented sooner than we thought, we can assume that the rate collector simply made a mistake in 1670. In 1671, the rate books note that collection for the house should come from 'Mrs Gwyn or present tenant'. Her name is not associated with the house after that.

Also anecdotal evidence from a correspondent, J How, to *Notes & Queries* (24 September 1881) confirms the south-side siting of the house. Mr How recalls watching Queen Victoria's coronation procession from St James's to Westminster Hall. He was the guest of his solicitors at a house in Pall Mall at the corner of King's Street (demolished in 1899 when it merged with Parliament Street, now Whitehall). The solicitors told him that 'they had possession for a client who had bought the property, and that among the deeds they learned that it had belonged to Nell Gwynne.'

The evidence surely removes the possibility that this house was on the north side and was part of the site that has been occupied by the Army & Navy Club (36–9 Pall Mall) since 1848. However, so strong is that belief that, over the years, 'the Rag', as the club is often known, has been bombarded with donations of many Nelly artefacts. These include: two portraits of her, one of which is a particularly attractive painting which, oddly, is not often reproduced; a silver fruit knife which is said to have been owned by Nelly, and with which no doubt she peeled her oranges; a miniature of Nelly with an assortment of alternative costumes, which can be slotted into the frame, and which Charles II is said to have carried about with him – even to his deathbed; and a four-volume scrapbook (although two volumes seem to have gone AWOL), including some of Nelly's household bills and other contemporary letters, built around Peter Cunningham's nineteenth-century biography.

However, Nelly had hardly unpacked in her new house before she was presented with the lease that Charles had paid for. Dr Heberden tells us that Nelly 'returned him the lease and conveyances, saying she had always conveyed free under the crown, and always would, and would not accept it until it was conveyed free to her by an Act of Parliament.'[3] The sheer charm of her stance won over the king. At this point, and undoubtedly with a little royal pressure (which in Charles's case probably included a few sweeteners), the earl of Scarsdale moved out of his new house. Nelly's rise was becoming irresistible. From lodgings in, or next to a brothel, she now moved in to a house fit for an earl, with the countess of Portland and Lady Raynelagh as neighbours. The freehold to the property was not finally conveyed to 'Mistress Ellen Gwinne of the parish of St Martin-in-the-Fields in the county of Middlesex, single woman' until 6 April 1677. And to this day the house is the only freehold property on the south side of Pall Mall. The rest are all owned by the Crown.

The house has had its share of history. Nelly's eldest son lived in the house until being forced to hand it over to creditors in 1694. The duke of Schomberg (whose father had acted as second-in-command to William of Orange in 1688) lived there between 1696 and 1698 while his own house was being rebuilt next door. In 1766, the drawing room witnessed the secret marriage between King George III's younger brother and the dowager countess Waldegrave. A tradition at the College of Physicians has it that the great Dr Sydenham also lived at this address. The house later came into the hands of Dr William Heberden who demolished then rebuilt it in 1770. That house was then also demolished and rebuilt as the present 79 Pall Mall in 1866–8 for the Eagle Insurance

Company. Today it serves as the head office of the P&O company and boasts a blue plaque commemorating its most famous owner.

The rate books of the time say that these houses had the advantage of 'gardens and mounts adjoining to the royal gardens'. In Stow's survey of 1720, Strype confirms this by saying the houses had 'raised mounts, which gave them the prospect of the [royal] garden and of the park'. So Nelly's garden wall backed on to the king's privy garden. This would be handy for chats over the wall or for Charles to scale it in order to make discreet visits to his mistress. On 2 March 1671, Evelyn met the king:

> . . . thence walked with him through St James's Park to the garden, where I both saw and heard a very familiar discourse between him and Mistress Nellie as they call the impudent comedian, she looking out of her garden on a terrace at the top of the wall, and the king standing on the green walk under it: I was heartily sorry at this scene: Thence the king walked to the Duchess of Cleveland's, another lady of pleasure and curse of our nation.

Charles had made a gift of Berkshire House in St James's to the duchess. In her usually rapacious way, Barbara Castlemaine had sold off much of the estate, but kept the mansion, renaming it Cleveland House in 1670. It was demolished in 1840–1 and replaced with Bridgewater House (which in 1980 was offered for sale for about £10 million). Barbara is commemorated in the area today by Cleveland Court, Square and Row. As well as being created duchess of Cleveland – as a sort of long service award – Barbara was also created Baroness Nonsuch of Nonsuch Park, Surrey. To go with that title, Charles also granted her the 'Tudor extravagance' of Henry VIII's magnificent old palace of Nonsuch and its park. Barbara cleaned the palace out and sold everything so that, by 1702, the palace that Henry had built so that none such could compare was a sad and bitter ruin.

As Nelly and Barbara prospered with their new homes, Charles's French mistress was firmly establishing herself somewhat extravagantly in her apartments at Whitehall. Little time was lost in proving, *s'il vous plâit*, that her taste was just as rich, if not more so, than Barbara's. In keeping with Charles's new-found tradition for his mistresses, Louise became a maid of honour to the queen. Nelly would also be so appointed but not until much later: she had the status of a mistress, all right, but not the breeding of a lady of quality. The haughty Louise's veins oozed with the bluest Breton blood available, while poor old Nelly's blood was as common as red could be. Louise believed it to be her right (by breeding alone) to be the king's only mistress. She sought to rule him completely, considering herself the uncrowned queen of England: she would rid the court of all challengers. But she seriously undertestimated the low-born ex-actress. For our English rose was about to lock thorns with the French fleur-de-lys. And how the petals would fly.

— *14* —

The War with France

[Nell Gwynne's] adventures were the talk to the town and
amused rather than shocked the good folks of London.

Colbert de Croissy, French ambassador in London to Arnauld de Pomponne,
the French foreign minister, 23 January 1672

[Louise de Keroualle] for fifteen years held Great Britain in
her delicate little hand and manipulated its king and statesmen . . . as she might have done her fan.

Louise de Keroualle, Henry Forneron, 1897

Nelly and Louise could not have been more different. One French,
highborn, Catholic, manipulative, greedy, hungry for power, and with a
great big long name: Louise Renée de Penancoet de Keroualle. Nelly
seemingly didn't know how to spell her last name. However, to be fair the
English in general had a problem with saying Louise's last name, never
mind spelling it. Those that tried to spell it offered 'Querouailles';
French genealogists plumped for 'Keroual'; Colbert de Croissy wrote
about 'Queroul'; in the charter donating lands to her, she is 'Keroel', the
old family papers, however, use 'Keroualle', as does Forneron in his
excellent biography. Louise, it is then.

Louise was born in September 1649 in the family château in Brittany,
about a mile or so from the port of Brest. Hers was an ancient family but,

as with so many, the proud nobility that filled the heart, mind and soul, filled the family coffers somewhat less successfully. Their treasure was in heritage alone. French snobbery was a class above that even of the English, and on her arrival in England, Louise brought over every single ounce of that finely honed snobbery with her. However, even before she had arrived, the nose that was used to look down on people was knocked seriously out of joint.

Louise's grand arrival was somewhat less auspicious than she would have expected. Charles II had sent his good friend and chief adviser, George Villiers, duke of Buckingham, to escort Louise safely into England. Buckingham, ever on the prowl for influence, saw it also as an opportunity to recruit the new mistress-to-be to his side. He met her in Paris, spending some three weeks with her, cultivating her to his causes back home. Then, having made preparations, he sent Louise on with part of his equipage to Dieppe, while he himself attended to some matters in the French capital. He would, he said, follow in due course and meet up for the crossing. Only he forgot and made his way back to England by Calais. Meanwhile, Louise waited for his grace to join her at Dieppe. And waited. Two days became two weeks until Louise finally received word that Buckingham was back in England.

Henry Bennet, earl of Arlington, came to her rescue and sent out a yacht to collect her. It was the start of a useful alliance for them both. Given these events, the assessment of Buckingham by the English ambassador at Paris, George Montagu, as the 'most inconstant and forgetful of men' seems adroit. One thing was for certain, all Buckingham's plotting and intrigue with Louise would count for naught: he had succeeded only in delivering this potentially most influential woman into the hands of his enemies. Louise would never forgive or forget this insult. Nelly, on the other hand, on being told the saga, would always retain a soft spot for my Lord Buck.

Despite this early setback as the forgotten passenger, Louise was a driven woman: she needed to rule the king as if his queen, if not actually be queen herself. Queen Catherine was no threat. Barren, ugly, squat and dull – how could she be? She had the pedigree, all right, but it was only Portuguese, after all. Catherine had by now accepted Charles for the man he was: and had grown to love him all the same. The hysteria that had been aroused by the openness of Charles and Barbara's long-standing affair had mellowed to a dignified acceptance of a woman's undignified lot in royal marriages. Indeed, the queen seemed to find Nelly almost acceptable.

Catherine once called unexpectedly on the king to see how he was, having heard that he had a chill. Charles was, at the time, being 'comforted' by Nelly. The ever diligent and reliable Mrs Chiffinch raced to his bedchamber and raised the alarm, causing a shocked Nelly to scramble under the bed. As the queen entered, she noticed Nelly's slipper on the floor. 'Ha!' she said, 'I will be off then. I see it is not you that has the cold.'

Catherine seemed contented that whatever the plotting or designs that skulked in the walkways at Whitehall, or whatever the infidelities of her husband; he was still that – her husband. And she was his and England's queen. So the arrival of yet another claim – albeit scheming and French – to Charles's heart and bed was no threat to Catherine. Not that Louise would see it that way, she believed that her ancient French name was ripe for the founding of a royal dynasty.

The wife could tolerate the mistresses. Louise could tolerate the wife but not the mistresses. By choosing his mistresses, Charles was exercising that dangerous prerogative: choice. Royal marriages are not based on choice, whereas the keeping of mistresses depends on it. Louise was sure: they all had to go. Charles's main mistresses at the time were Barbara and Nelly, both of whom had provided the king with children – a bond tough to break and one to be equalled. However, Barbara's star had long since lost its sparkle, although Nelly's was still burning defiantly brightly. But both were to be outshone by the ascendant French star. It was soon very clear to Louise that Charles cared and bothered little with Barbara, but tolerated her presence for old times' sake. So, not a threat then – other than that uncomfortable feeling that only an ex on the premises can stir. As for Nelly, well, a low-born strolling actress – just a fad, a phase: a bit of rough. Class will out and class will tell. Louise was home and dry. Or so she thought.

George Savile, later marquess of Halifax, wrote that Charles II's 'mistresses were as different in their humours as they were in their looks'. Certainly their characters were different: Nelly was witty, selfless and happy; Barbara was hysterical, rapacious and tactless; and Louise was scheming, aloof and heartless. Again certainly all three looked different, but not that you would notice if left to judge from the paintings of Sir Peter Lely. Although Nelly was pretty, Barbara was undoubtedly the best-looking of the three: her looks were as famous as she herself was infamous. On seeing a portrait of her ('a most blessed picture') Pepys declared it 'one that I must have a copy of'.[1] Louise was less obviously attractive than the other two. John Evelyn described her as having a 'childish, simple and baby-face'.[2] She was also round-faced and Charles gave her the pet name 'Fubbs' – an amalgamation of 'fat' and 'chubby'.

While Barbara affected her laugh, and Louise affected her tears, Nelly simply affected those around her. With Barbara's tantrums and outrageously false and loud laugh, and Louise's regular and very controlled public bouts of uncontrollable sobbing (Nelly called her 'the Weeping Willow'), it's little wonder that Charles sought sanctuary with the down-to-earth, what-you-see-is-what-get Nelly. Not only was the sex good, she also had the priceless ability to make him laugh, as *The Lady of Pleasure* describes:

> She knew so well to wield the royal tool,
> That none had such a knack to please the fool.
> When he was dumpish, she would still be jocund
> And chuck the royal chin of Charles y[e] Second.

Charles certainly enjoyed sex and indeed seems to have been well equipped for the task. Rochester tells us:

> . . . his gentleness is such
> And love he loves, for he loves fucking much.
> Nor are his high desires above his strength:
> His sceptre and his prick are of a length.[3]

The same poem also informs us that Nelly, too, shared Charles's devotion to the business of the bedchamber and delighted in his extravagant tool of his trade, although sometimes she had to work at it:

> This you'd believe if I had time to tell ye
> The pains it costs to poor, laborious Nelly,
> Whilst she employs hands, fingers, mouth and thighs,
> Ere she can raise the member she enjoys.

All his mistresses performed in the bedchamber, but it was Nelly's humour that set her apart for Charles. No mean wit himself he loved to be surrounded by people who could make him laugh – the Rochesters, Buckinghams, young Killigrews and Baptist Mays of his world. Almost inevitably these companions were almost always men. Nelly was the only woman who could regularly or even presume to make the king laugh. Although being a mistress of the king was by no means a hindrance, her humour genuinely endeared her to the court. Her mimicry was spot on. It was a talent shared by Buckingham, whose execution was so deceptive and subtle that the people being ridiculed laughed along, not realising they were being sent up. Nell's mimicry, as befitting such a public performer, was never understated when it could go marauding shamelessly over the top. Naturally, Louise was her favourite target (her very broken English, for example, provided easy pickings), not only for the laughs she obtained at her cost, but also for the outrage and horror she could pluck effortlessly out of her rival.

Nelly's attacks on Louise weren't always inspired by a sense of fun or satire: very occasionally they were laced with undiluted venom. However, mostly they were basted with humour even if cooked with contempt. Towards the end of 1674, news reached Louise of the death of Louis, chevalier de Rohan. He had fallen from grace at the French court and, in an attempt to revive his fortunes, he had entered into negotiations with the Protestant Dutch, the sworn enemy of the Catholic French. Unfortunately for Louis de Rohan, his treason was discovered and his life ended as his head departed the rest of his body outside the Bastille on 27 November 1674. The de Rohan family, like Louise's, was an ancient and noble one. Louise, draped in deepest black, went into a very public mourning for him. A letter by the poet Andrew Marvell, dated 19 December 1674, describes that Louise 'is in deep mourning for the Chevalier de Rohan, as being forsoothe of kin to that family.'[4] However, their families were not related (they didn't even know each other) but Louise believed that because of her ancient nobility she had the *right* to mourn. She wailed at her great loss.

The following day, Nelly, also draped in deepest black, entered the court, mimicking Louise's performance the day before – shedding tears and moaning dolefully. When asked by a bemused courtier, within the presence of the king and Louise (who was still in black and tearful), for whom she was mourning, Nelly replied 'Why, have you not heard of my loss in the death of the Cham of Tartary?'[5] And, what relation, pray,' the questioner continued, 'was the Cham of Tartary to you?' 'Oh,' replied Nelly, a smile emerging on her face, 'exactly the same relation that the Chevalier de Rohan was to Cartwheel.' Louise was furious and stormed out at the insult. Charles and the court roared with laughter, and Nelly took her curtain-calls triumphantly. The rivalry became the talk of dinner tables the nation over. Lady Russell wrote of the 'great talk of [Louise's] and Mrs Nell Gwynne's doings'.

A celebrated contemporary account comes from the prolific letter writer Madame Marie de Rabutin-Chantal, marquise de Sevigne, who wrote to her daughter on 11 September 1675 explaining Nelly's reasoning for her treatment of Louise:

> 'This Duchess,' says she, 'acts the fine lady; she says she is related to everyone in France; as soon as any great nobleman dies she goes into mourning. Right, if she is of such nobility, why is she a whore? She ought to die of shame. As for me, it's my trade, I don't set myself up as anything better.' This creature boldly pushes herself forward and outstares and embarrasses the Duchess to an extraordinary degree.

Despite the humiliation, Louise would continue to mourn the loss of any European potentate, or anybody else of a suitably high and ancient pedigree for that matter. Nelly responded each time, even to the extent of making up the names of such potentates – 'The Boog of Oronooko', for example. On one occasion Louise went into deep mourning for the death of the king of Sweden. Handily for Nelly, the next day brought the demise of the king of Portugal. So, dressed in the identical clothing of woe and loss that bedecked the pompous Louise, Nelly suggested that such were the number of deaths that perhaps they should consider dividing the world up: Louise could have the kings in the northern hemisphere, while she would take care of those in the south. Not unusually, Louise was the only one who was not amused.

Nelly's sense of theatre stood her and her japes in good stead, and on one occasion she brilliantly lampooned Barbara's extravagance. A horse-drawn carriage was a symbol of wealth and status (Pepys, for example, was beside himself with pride when he was finally able to afford one). To have a single drawn carriage was the low end of the market; to have two or even four horses for the job was admirable. To have six horses was considered the height of extravagance or the reserve of royalty. Barbara's new carriage was drawn by eight horses. Such a bout of ostentation could only inspire Nelly. She turned up at court with a carriage drawn by eight oxen, crying 'Whores to market! Ho!' Such acts caused the self-serving historian Bishop Burnet to comment that Nelly, to whom he was no friend, was 'the indiscreetest and wildest creature at the court'.

Madame de Sevigne, in the same letter quoted above, provided a telling description of the rivalry between Nelly and Louise:

> Mademoiselle de K— has not been disappointed in anything she proposed . . . she amasses treasure, and makes herself feared and respected by as many as she can. But she did not foresee that she should find a young actress in her way, whom the king dotes on; and she has it not in her power to withdraw him from her. He divides his care, his time and his health between these two. The actress is as proud as Mademoiselle: she insults her, she makes grimaces at her, she attacks her, she frequently steals the king from her, and boasts whenever he gives her the preference. She is young, indiscreet, confident, wild, and of an agreeable humour: she sings, she dances, she acts her part with a good grace . . .

The image of little Nelly pulling faces at the haughty Louise is a pure delight, capturing the essence of them both perfectly. It illustrates just how confident Nelly was – confident in her position to be able to get away with such things, as well as having the devil-may-care confidence to actually say or do them in the first place. As does her habit for giving people nicknames: Nelly, in addition to 'Cartwheel' and 'the Weeping Willow' also called Louise 'Squintabella' because of an apparent squint in one of her eyes. More striking is the fact that she labelled the king's brother, James, duke of York, on account of his lack of humour, 'Dismal Jimmy'.

Nelly's popularity extended beyond the court. There was a general hatred of all things French and Catholic, which didn't give Louise much of a chance of winning the hearts of the populace, even had she not been so highhanded and overbearing. Nelly remained at heart just one of the people, whereas Louise was kept imperiously upright by a spine of pretentiousness.

Nelly had no qualms about her status – she was a whore; she knew it and didn't care who else knew it either. This is not to say she was a prostitute, which is our general understanding of 'whore' today. In Restoration England the word 'whore' meant a kept woman, an adulteress (seriously shameless and society-shocking all the same). And, indeed on those grounds, she *was* a whore. Indeed, Nell probably considered that she was a prostitute in a sense: she slept with the king and took his money, after all. However, despite the many transactions, there was just the one client. She may have taken his money, but he had taken her heart. Nelly traded openly with her whoredom. Organising a party at Pall Mall to celebrate the king's birthday, Charles asked whether he should invite the notorious adulteress the Countess of Shrewsbury. 'Oh, I shouldn't think so,' replied Nelly, 'I think one whore's enough for you, sire.'

Most famously, she had taken loan of Louise's carriage and travelled to Oxford in 1681. On her way to meet the king, some citizens noticed the initials of the carriage's owner and assumed that Louise was inside. A small crowd hurled insults and began to push the carriage of the hated French Catholic. Nelly pulled back the curtain, stuck her head out to the protesters and cried: 'Pray, good people, be civil: I'm the Protestant whore!'

An anecdote from the spurious Smith 'biography' and recast in Henry Fielding's *Tom Jones* is worth noting. Of doubtful authenticity, it does capture Nelly and the times well. On hearing a commotion in the street, Nelly opened her windows to investigate and saw her footman fighting. Calling him to stop, she asked the reason for the brawl: 'He called you a whore, madam,' replied the footman. 'You blockhead!' yelled Nelly, 'in future defend what is wrong, not what is right! I am a whore!' 'That's as may be, madam,' came the reply, 'but I'll not be called a whore's footman.'

For the people the battle between Nelly and Louise was England versus France: so the crowd loved Nelly and despised Louise all the more. On one occasion a crowd had gathered outside a goldsmith's shop wherein the owner was making a plate for Louise as a gift from Charles. On seeing the extravagance and beauty of the plate, the crowd wished a thousand miseries on Madam Carwell and hoped that the gold be melted and poured down her throat. They also sighed a thousand pities that his majesty had not bestowed it on Madam Ellen.

Towards the late 1670s, Nelly's popularity soared: she was having books and plays dedicated to her. Thomas Duffet set the ball rolling, dedicating his play *The Spanish Rogue* to her in 1674. In the adulatory tones that marked such occasions, Duffet felt no need to hold back, referring to Nelly as 'the most perfect beauty and the greatest goodness in the world'. In 1678, Robert Whitcombe dedicated his book *Janua Divorum, or, The Lives and Histories of the Heathen Gods, Goddesses and Demi-Gods* to 'the illustrious Madam Ellen Gwin'. And he was unstoppable:

> I knew that curious Nature had extended her endeavours in the formation of your delicate body, enjoined both it and every limb about you to an exact symmetry and pleasing proportion...Apollo told me that in you only he

should meet with his primitive wisdom. Mercury, with his pristine wit. Juno, with her old sovereignty or greatness of mind. Venus, with her delicate beauty. And Alcides, with his godlike courage and brave spirit. And, in short, they affirmed, that all those noble qualifications for which they were formerly deified, were only concentrated in yourself.

Most significantly, perhaps, the novelist and dramatist Aphra Behn dedicated her play *The Feign'd Courtesans* to Nelly in 1679. Behn (1640–89), who was the first English woman to make a living out of writing, said:

> I with shame look back on my past ignorance which suffered me not to pay an adoration long since where there was so very much due... Besides all your charms, the attractions and powers of your sex, you have beauties peculiar to yourself – an eternal sweetness, youth and air which never dwell in any face but yours. You never appear but you gladden the hearts of all that have the happy purpose to see you, as if you were made on purpose to put the whole world into good humour.

The odes and dedications flowed: she was now 'the darling strumpet of the crowd' who

> Forgets her state and talks to them aloud;
> Lays by her greatness and descends to prate
> With those 'bove whom she's rais'd by wondrous fate.[6]

Even the satires that attacked the king for devoting his all too precious time and keen ability to affairs of the bedchamber rather than those of the state, somehow softened their rage when it came to Nelly. Andrew Marvell's 'Royal Resolution' articulates a view of Charles:

> I'll wholly abandon all public affairs,
> And pass all my time with buffoons and players
> And saunter to Nelly when I should be at prayers.

Another aspect of her character that fed her popularity was that she, unlike the others, actually loved the king for the man himself and not for what she could get out of him. Nelly was loyal to the king as his subject and his lover. She may have mimicked the other mistresses and gloated when she was preferred over them, but she was never jealous of Charles's other lovers. Unlike them. During one of her trademark furies, Barbara screamed at him: 'I am the one woman in England who least deserves your reproach. If you want to satisfy your base desires you need only stupid geese like Stuart and Wells and that little slut of an actress you've recently taken up with.' On 27 December 1674, the French ambassador Courtin wrote to the French minister of state Louvois: 'I tell you privately, and in the hope that it will not travel further, how three days ago [Louise] in my presence attacked the king about his infidelities. She did not hide from me what she had suffered two years ago from his misconduct with trulls; and he himself then described to me how his head doctor had prescribed for her.'

Nelly was never jealous of Charles's indiscretions. She was simply and truly overjoyed at whatever time he chose to spend with her. In that king's reign, Nelly would never lack a friend in court, town or country: hugely popular, she could go anywhere and find nothing but warmth from people. However, as for her love, it was only safe with one man: it had no need or wish to go elsewhere.

Although her constancy was known, this didn't stop people trying their luck, testing her waters or chancing their arms. Even the all-conquering Buckingham was rebuffed. On 9 December 1672, Girolami Alberti, Venetian secretary in England, wrote to the doge and senate: '...Buckingham is now in disgrace with the King for an audacious attempt on his Majesty's private pleasures...' In a letter to Louis XIV, on 23 January 1673, Colbert de Croissy also described how Buckingham, intent on discussing state affairs, had found Nelly in the king's private apartments. In attempting to snatch a kiss (or 'some gallantries' as de Croissy called it) all he received in return was a 'sound box on the ears'. Nelly's view of life was, perhaps, captured by the inscription on her bedpan: 'Fear God, Serve the King'.

Much later, after Charles had died, she still remained faithful to him. At a divorce trial in 1692 (five years after Nelly herself was dead), evidence was given against Sir John Germaine who was accused of adultery with Mary, duchess of Norfolk. The court heard that in 1686 Nelly had some gambling debts with Germaine. Recognising her difficulty in paying he suggested that the debt be wiped clean should Nelly have sex with him. She refused, claiming 'that she would not lay the dog where the deer laid...' A contemporary satire has 'Madam Gwin' uttering the following to Louise:

> Let Fame that never yet Spoke well of Woman,
> Give out I was a Stroling Whore and Common,
> Yet have I been to him since the first hour,
> As constant as the Needle to the Flower;
> Whilst you to your Eternal Praise and Fame
> To Forreign Scents betray'd the Royal Game.[7]

The satire *The Lady of Pleasure*, in its explicit and inelegant way, confirmed Nell's faithfulness:

> Nor wou'd his Nelly long be his survivor;
> Alas! who now was good enough to swive her?
> She was too generous to let subjects dabble
> Where she had so oft had soaked the royal bauble.

This did not prevent gossip that Nelly had married, however. The diary of Thomas Isham of Lamport records on 6 May 1673 that 'the Earl of Newport has married Nell Gwynne'. The earl was actually even madder than the rumour. Even if true the marriage would not have lasted too long as the earl was buried at St Martin-in-the-Fields on 20 March 1675 and was, according to *Complete Peerage*, 'an idiot and unmarried'.

One aspirant MP thought it might aid his prospects if he were to suggest that he had married Nelly. However, it didn't help Slingsby Bethel triumph at the borough of Southwark election in 1681 as this contemporary account shows '...the rumour of his being married to Nell Gwynne did never obtain to his prejudice, and had ended with the poll, had he not afterwards taken so much pains at the Amsterdam Coffee-House to purge himself in that matter.'[8]

The other mistresses, however, were rather less than faithful. Barbara and Louise were branded:

> A brace of cherubs, of as a vile a breed,
> As ever was produced of human seed.[9]

Born in 1641, part of the influential Villiers clan – her father was killed fighting for the Royalists in the Civil War – Barbara was unquestionably beautiful. Grammont records that she was 'a lively and demanding woman' with it. And it was money that she mostly demanded. She could launch into hysterical tirades at will; Charles often suffered her tantrums publicly. Regularly she would threaten to burn down her house or kill her children, often by stabbing them, if she could not have whatever it was she desired. That, and a lot of sex.

Adultery, sex scandals and the like were so rife it almost became a scandal if a couple were faithful to each other. It was *de rigueur* to indulge in extra-marital activity.

For a woman to be equally promiscuous, society's wrath and shock would be vicious, unrelenting and unforgiving. The men were rakes, fops and gallants. The women simply whores, slatterns and bitches. The language may have changed somewhat today but the sentiments remain, as solid and as uncompromising as ever. It seems the gander's goose is for ever cooked. So women like Barbara ('The damned, dirty duchess') and the countess of Shrewsbury were easy targets for the scurrilous ink of the satirists. These vile women, as they were known, were held up in scorn by a society desperate for a comfort zone into which they could lie smugly and think that no matter how dishonest or unfaithful they were, they were never as bad as that.

Barbara, in particular, had a sexual appetite that many men tried, unsuccessfully it seems, to sate: 'Full forty men a day provide this whore/Yet like a bitch, she'll wag her tail for more' suggested the *Satyr* of 1677. In his *Signior Dildo*, Rochester called her 'that pattern of virtue [who] has swallowed more pricks than the ocean has sand'. She slept with people for revenge, for money, for the sheer bad taste of it, for the hell of it and for the fun of it. As well as Nelly's ex-lover, the actor Charles Hart, other conquests included Jacob Hall, a rope-dancer from Bartholomew Fair, the playwright William Wycherley and the notoriously ugly actor Cardell Goodman. Indeed his lack of looks was acknowledged thus:

> Pardon me, Bab, if I mistake his Race,
> Which was Infernal sure, for tho' he has
> No cloven foot, he has a cloven face.

Barbara's most notable young sexual protégé was John Churchill, later duke of Marlborough. Now Churchill *was* a whore: he slept with Barbara for money and reward. On being disturbed by Charles, who called to Berkshire House to visit Barbara, Churchill leapt out of the window and made his escape across the grounds. Charles, long since unperturbed at

Barbara's activities, cried out after him: 'Nay, hasten not, I know you only do it for money.' Alexander Pope wrote of Barbara's and Churchill's affair:

> Who of ten thousand gulled her Knight
> Then asked ten thousand for another night.
> The gallant, too, to whom she paid it down
> Lived to refuse his mistress half-a-crown.

Churchill became, through shrewd investments (for example, Barbara gave him £5,000 for clothes which he used to buy an annuity instead), a wealthy man. But one who, as Pope suggests, was very cautious with the spending of it. On being mistaken for him, Lord Peterborough is said to have replied: 'I can convince by two reasons that I am not the Duke. In the first place, I have only five guineas in my pocket, and in the second, they are heartily at your service.'

On another occasion, Charles had called on Mary Knight at her house in Pall Mall, just down from Nelly's. The house was also being used by Barbara for her assignations with Wycherley. On climbing the stairs, Charles was met by a young man disguised by a muffle scampering downwards. Charles let him by and entered Barbara's room. He found her unclothed in bed but she explained that she was staying at Mary Knight's house in preparation for Lent, having converted to Catholicism. Charles replied, with his usual glint, that he was sure then that he must have just passed her confessor on the stairway.

Louise would also be unfaithful (despite her protestations over Charles), but only if it would serve her interests. Nelly even commemorated her rivals in an awesome silver bedstead she had specially made. The bed was decorated with carvings and engravings, one of which was a dancing Jacob Hall to mock Barbara. Another had Louise in a grave with an unnamed eastern potentate.

— 15 —

Title Bouts

The misses take place, each advanced to be duchess
With pomp great as queens in their coach and six horses;
Their bastards made dukes, earls, viscounts and lords,
And all the high titles that honour affords.

'A Dialogue Between Two Horses', Andrew Marvell[1]

This making of bastards great
And Dutchessing every whore.

Song, anonymous, c.1673

In her grand plan to ensnare the king, Louise had clearly done her homework. She knew that the way to his soul was through his sexual frustration. A study of the king would reveal that in the mid-1660s the grip Frances 'La Belle' Stewart[2] had over him tightened because she refused to sleep with him. Charles became obsessed. However, Frances wasn't using her sexual prohibition to plot, intrigue, gain wealth or advantage – she just didn't fancy him all that much. Louise wasn't blind to the possibilities – indeed, her eyes could not be more open and all-seeing. To plan, she became a virgin. And to plan, Charles became obsessed. The peaceful king had to go a-conquering again – and it would take him nearly a year to succeed.

Advised strongly by Colbert de Croissy that the time for surrender was nigh, Louise had arranged in October 1671 to stay at the seat of the Arlingtons, the impressive Euston Hall, in Thetford. Charles would, as usual, be at nearby Newmarket for the races in October. Also, and again as usual, he would attend a large party and stay over at Euston – it being far more comfortable than his own modest palace at Newmarket. Perhaps just as importantly, Nelly would not be around. She had remained in London, seven months pregnant with her second child. And with Barbara off the scene, the pieces were fitting together neatly.

It was during her two-week stay at Euston that Louise granted Charles the favours he had so desired. Colbert wrote to Louvois on 22 October 1671:

> The king comes here for his repasts; and after eating he passes several hours with Mlle Keroualle. He has already paid her three visits; and he invited us yesterday to Newmarket to see the races. We went, and were charmingly entertained, and he seemed more than ever solicitous to please Mlle Keroualle. Those small attentions which denote a great passion were lavished on her; and as she showed by her expressions of gratitude that she was not insensible to the kindness of a great king.

Colbert added that he now hoped that Louise would so behave 'that the attachment will be durable and exclude every other'.

Writing to Lord Preston on 19 October 1671, Joshua Bowes describes what appears to be Charles entertaining and showing off his latest conquest: 'Madam Carwell went to Newmarket with the French ambassador, and was received there in great state; she came in her Majesty's coach [now Louise would have loved that], with two other coaches attending her, and my Lord Arlington and another Lord Lieutenant accompanying her, and so returned again to her lodgings.'[3]

The union was a blessing to gossips and pamphleteers who suggested that a mock wedding ceremony had taken place to mark the occasion. Louise is reputed to have said after the event in her shattered English: 'Me no bad woman. If me taut me was one bad woman, me would cut my own trote.'[4] Certainly such a ceremony would have appealed to Louise: better to be a mock queen than no queen. One of the guests of the Arlingtons was John Evelyn. On arriving at Euston, he wrote:

> I found Monsieur Colbert & the famous french maid of honor, Mademoisell Quierovil now comeing to be in grate favour with the K—: ... It was

universaly reported that the faire Lady – was bedded one of these nights, and the stocking flung, after the manner of a married Bride: I acknowledge she was for the most part in her undresse all day, and that there was fondnesse, & toying, with that young wanton; nay 'twas said, I was at the former ceremonie, but tis utterly false, I neither saw, nor heard of any such thing whilst I was there.[5]

It was a happy time for all involved. Colbert de Croissy was almost as relieved as Charles. Louis XIV was delighted at the match (at last). So much so that he sent Lady Arlington a diamond necklace as a token of thanks for her role as matchmaker. Whatever the circumstance of that first union, it was certainly an unprotected one for, exactly nine months later, on 29 July 1672, Louise gave birth to a son. Young Charles (the fourth to take his father's name) would be Charles II's last acknowledged child. All three mistresses now had children: Barbara leading the way with five (although at least two were not definitely Charles's, despite his acknowledged paternity), Nelly with two and Louise with one. The battles between mistresses were mere skirmishes compared to those to come in the war of mothers.

Nelly's youngest son was born on 25 December 1671. She called him James, after his uncle the duke of York. It was a courtesy that James wouldn't forget. Despite her mimicry of him and his general aloofness, there must have been some affection between them. Although born on Christmas Day, there was no national celebration and no bonfires were lit to mark the birth of the king's eleventh child. The court marked the occasion, however, Charles and James called to see the mother and baby, as did Lord Buckhurst, and the French ambassador complained that political business of the court all but stopped in order to celebrate the birth.

Louise, although unquestionably Charles's main mistress, was unhappy that she didn't have a more substantial and permanent title to reflect her status. Particularly so, as Barbara had been created duchess of Cleveland on 3 August 1670, officially in consideration of her noble descent and 'her own personal virtues'. Realising that no such title was possible for a foreigner, Louise appealed to Louis XIV, through the ambassador, for leave to become a naturalised English subject 'as a necessary means to profit from the gifts which the King of England might have the kindness to lavish upon her',[6] Louis agreed. Just over a year after she gave Charles his final son, his kindness seemingly knew no bounds and the king well and truly lavished his French favourite with a thundering roll of honours. On 19 August 1673, she was created Baroness Petersfield, countess of Fareham and duchess of Portsmouth. It has been said that originally the ducal title was to have been Pendennis, but this was changed. Later on in the year Louise was sworn a lady of the queen's bedchamber.

Being made an English duchess made Louise, impossible though it may seem, even more unbearably pompous. But, as Charles could testify, Nelly had a tongue that could hit the spot. On seeing Nelly dressed in all her finery, Louise mocked: 'Why, Nelly, you look fine enough to be a queen.' Nelly retorted, 'Aye, Carwell, and you look whore enough to be a duchess.' Louise complained bitterly to the king, who didn't help matters by laughing out loud. Charles, ever seeking comfort and compromise, once even arranged a meal with just Nell and Louise as guests, in an attempt to build bridges between the two big loves in his life. Louise, who had two pieces of chicken on her plate, declared that she had in fact got three pieces of chicken. 'How so?' asked Charles. Louise, giggling with childish satisfaction, pointed to her plate and said, 'One piece, two piece; and one and two piece makes three piece!' Unamused, Nell leant over and picked up Louise's two pieces of chicken and said, with the usual mischief in her eyes: 'If that's the case, then I'll have one piece, Charles can have one piece, and you can have the third piece for yourself!'

Now that Louise had been elevated by right she turned her attentions, influence and intrigue to her son. There was a clear precedent for Louise to pursue: Charles's eldest acknowledged son, James Crofts, had been created duke of Monmouth in 1662. Barbara's first son but second child, Charles Fitzroy, had taken the title of Lord Limerick, that being the subsidiary title of the earl of Castlemaine (his mother's husband Roger Palmer having been passed off as his father). All the others – Catherine Pegge's son Charles Fitzcharles (commonly known as 'Don Carlos' because of his popularity and amiability at court), Barbara's second son, Henry Fitzroy, Nelly's two sons, and, of course, Louise's son – had yet to receive any ennoblement.

There is some irony that the title allotted for Louise's child should be that of Richmond. The previous duke died at Elsinore, Denmark, in December 1672. He was married to Frances Stewart whom the king had chased remorselessly, and it was Frances's rebuttal of Charles that Louise had adopted as her tactic for gaining influence over the king. With no issue that very title was now at the browbeaten king's disposal to grant to the child of Louise de Keroualle. Even more remarkable is that Louise's son was only three years old. James Crofts, being the first son, had a special place in Charles's heart and even he was 12 before being created a duke. Barbara's two other sons – Henry and Charles Fitzroy – were also vying for titles but were nine and ten years older than Louise's son.

Nelly was furious. 'Even Barbara's brats were not made dukes until they were 12 or 13, but the son of a French spy is given that title when he is hardly out of long clothes' she fumed. Why was Charles doing this? Louise had brought great pressure to bear and Charles had simply given in. And it was important that her son was ennobled before Barbara's because, crucially for the aristocratic Louise, ducal precedence was at stake. This would give her son the right to precede Barbara's in ceremonies and social formalities.

So, with Nelly seething in Pall Mall, the battle lines were drawn and with no quarter asked or given, the two duchesses unleashed their deadliest weapons first: influence over Charles. Charles, tugged from one side to the next, promised both whatever they wanted. Then realising this was impossible, in another fit of compromise, Charles suggested that both children be ennobled at the same time. A bloody but squared battle seemed the outcome. But neither Charles nor Barbara had reckoned on the resolve of Louise.

Drawing on her cultivated friendship with the lord treasurer, Thomas Osborne earl of Danby, she procured the information she needed: even if both sons were ennobled on the same day, the one whose patent was sealed first would, indeed, hold precedence. Louise also discovered that the patents could not be signed on the date given because Danby was actually leaving to take the waters at Bath at midnight and would not be back for a month – so they could not be sealed until his return.

However, Louise organised her lawyer to be at Danby's apartments before midnight so that before he left the warrants could be signed. By the time Barbara's lawyer arrived later that morning to inquire about due process, Danby was well on his way out of London. So on 9 August 1675, Louise, duchess of Portsmouth, was the proud mother of Baron Settrington, earl of March and duke of Richmond (the first and last of his titles coming from Yorkshire). This battle of precedence caused great amusement to the court, particularly the gossip that Louise had secured

Danby's support through the diplomacy of the bedchamber. For the record, Charles (Palmer) Fitzroy was created, duke of Southampton on 10 September 1675 and Henry Fitzroy created duke of Grafton the next day.

And, as if all that wasn't enough for Nelly and Barbara to bear, on 9 September 1675, Louise's son was also created Baron Methuen of Tarbolton, earl of Darnley and duke of Lennox in the peerage of Scotland. To this day, Richmond and Lennox have precedence over Southampton and Grafton. Louis XIV followed suit and created Louise's son duke of Aubigny in remainder to his mother (which meant that should her son die before her, Louise had the right to the estates). Charles Lennox, as the child became known, had so many honours showering down on him that it's a wonder he wasn't always rushing for cover. At nine he would be made a knight of the garter and appointed governor of Dumbarton Castle: and a year after that he would be master of the horse. If there was a doubt, it was now history: Louise de Keroualle, the small, pouting, sulking, chubby Frenchwoman was a duchess, the king's main mistress (the *maîtresse du titre*): more than that, she was queen in all but name. And how she knew it.

Nelly felt, literally, out of her class. Evidence suggests that Nelly did seek a title from Charles, despite her well-known modesty and altruism. The possibilities were investigated and the title of countess of Plymouth was being considered around the same time as Louise was being ennobled. In a letter to secretary of state Sir Joseph Williamson on 25 August 1673, civil servant Henry Ball in Whitehall wrote:

> My Lady Duchess of Portsmouth's patent has much troubled the people, they reporting it stopt, because shee was not naturalised, but her denization cleered that point. The people say, Madam Guinn complains shee has no house yett, and they will needs have it shee is promised to be Countess of Plymouth, as soon as they can see how the people will relish itt; so accordingly it's reported shee is so made, but how farr this motion is gone, I cannot learne.[7]

In his 'Signor Dildo', written about December 1673, Rochester refers to Nelly in the lines:

> The countess o' th' Cockpit (Who knows not her name?)
> She's famous in story for a killing dame...

With his usual, highly tuned humour, Rochester baits Nelly's aspiration with her reality: the Cock Pit was the small theatre at Whitehall. But even so, he fondly comments on her popularity and fame. It seems that any plans were scuppered by Danby, who argued against the ennoblement of a commoner. Nelly wouldn't forget or forgive this opposition. A later satire, in 1680, called 'Flat-foot ye Gudgeon taker' shows that Nelly still harboured hopes:

> Her brother Buckingham shall be restor'd
> Nelly a countess, Lory be a Lord.

'Lory' was Laurence Hyde, a friend of Nelly's, who would become earl of Rochester after the death of John Wilmot. Later on it was thought that Nelly was being lined up to become countess of Greenwich, but was thwarted by the death of Charles. In a manuscript book, *The Royal Cedar*, in 1688, Frederick Van Bassen wrote that 'Hellenor or Nelguine...who should bein advanced to be Countes of Greeniez, but hindered by the king's death...'[8]

However, whatever or whoever she was, her children's father was the king of England. And that must surely count for something. How could she just sit by and watch her rivals lord and lady it over her? She harangued and mother henpecked the king in the manner of Louise and Barbara, but had to wait until the end of 1676 to collect the fruits of victory.

As befitting Nelly's character, anecdotes suggest that it was Nelly's wit and sense of drama rather than relentless whingeing and pestering that forced the king to elevate her children. Annoyed that they had not even been granted a surname, let alone a peerage, Nelly decided to shame the king. One day in court, Charles, ever the affectionate father, asked to see his children. As Nelly's eldest son appeared she cried out to him 'Come here you little bastard and see your father!' The court was stunned into silence at this ungracious outburst. Charles was mortified. 'Why, Nelly,' he asked, 'do you call our son so?' 'Well, I've no other title for him,' came her calm and cutting response. This greatly amused Charles and he ordered Danby to attend to it.

However, progress was slow and this frustrated the quick-witted Nelly. She decided to take a more dramatic approach. The king and his brother called on Nelly at Pall Mall, only to be greeted by her shouting out of a top-floor window. As they looked up they saw that Nelly was dangling

Master Charles out of the window, threatening to drop him if he was not granted a title. A shocked Charles quickly responded: 'God save the Earl of Burford!' he cried. It's unclear whether this incident actually took place (and even if it did, it's equally unsure where: Lauderdale House in Highgate, for example, also claims to be the setting). But as with so many stories and anecdotes relating to Nelly's life, it is dressed in authenticity because it would be so like her to behave thus. There is an alternative version to the story: while Charles was out fishing Nelly submerged young Charles's head in the pond threatening to let him drown if no title was forthcoming. However, such cruelty is unlike Nelly. It's easier to imagine that she only forced her son's head and torso out of the window while making sure that he was safely in her hands.

Whatever the truth the outcome is undeniable. A warrant for the grant of dignities dated 21 December 1676 came into force six days later. The poor child who had scraped a dangerous living in the slums of London had seen her son created Baron Headington and earl of Burford. It was pure pride that pumped the blood around her veins that Christmas: her mother's heart was fit to bursting. Master James was not forgotten either. On 17 January 1677 a royal warrant assigned arms to him and his elder brother which, curiously, gave James the place and precedence of the eldest son of an earl. The arms included the 'baton sinister' which denotes illegitimacy. A motto was also chosen: *Auspicium Meloris Aevi* – 'A Pledge of Better Times' which would, in 1818, be adopted as the motto of the Order of St Michael and St George.

The granting of titles also meant that Nelly's boys were at last given a surname, that of Beauclerk (pronounced Bo-clare). James was granted the title 'Lord Beauclaire'. The choice of name is interesting. Charles was infamous for the number of children he sired outside the royal marriage. His unofficial royal family would total 13 (although there is some dispute over whether Catherine Pegge also gave birth to a girl, about whom little is known). Buckingham had once referred to Charles 'as the father of his people', adding under his breath 'of a good many of them, at least'. In *Absalom and Architophel* Dryden casts Charles II as the biblical King David:

> Then Israel's monarch after Heaven's own heart,
> His vigorous warmth did variously impart
> To wives and slaves: and, wide as his command
> Scattered his Maker's image through the land.

Henry I (1100–35) was known as the 'Lion of Justice' but he later acquired the nickname 'Beauclerc' in recognition of his education. However, Henry also holds the record of most acknowledged children with mistresses than any other English king. He also failed to leave a legitimate male heir to the throne. So the name was somewhat apt, whether intentional or not. Nelly, we can rest assured, would have approved of that.

News of young Charles's elevation spread widely and quickly. A letter to Laurence Hyde at Nijmegen dated 26 December 1676 (a day before it occurred), informs him that 'Mrs Nelly's son is now Earl of Burford'. Also, early in 1677, John Verney wrote to Edmund Verney that 'Nell Guin's son Charles is made of Earl of Burford, and, in want of heir male, to go to his brother James and his issue.'

However, with the battles for titles all but over, new game plans were being laid. The simple truth was that to be a king's mistress was expensive enough, but, add to that the responsibilities of being a mother of newly created members of the aristocracy and the costs would spiral out of control. Completely.

— *16* —

Money, Money, Money

For this Old Rowley gave 'em coach and horses,
Furnish'd them palaces and stuffed their purses.

'The Lady of Pleasure', anonymous, 1687

While these brats and their mothers do live in such plenty,
The nation's impoverished, and 'Chequer quite empty;
And though war was pretended when the money was lent,
More on whores, than in ships or in war, hath been spent.

'A Dialogue Between Two Horses', Andrew Marvell

Although resenting his lack of financial independence Charles II did consider it better to be a poor king than no king. Rochester famously labelled him 'a merry monarch, scandalous and poor'. Charles regularly needed to go cap in hand to Parliament, to supplement his secret French money. Of course, kingly poverty is all relative. He may have had debts but it didn't stop the extravagance – a characteristic adopted by those around him, including his mistresses – or restrict his natural generosity (somewhat enhanced when it's not really your own money you're spending). This soft-hearted king was also a soft touch and his lifestyle was thus expensive. The people, although genuinely fond of their restored king, despaired at how he chose to spend his (that is, their) money.

Particular resentment was reserved for the free-spending mistresses.

But while they all certainly knew how to dispose of a pound or two, it is Nelly who emerges, so to speak, with most credit. Undoubtedly guilty of extravagance, particularly when compared to what her purse might have contained had she not caught the eye of a king, Nelly still proved markedly less burdensome on the taxpayer than the others. Bishop Burnet considered her expenditure to be above £60,000 in total.

Indeed, Charles's expensive dalliances would cost him (that is, the state) dear: threatening even his carefully cultivated (and, to be fair, mostly warranted) popularity. Paolo Sarotti, a Venetian resident in England, wrote on 16 August 1675 that the elevation of three of his natural sons 'has increased to no small extent that the murmurs of the ill-affected because of the great sums of gold which his Majesty is constantly consuming to satisfy his numerous favourites and in providing for his children what is needed for the maintenance in a becoming manner.'[1]

The king liked to indulge his mistresses. They would ask, he would promise: 'I shall attend to it' almost became his catchphrase. In all likelihood, the promises were genuine but he rarely kept any. He revelled in generalities and disliked the detail that would make anything a reality.

Given the promiscuity of the times, primitive protection and underdeveloped health care, pleasure had its price: sometimes a doubtful paternity or an unwanted pregnancy, but usually the true cost was the pox. As would be expected, when the king's passions were so liberally shared, the mistresses and the monarch were often infected. The affliction picked more readily on Louise than Nelly, which would suggest that Louise, despite her protestations at Charles's infidelities, enjoyed to some extent at least the life of an avenging gander – 'not by Charlie is her own admission/cos the pox-filled wench is out of commission' as one not overly subtle contemporary ballad had it. For those who could afford it, a vacation to take the waters was the lonely penance for the reward of health again. However, on one such occasion, the pox brought another reward for the suffering Louise.

On 14 May 1674, the then French ambassador, Ruvigny, wrote to his minister Pomponne:

I have a thing to tell you, Monsieur, for the king's information [Ruvigny would refer to Louis XIV as 'the king', Charles would be the 'King of England'], which should remain secret as long as it pleases his majesty to keep it so, because if it gets out it might be a source of unseemly raillery. Whilst the king was winning provinces, the King of England was catching a malady which he has been at the trouble of communicating to the Duchess of Portsmouth. That prince is nearly cured; but to all appearances the lady will not so soon be rid of the virus. She has been, however, in a degree consoled for such a troublesome present by one more suitable to her charms – a pearl necklace worth four thousand jacobus [about £4,400, equivalent to about £335,000 today], and a diamond worth six thousand [about £6,600 – equivalent to about £502,500 today], which so rejoiced her... [2]

However, whatever the generous gifts did for Louise's morale, her pride was soon delivered another (for her) devastating blow. Her doctors advised trying the water at Tunbridge Wells. On arrival she found the marchioness of Worcester settled in for the season in the house Louise had hired. In her most engaging way, Louise explained that the marchioness was in the wrong, the law was against her and that she should make way, anyway, being as Louise was a duchess and above her in the peerage. The marchioness replied that people whose titles had been earned by prostitution had no sway over 'persons of quality and sense'. And then proceeded to taunt Louise about her past indiscretions with the likes of comte de Sault (son of the duc de Lesdiguières, a debauched French courtier) and Anthony Hamilton. Charles swiftly arranged for Louise to lodge at Windsor. It can only be hoped that the marchioness enjoyed the rest of her summer. Still, even by Louise's exasperating standards, the pox and public humiliation were handsomely compensated with the equivalent today of almost a cool million's worth of jewels. Little wonder that Ruvigny thought 'that I should not wonder if, for the price, she were not willing to risk another attack of the disease'. [3]

Despite generous settlements on them all, payments were often problematic. On 28 September 1673, Dr Henry Stubbes wrote to the earl of Kent that 'neither Madam Kerwell's, nor the Duchess of Cleveland, nor Nell Gwynne's warrants would be accepted'. Thomas Osborne, who had been at the treasury, became lord treasurer in 1673 (and would become earl of Danby the following year). Evidently his main task was to get to grips with the king's finances – and this would mean reviewing all payments – mistresses included. He would need tough hands to rein in this crowd.

At times Charles simply ran out of money. The mistresses may have moaned about late payments but none had to wait as long as others on his payroll. For example by midsummer 1665, '42 musitians' had remained unpaid for three and a quarter years: his Majesty's debt to them being £2,017.8s. Despondent that he was, and probably never could be selfsufficient, Charles brooded over the prospect of facing Parliament to request financial help. Indeed, when once asked why when he spoke to Parliament he would read from a script and never look up, he replied: 'I have asked the two house's so often and for so much money, that I am ashamed to look them in the face.' At these low times, and as ever, Nelly was brimming over with advice.

On one occasion she had the court in uproar: 'Nell Gwynne told ye King shee desired money of him, who replied he had not none; said shee I will tell you how you shall: Send ye French into France again, sett me on the stage again & lock up your codpiece!'[4] A second piece of advice also cheered Charles up. A contemporary letter tells the tale: 'I am told that his Majesty complaining he wanted money, Nell Gwyn should make answer, if he would take her advice she doubted not his Majesty would be supplied; he asking which way, she told him his Parliament being to sitt, he should treat them with a French ragoe, Scotts collopes, and a calves head; at which his Majesty laughed and was well pleased.'[5] Nelly had identified the three people Parliament disliked the most: Louise (the ragoe), Lauderdale (the collopes – he was Scottish) and Robert, earl of Sunderland, who was in league with Louise and was thought to have favoured a return to the policies of Charles I, whose execution the Whigs labelled mockingly 'Calves Head Day'.[6]

However, when England proved a difficult source of income, another target for raising money lay across the sea to the west. Pensions out of Ireland were paid to, among others Rochester and Buckingham. Arthur Capel, earl of Essex, was a largely unsuccessful viceroy during his tenure as lord lieutenant of Ireland between 1672 and 1677. He did, however, have more success (from the Irish point of view, at least) in frustrating settlements on the royal mistresses. Barbara never received Phoenix Park and Louise was refused £4,000 much needed to help bolster her obviously flagging jewellery collection. However, the latter 'victory' was short-lived as the 1676 Irish estimates include a payment of £7,600 for the redemption of jewels pawned by Louise. Essex, writing in 1675, likened the treatment of Ireland as 'nothing better than the flinging the reward, upon the death of a deer, among a pack of hounds where everyone pulls and tears what he can for himself.'[7] The complexity of land titles has been described as 'the curse of Ireland at the time'.[8]

Grants of land and titles were made, perhaps innocently, perhaps not, without any regard as to whether they were already legally owned. And so the battles for rights and pensions began. Nelly, as to be expected, was also granted a pension out of Ireland. The country's chief industry was its livestock and it was against the farmers that Nelly was to make her claims.

Even her mentor and friend Rochester attempted to exert influence to obtain her Irish pension. His letter, in his own hand, to Essex is in the British Library:

> The bearer of this being to present y^r Excellence with a preference from y^r King, wherein my name is to appeare, it becomes my duty to lett you know that I am made use of only as a trustee for Mrs Nelly & that by a particular direction y^r favour is humbly begg'd and much rely'd upon by her in this Affayre & my part is noe more but to advice her (as I wont) all I wish well to, I by any meanes to bee oblig'd to y^r Excellence if they can, since there is noe where be found a better friend or worthyer patron, how sincerely this is my opinion you would not doubt my Lord, could I make appeare to you, wth how much zeale & faithfullness I am, & wish ever to continue
>
> y^r humble servant
>
> Rochester[9]

However, it was after Essex's removal that the playwright, Sir Robert Howard, now serving the state rather than the theatre, acted as Nelly's trustee. He had replaced Sir George Downing (an unloved bully who, in about 1680, built the cul-de-sac of houses in the famous London street that takes his name) as secretary to the commissioners at the treasury. Howard corresponded frequently with James Butler, duke of Ormonde, over the settlement of an £800 annual pension on Nelly. Ormonde, who from 1677–1684 was appointed for the second time lord lieutenant of Ireland, wrote to Howard on 20 November 1677 'concerning Mrs Gwin's concernment' explaining that a number of patents preceded hers and that he didn't want to 'bring on noise and murmur' by moving her nearer to the top. Howard's reply, dated six days later, shows a typical side of Nelly's character:

> Mrs Nelly has commanded me to present her among the number of your true servants...that unless within a little time you command her something that

she may serve you in, she swears she will pick a quarrel with you, for she vows she loves you entirely... I presume to present her own words to your Excellency...

Ormonde wrote to his son Richard, the earl of Arran, on 24 January 1678 desiring him to 'make a visit to Mrs Gwin, and assure her of my readiness to serve her'. However, despite all the readiness to serve, the readiness to deliver was some way off. Nelly, it seems, was getting desperate for the money – offering even, to pay a higher commission in the hope that that might sweeten the way to her pension being advanced. Writing to Ormonde on 25 February 1678, Howard informed him: 'Mrs Gwin... cannot get the money due on her pension Michaelmas last... she has intimated that if she give 12 pence in the pound she may have it advanced, that is, besides the usual fees in the Exchequer.' However, it is made clear that Nelly wouldn't be paid until the 'civil and military lists were satisfied'.

On 16 March 1678, the earl of Arran wrote to Ormonde:

Mrs Gwyn sent for me the other day and desired my advice concerning money she should receive out of Ireland. Mr Mulys [Melish], one of your servants, is her agent in the matter; but Sir Robert Howard not being in town, I am to be informed from him, when he returns, out of what funds he is to be paid, for she could not inform me, and I don't find hers nor Sir Robert Howard's name in the list of pensioners who she says is her trustee in the business. She says she hopes to have your favour when you are applied and better instructed in the matter.

Ormonde replied from Dublin ten days later telling the earl that he 'may assure Mrs Gwyn that I understand her affair here very perfectly, and that she shall be very punctually paid, whoever is not, as long as I am in this place.' However, it seems that any notion of a punctual payment was about as solid as Irish mist. Sir Robert Howard ups the ante on 21 January 1679. He tells Ormonde that the king's secretary of state Williamson has issued a warrant:

to Mr Attorney general for the prosecuting of a suit against the possessors of Dundalk and Carlingford, which was begged upon discovery made of the deficiency of the title by Mrs Gwyn. The King took the opportunity of it to cause the benefits she is to have to be added to some other things to buy an estate in land for my Lord Burford.

Howard was to take care of buying the land. It seems that some payments were made eventually but apparently without regularity. A letter sent and signed by Nelly (but not written in her hand) on 4 September 1682 confirms this:

> This is to beg a favour of your Grace which I hope you will stand my friend in. I lately got a friend of mine to advance me on my Irish pension half a year's payment for last Lady Day, which all people have received but me, and I drew bills upon Mr Laurence Steele, my agent, for the payment of money, not thinking but long before this, the bills had been paid; but contrary to my expectation I last night received advice from him that the bills are protested, and he cannot receive any money without your Grace's positive order to the Farmers for it.
>
> Your Grace formerly upon the King's letter, which this enclosed is a copy of, was so much mine and Mrs Forster's [Nelly's sister] friend as to give the necessary orders for our payments notwithstanding the stop. I hope you will oblige me now, upon this request, to give your directions to the Farmers, that we may be paid our arrears and what is growing due and you will oblige.
>
> My Lord,
>
> Your Grace's most humble servant to command,
>
> Ellen Gwin.

Apart from showing that her sister Rose was also benefiting from Ireland, it's also clear that Nelly was still spending more than she was receiving, having to take loans out in advance of payments to help cover her debts. Little action followed this causing Nelly to write to the earl of Arran on 26 November 1682 informing him that the lords of the treasury had given an order 'to cause the arrears of my pension stopped in Ireland to be paid what is due to me to last Michaelmas with my sister's, Mrs Forster's, and the others whom their letter mentions.' No other correspondence has emerged, so we can guess that the pension payments resumed.

The mistresses got their money from pensions paid each English quarter day, which were Lady Day (25 March), Midsummer Day (24 June), Michaelmas (29 September) and Christmas Day (25 December). In addition there would be occasional payments ('bonuses'). As well as gifts from the secret service there was always the potential of more lucrative payments from taxes, duties and so on.

To put the extravagance of all the mistresses into an economic perspective, it's worth noting that it has been estimated that to maintain a middle-class lifestyle in Restoration England would require about £40 per year.[10] Nelly received £4,000 a year (today worth about £300,360), which wasn't bad for a state pension. However, with her son being ennobled, Nelly received a pay increase: 'The King directs that £1,000 per.an. shall be added to the £4,000 per.an. already paid to Maddam G to make that yearly payment of £5,000 per.an. and that this £1,000 per.an. shall begin from Christmas last.'[11] Interestingly, Nelly was the only mistress who received payments directly for her children. Money for Barbara's and Louise's children was paid to trustees. Perhaps, of the three, only Nelly could be trusted to actually spend the money on her children.

Nelly supplemented her allowance with her Irish pension, the patent of the grant of logwood – the passing of which on 24 November 1676 chopped her debts down by £162.5s. – and, of course, the occasional gifts of 'royal bounty'. An instruction, dated 21 January 1675, to pay a further £500 to 'Mrs H G' explained that 'the 500 guinnyes she formerly received being intended extraordinary for hangings [curtains, tapestries, drapery with which the bedstead and walls are hung].[12] This was duly done on 15 February 1675 and was not to be 'accompted any part of her allowance'. Nelly's local draper probably danced a jig to rival one of her own on hearing that news.

However, Nelly's approximate £6,000 a year was still less than paid to the others. In 1677 Barbara received a £6,000 a year pension (and £9,000 a year for her children) paid out of Post Office moneys. She also had the rights to the lucrative wine licences which brought in another £8,000 a year and, with various other duties and allowances, was estimated to be in receipt of about £30,000 a year. In today's money Barbara would be receiving over £2.25 million a year. Add to this her ruthless acquisition and pillaging of land and property grants for debt settlements and you can safely consider that she was doing very nicely out of the state thank you very much.

But even Barbara was surpassed by Louise, whose pension rose from £8,600 (to be paid out of Irish funds) a year in 1672 to £17,000 by 1680. To supplement this, Louise ('our right beloved cousin') and Charles, duke of Richmond and Lennox ('our right trusty and beloved son') were to receive 'the several sum of 12d. payable... by the governor, Stewards and Brethren of the Fellowship of the Hoastmen of Newcastle [upon every chaldron of coal] sold in England.'[13] This was also hugely profitable. As with Barbara, the wine licences also proved a substantial source of income for Louise. Andrew Marvell wrote in a letter from Westminster to Sir Henry Thompson on 19 December 1674: 'You have heard doubtlesse that the Duchesse of Portsmouth has £10,000 a yeare settled out of the Wine Licences...'[14]

The secret service money received by Louise between 27 March 1676 and 14 March 1679 amounted to £55,198 7s. 11d. (over £4.2 million today). This is an amount, wrote Danby to Charles on 28 April 1679, 'wch certainly bring her upon ^ye stage' – meaning that Charles would have to answer for it. During the same period, Nelly received £16,041 15s. – less than a third given to Louise. One payment alone to Louise, on 21 July 1677, amounted to £11,000. Although including some back payments from the previous year, the secret service accounts reveal that Louise, in 1681, received the colossal amount of £136,000 (over £10.3 million today). All of this, well known to the people, was not lost on visiting dignitaries either. The Venetian diplomat, Paolo Sarotti, wrote to the doge and Senate on 29 November 1675: 'The more politically minded dwell upon the quantity of gold which the King has given and which he lavishes daily upon his favoured lady, who is a Frenchwoman.'

Although she was never as rapacious as Louise and Barbara, Nelly was fully aware of the unfairness of it all. She complained to secretary Sir Joseph Williamson in January 1674 that she was not being as well treated as her rivals, young and old.[15] This is perhaps also another significant indicator of Nelly's age. Her only serious rivals were Louise and Barbara. But if we accept the 1650 birthdate for Nelly, she would be younger than them both, leaving her with no 'younger' rival. Barbara was born in 1641 and Louise in 1649: for one to be older and one to be younger, Nelly would need to be born between those two dates. Once again, 1642 could fit the bill.

So, what did they all spend the taxpayers' money on? Spending money did not tax them unduly as we shall see. They furnished their houses with luxury, furnished themselves with jewellery, lost heavily at gambling, delighted at entertaining, and bought services and favours.

The sight of jewellery brought a sparkle to their eyes. Evelyn commented that one night Barbara wore jewellery 'esteemed at 40,000 pounds and more: & far out shining the Queene'.[16] On 11 July 1677, Charles Bertie, secretary to the treasury, wrote to the commissioners and receivers of the excise, to pay Louise £8,385.7s. 6d. 'to redeem her Grace's jewels'. Seemingly, hocking her jewellery for loans was quite a pastime for Louise. Nelly, as we have already seen, paid handsomely for the 'Ruperta necklace'. However, that undoubted extravagance seems to have been Nelly's only one on jewellery. She maybe felt the need for variety and was known to have loaned jewellery, which could also prove cost effective, as this receipt shows:

19 March 75
rec^d of Madam Gwin at ye hands of Thomas Groundes ye sum of five pounds for the use of a parcell of jewels wc^h I form^{r}ly lent to her, and do hereby acknowledge yt I have rec^d them all back againe, I say rec'd
by me John Marlowe

Louise's 'glorious Appartment at Whitehall' was as luxurious as she was notorious, and because of its location, she became known as 'the lady at the end of the gallery'.[17] Once again, Evelyn is our eyes: 'I was Casualy shewed the Dutchesse of Portsmouths splendid Appartment at Whitehall, luxuriously furnished, & with ten times the richnesse & glory beyond the Queenes, such massy pieces of Plate, whole Tables, Stands &c: of incredible value &c.[18] His later visit, although uncomfortable in the presence of the king and his 'gallants' conversing openly with the part-dressed Louise, found him no less impressed:

... but that which ingag'd my curiousitie, was the rich & splendid furniture of this woman's Appartment, now twice or thrice, puld downe, & rebuilt, to satisfie her prodigal & expensive pleasures... Here I saw a French Tapissry, for designe, tendernesse of worke, & incomparable imitation of the best paintings; beyond any thing, I had ever beheld: some pieces had Versailles, St Germans & other places of the French King with Huntings, figures and Landscips, Exotique fowle & all to the life rarely don: Then for Japon Cabinets, Skreenes, Pendule Clocks, huge Vasas of wrought plate, Tables, Stands, Chimney furniture, Sconces, branches, Braseras &c they were all of massive silver, & without number, besides of his Majesties best paintings...[19]

He later that evening lamented: 'Lord, what contentment can there be in the riches & splendor of this world, purchas'd with vice and dishonor.' As far as the mistresses were concerned, great contentment indeed, one imagines. The teeth of hungry satires were biting:

To pay thy debts, what sums can'st thou advance?
Now thy exchequer is gone into France
To enrich a harlot, all made up of French,
Not worthy to be call'd a whore, but wench.[20]

Nelly certainly was untroubled by vice and dishonour and felt reasonably recompensed for it all, although undoubtedly distressed at the apparent financial inequality dished out to her among the main mistresses. She may have been less ostentatious than the others, but she was still extravagant. Although draped with her trademark humour, the example of Nelly's bed is testament to her extravagance. She planned and bought a most remarkable silver bed, weighing nearly 200lbs. Her silversmith's bill for silver ornaments for her bedstead (and for one or two other things) came to an astonishing £1,135. 3s. 1d. It was a good job she had somewhere to lie down when she received the paper headed: 'Work done for ye righte Honble Madame Guinne. John Cooqus, siluersmyth his bill.' John Coques was also a neighbour of Nelly's living on the north side of Pall Mall. The ornaments included the king's head, eagles, crowns, and cupids (possibly her sons). The bill also included an item 'Paid for iacob haalle [Jacob Hall] dansing upon ye robbe [rope] of Weyer Worck [wicker-work]' and 'ye other figure with ye caracter' which was Louise lying in a grave with an unnamed eastern potentate. One silversmith conservatively estimated that for a similar bedstead to be made today (dependent upon the intricacies of the carvings) the price would be around £250,000.

Nelly was evidently so pleased with the work that the bill included a £2 tip 'given to me Journey man by order of Madame Guinne'. The Alfred Morrison MSS show from 31 December 1674 to 30 April 1675, Nelly's secret service payments amounted to £2,000. On 4 February, £1,000 was paid 'to M^{ris} Hellen Gwyn', and the same amount again on 25 March. Also under 'More ordered and to be paid' a further £500 was granted to 'M^{ris} Gwin'. Well, that's the cost of the bed covered. Nelly had a taste for silver and gold: bills show a charge for 'mending ye goold hower glass' (2s. 6d.) and two silver bottles 'weighing 37 ounces 17 dweight' (£15.2s. 9d.). And just as she signed herself with her initials, so she would mark her silver plate. However, it would seem that others had a fancy for her plate as well, as the following was advertised in *The London Gazette* on 3 January 1678:

All goldsmiths and others to whom our silver plate may be sold, marked with a cypher E.G., flourished, weighing about eighteen ounces, are desired to apprehend the bearer thereof, till they give notice to Mr Robert Johnson, in Heathcock Alley, Strand, over against Durham Yard, or to Mrs Gwin's porter in the Pell Mell, by whom they shall be rewarded.

Getting around Restoration London was a demanding affair (some things rarely change). Walking was potentially hazardous, particularly in the pitch blackness of night. To light your way around you could buy a link – a torch made of tow and pitch – or hire a link-boy to see you home. Nelly's household bill for Christmas 1675 includes a payment of 3d. 'for a linke'.[21] Alternatively, you could hire or buy your own sedan chair and be carried, or hire a hackney coach or carriage. As there were only 400 licences for such coaches they were valuable items to have. Hire charges were set at up to 1s. 6d. for the first hour and 1s. thereafter; the maximum daily rate was 10s.[22] One of Nelly's household accounts includes a payment of 6d. 'for a hackne Cochman'.[23] However, *the* way to travel was by private coach as it was a luxury few could afford. But those few included the king's mistresses.

Nelly had a coach and four horses. A bill dated 23 September 1675 includes 'iron workes for the body of the carriage' and 'embellishments to roof, door and wheels': the cost being £146.5s.[24] But carriages didn't pull themselves and while horses could be hired it seems that Nelly preferred to have her own. The Treasury Minute Book on 24 November 1676 records that 'Mrs G' was 'to have £200 for horses'.[25] Her coachman, one Thomas Johnson, received £4 a year 'standing wages'.[26] It cost a lot more more than that to feed the horses. One bill shows that 'one load of hay bought when we come from Winsor' cost £1.16s. Between 6 July and 8 August 1675, 'Madam Gwynne's Bill for Horsemeate', which included 'oates', hay, straw and packs and bushels of 'beanes', came to over £21. Given that this was a typical monthly bill, it would cost Nelly over £250 per year just to feed her horses: nearly £19,000 a year in today's money. The carriage was embossed with a coat of arms and the initials 'EG'. Nelly liked to have her initials on things: her napkins and her windows. There still exists a bill for 'diament cutting' her initials on to '17 & 12 & 15 inche glasses and polishing the staines out of them . . . for putty and putting the glasses into the shapes'. Other costs incurred by her coachman, John Cooke, included 'greasing the coach', bringing the horses to the farrier, and even buying the farrier a 'drinck' while he went about his business.

Earlier in the year Nelly had treated herself to a sedan chair, which would just have to be embellished in her favoured silver and gold. It had 'the best neats leather to cover the outside', glass windows and was studded with thousands of nails 'guilt with water gold'. The delicious ostentation came to £34.11s., of which £2.10s. was for 'workmanshipe, the chaire inside and outside'. However, her steward Thomas Grounds settled the account (on 13 July 1675) for only £30 'in full discharge'. Nicholas Wandell signed a receipt on 12 April 1675 for £16.4s. 'for silvr worke for Madam Guin's sedan'. However, despite having her own sedan, she didn't always use it. A bill settled on 13 October 1675 was for services rendered by one William Calow is detailed below:

	£.	s.	d.
For careing you to Mrs Knights and to Madam Younges, and to Madam Churchfillds, and waiting four oures		5	0
For careing you the next day, and waiting seven oures		7	6
For careing you to Mrs Knights, and to Mrs Cassells, and to Mrs Churchills, and to Mrs Knights		4	0
For careing one Lady Sanes to ye play at White Halle and wayting		3	6
For careing you yesterday, and wayting eleven oures		11	6
ye some is	1	11	6

Most notable is the waiting times endured while Nelly gossiped and supped with her friends. Typically, Nelly allowed 'Lady Sanes' (probably her friend Lady Lucy Sandys) to use her sedan and picked up the tab. A household bill for 19–26 January 1676 also includes a charge of 2s. 6d. for carrying Nell's eldest son: 'for chare man brought mr [master] Charles' .

Nelly, the mistresses and their extravagance were cheap fuel to keep rumours burning around town. Henry Ball, writing to Sir Joseph Williamson on 14 July 1673, related one such rumour:

A pleasant rediculous story is this weeke blazed about, that the King had given Nell Gwinn £20,000, which angrying much my Lady Cleaveland and Mademoiselle Carwell, they made a sopper at Berkshire House, whither shee being invited was, as they were drinking, suddainly almost choked with a napkin, of which shee was since dead; and this idle thing runs so hott that Mr Philips askt me the truth of it, beleiving it, but I assured him I saw her yester night in the Parke. The people say there has been £100,000 given away within these last five weekes, so ready are they to blaze pernitious lyes.[27]

Another great expense for Nelly, but as ever not quite in the same league as Louise and Barbara, was her houses. Indeed, had she really owned all the houses that tradition suggests, she may well have surpassed her rivals. Pall Mall was Nelly's main home – her town house. She also had houses where the court often travelled, in Windsor and Newmarket.

Bagnigge Wells, near King's Cross, an area a touch more idyllic in the seventeenth century than today, was reputed to have been her summer retreat, and perhaps was. Demolished in 1841, when it had become a place of public entertainment, one frequenter recalled:

The long room, originally the banqueting room of the old residence...was about eighty feet long, rather narrow in proportion to its height, and with a low ceiling ornamented at one end. The walls were panelled, and the bust of Nell Gwyn was over an ornamental fireplace. It was in alto–relievo, let deep into a circular cavity in the wall.'[28]

Thornbury wrote that 'near the Fleet, and amid fields, she entertained Charles and his saturnine brother with concerts and merry breakfasts in the careless Bohemian way in which the noble specimen of divine right delighted. The ground where the house stood was then called Bagnigge Vale.'[29]

Another house touted as a possible summer retreat is Lauderdale House in Highgate. This house belonged to John Maitland, earl of Lauderdale, secretary of state for Scotland, and that country's virtual ruler. As he spent a lot of time in his native land, he may well have lent the house out. But the big, rough Scotsman, whose tongue was too big for his mouth causing him to 'bedew all he talked to', was no great friend of Nelly's – all they really had in common was red hair – so it would appear unlikely that she did live here. Charles may have stayed here, of course (there is a room known as 'the king's chamber'), in which case Nelly may well have joined him.

Tradition also links Nelly to Sandford Manor House, near the King's Road, Fulham. However, during Nelly's time the house was owned by the Maynard family and there is no evidence supporting the idea that she lived here, despite Faulkener's claims in his *History of Fulham*.

Houses claiming a Nelly connection (with the statutory secret passage) have reached almost Queen Elizabeth and Cromwellian proportions. A typical example comes from the London *Evening Standard*, on 31 August 1967 which ran a story that the composer Ron Grainer (who wrote the themes to *Dr Who* and *Steptoe and Son*) had 'rented a small period house in Hornsey Lane, Highgate which dates from the time of Charles II. "The story goes that it was used by Nell Gwynne for her ladies-in-waiting, or maybe for a few of the king's other lady friends!" said Ron Grainer.' Well, Nelly didn't have any ladies-in-waiting and, while she was not jealous of her rivals for the king's attentions, she certainly wouldn't have organised his sessions for him. Other claims have been made for Littleberries in Mill Hill,[30] and a 'two-storied, bow-windowed house, nearly opposite the… vicarage' in Leyton, Essex.[31] The same county is again put forward in an etching in the Mander and Mitchenson theatre collection of 'Nell Gwynne's house in Newport, Essex'.

The claims of a house in Hodge Lane (later identified as 38 Princes Street, and later becoming 53 Wardour Street) are more likely. A deed of covenant discovered among the papers of the house required the covenanter to produce a patent of 'Indentures of lease and release between William Chaffinch and Martin Folkes of the first part, Henry, Earl of St Albans of the second part, and Mrs Ellen Gwynne, John Mollins & Thomas Grounds, gentlemen, of the third part'.[32] It is, however, unlikely that she lived there but rather simply enjoyed spending the rent it made.

As she did with Bestwood Lodge in Nottinghamshire. Bestwood was founded by Edward III and had been the resting place for Richard III on his way to battle with Henry Tudor at Bosworth. The legend of how Nelly came to own it is certainly more interesting than the truth. One day while staying at the lodge, and mocking Nelly for her poor riding skills, Charles is supposed to have said that whatever land Nelly could ride around before breakfast would be hers. Thus she received the lease for most of Bestwood Park. Documents refer to the leaseholder as 'Lady Elinor Gwynne of the parish of St-Martin-in-the-Fields'. Although wrongly assigned, it was probably the closest Nelly came to a title. The truth is that Nelly probably never even visited the place let alone galloped around it in the early hours of the morning. The link was purely financial, not emotional: she was a landlady and the rents could be spent.

It's safe to say that not a penny of Nelly's allowances was spent on actually buying any of her houses. The state took care of that. All her spending would be on furnishing and decorating them. The two homes that certainly cost her money were Pall Mall and Windsor. Pall Mall was expensive to keep. Pennant described how the 'back-room on the second floor was (within memory) entirely of looking-glass, as was said to have been the ceiling. Over the chimney was her picture; and that of her sister was in a third room.' A bill from Anne Traherne included 'glass for dressing room' charged at £7. The same bill, again shows Nelly's love of gilding, as a charge is made for £3.10s. 'for gilding the hinges and nayles' of a bedroom cabinet.

An original order dated July 1678 for the payment of £5,000, for the rebuilding and repairing of the lodgings for the king and the duke of York at Windsor, was actually used to build Nelly her house, which she called Burford House, and Charles a tennis court. As with Pall Mall, Nelly would later extract a freehold for Burford House. The lease of 14 February 1680 would be superseded by a royal warrant dated 7 February 1683, which decreed:

> The new erected capitall messuage or mansion house now called or knowne by the name of Burford House with the gardens orchards out houses stables and appurtenances thereunto belonging situate and being in New Windsor in the co. of Barks and by the s^d deeds the same are declared to be in trust for Ellen Gwyn for and during her life and after her decease in trust for Charles Earl of Burford and the heirs males of his body.

The warrant also made provision that should there be no male heirs, then female heirs would inherit the property. Nelly's ex-lover and still good friend, Charles Buckhurst, by then earl of Dorset and Middlesex, was one of the trustees to the warrant. The house would only stay in the family until 1775, when it was, as one historian and apparent keeper of the nation's morals put it, 'bought by chaste George III for his (legitimate) daughters, and later home of the *married* quarters of the Guard'.[33] The house, although now once again called Burford House, is but a shadow of its former self. It is now part of the Queen's Mews.

In Nelly's time the house and grounds, however, were clearly remarkable. Writing his *History of Windsor Castle* in 1749, Pote commented that 'on the East side of the Town his Grace the Duke of St Albans [this would be the second duke, Nelly's grandson] has a stately and handsome seat with beautiful gardens that extend to the Park wall...'[34] Evidently, the magnificent staircase was embellished, at the king's request, by the Italian decorative painter Antonio Verrio (*c*.1640–1707), who decorated Windsor Castle for Charles and Hampton Court for William III. Work continued outside as well. A bill of £30.12s. 8d. 'for building a pump for Mris Gwyn at Windsor, viz £41.19s. 8d. to Edward Jordan, carpenter; £4 to Davis Smith and £21.3s.7d. to Alexander White, plumber' and another for rebuilding the garden wall show her taking a keen interest in personalising her gardens. Indeed, another bill from the 'bricklere' Francis Brookes details 'worke done for Medem Gwin' in her garden at Pall Mall. This includes 3s. for 100$^1/_2$ bricks and labour charges of 5s. 'for myselfe' and 3s. 'for my mann'. Nelly was very proud of her huge garden at Burford House, which took up many acres and hours, complete as it was with bowling greens and, perhaps somewhat symbolically, her own orangery.

Nelly, as befitting her status, had household staff. The most important and expensive of whom was her steward ('her man'), Thomas Grounds who simply took care of everything: the staff, ordering, paying, managing the accounts (as far as was ever possible with Nelly at the purchasing end of the business). A good steward was pivotal to a successful household and Nelly had good grounds to be thankful to have Thomas at the helm in the mid 1670s.

Although good stewards cost money the amounts were modest compared to Nelly's income. It has been suggested that Grounds was a £100-a-year man but this is unlikely.[35] A steward at Woburn Abbey at this time cost only £40 a year.[36] The next most important member of the household, who would expect to earn about half the salary that the steward commanded, was Nelly's 'lady' who would act as her personal maid, clerk and confidante. As Nelly couldn't (or chose not to) write, her lady would also take dictation. There would be a number of footmen (probably five) who were chiefly employed to attend the carriage and serve the table. Other staff included a cook, kitchen maid, coachman and porter. There would also be pages (probably about four) – young men who would run errands and so on – who sat patiently on the bottom rung of the domestic staff ladder. They were often unpaid and hoped for promotion to one of the paid duties. Other people, such as doctors, lawyers, auditors, attorneys and so on, were kept on retainers or paid gratuities. Two collectors (Obadiah Neale and William Lawne) on 22 December 1675 signed a receipt for 'twenty shillings wch is Maddam Gwin's gift to Dr Meriton for one yeare ending at Our lady Day...'

All domestic staff, bar the steward, were given board and lodging. They were also entitled to liveries – clothing and badges – a sort of household uniform. Nelly made sure her staff were well turned out and looked the part. A bill dated 24 April 1675 includes charges 'for 5 french hatts for ye footmen at 10 [shillings] a piece' and 'for 4 English hatt for ye other men at 7 and 6 [shillings] a piece'. This, of course, suggests that Nelly had nine male staff in her house.

Nelly herself always looked the part. Her hairstyle and clothing saw the former cinder girl set the London fashion scene ablaze '...some of your news I heard,' wrote Ursula Wolryche to her daughter Lady Wrottesley, 'as concerning Nell Gwine. They say there is the greatest gallantry maybe in towne; silver and gould lace all over peticotes and the bodies of their gounes; but sleeves and skirts blake; abundance of curles very small on their heads, and very fine their heads dressed.'[37] Indeed, one bill includes what may well be a reference to head-dress: 'a large cround allamode', which could be a large crown of the type in fashion (à la mode). Certainly to be à la mode, or rather mode-setting, you had to spend money. And that was something Nelly did rather well.

Nelly was fond of silk, lace and satin and just as fond of buying it for others as well. One bill shows Nelly paying £6.12s. (about £160 each) for three pairs of 'silke' shoes: 'one for yourself, another for ye sister and another for yor woman'. A bill from Charles Rise asked £1.18s. for 'two pair of pearle colour hose for Madame Gwynne'. A pair of 'gold buckels' set her back £4.3s. There are numerous receipts for gold and silver silk and lace, 'peticots', 'night gounds', and she'd buy yards of 'fine greane sattin'. Indeed, she might as well have been invoiced by the mile rather than the yard. Nelly's sister ('Rose Caslas') would shop for her and do some sewing for her. One of her bills is for 24 yards of Colbertine (French lace) for 'skirts' (the price is missing but it must have been at least 2s. a yard), '50 yards of narrow to ruffle' (at 6d. a yard), '3 yards of broad for the boddy of ye coate comes to 12d., 18 yards of pinck colored ribbon at 5d. the yard'. Evidently, even the shops couldn't keep up with the demand. The same invoice contains the following (sadly damaged) message: 'I have sent you the rest of the ribbon that was left. I was in twenty shopps in looking for cheper but could [not find any] for my life.'

Nelly was very fond of expensive materials: she particularly liked sarsenet (or 'saracen cloth') a very fine and soft silk material, now used chiefly for linings. Elizabeth Bowman provided '2 white sastnet hoods for child (7s.); 1 dus of children half hands (6s.); 6 paire of whit fingered gloves (6s.); 2 white sasnet hoods with scarvs (11s.)'. Nelly extended her peculiar penchant for satin and lace shoes to her children. An extraordinary bill includes 'scarlett sattin shoos with silk lace', pink satin shoes with black and silver lace, black lace shoes, green lace shoes with gold silk and black lace, and green satin shoes for Nelly herself and 'sattin shoos lace and gold' for Master Charles and for 9s. two pairs of children's shoes in pink lace.

All these invoices were paid by Thomas Grounds, although (as said) not before haggling for a best price. One bill of Henry Robins for £1.8s.9d. for '1 yd ³/₄ of gold & silver lace at 50d yd and 12 yds of gold, & silver & silk lace at 20ᵈ@ yd' was signed 'Rc'd – six + twenty shillings and six pence... in full of this bill.' The dependable Thomas wangling an eight and a half per cent discount for cash.

On 14 August 1675, 'Madam Guyn' received 'two silver indian cupps' for £2.15s. and a teapot for 16s. So, all she needed now was the tea itself: and sure enough on the same bill is a charge of 14s. (over £50 today) for 'half a pounds of tea'. Tea was a luxury item: at those prices tea bags would retail at 74p each today. On 25 April 1675, she thrust 19s. into the hands of Thomas Hawgood for 'two rapiers with gilt handles'.

Of course, Nelly's expenditure also included the more everyday household items. Collections of preserved bills offer a fascinating insight into the times.[38] Clearly part of the fascination is comparing the cost of items. In February 2000, the Bank of England estimated that £76.14 would be needed now to have the same purchasing power as £1 between 1670 and 1680. This means that a penny (240 to the pound) then would be equal to about 32p today and a shilling (twelve pence) would be equal to about £3.80. So a 'pidgon pey' bought by Nelly on 26 August 1675 at 2s 6d. would cost £9.52 today, and a 'creme cheese' at 1s 6d. would be the equivalent of £5.71 today. A sumptuous dinner was clearly being prepared on 14 March 1676, for that day was delivered: 6 ducklings (£1.10s.); 4 geese (£2); 6 fat chickens (12s.); and 6 rabets (7s.). She certainly kept a good table.

However, Christmas, inevitably, meant the biggest shop of the year, it being Master James's birthday also. Between 23 and 29 December 1675,

Pall Mall household accounts include payments for 'a dusen of oringes' which at just 1s. – that is a penny each – were markedly cheaper than the 6d. charged for one at the theatre; although Nelly ordered alcohol separately she obviously needed to top-up with 'a pint of brandy' for 8d. – clearly, Nelly's mother was planning to stay. And just in case the brandy ran out, deliveries had been taken of vinegar (3d.) and elder vinegar (5d.); other drink included 'strong waters' for 6d. and 3 pints of 'sack' or sec – Spanish white wine.

William Scott presented his 'poulter's bill', which included chickens, larks, 'a hen with eggs', a pullet and a snipe; Wilf Thompson presented his 'bucher's bill', which included a shoulder of mutton (the king's favourite, so it was probably apt that his cook was called Lamb), a side of 'lame', 'a legge of veale', an ox head (2s. 8d.) and two orders of beef totalling 14½ stone (for £2.4s.7d.); the '4 pound and a halfe of butter' (3s. 4d.) must be a better quality than the 'barill butter', four pounds of which cost 2s.; the only gesture towards vegetables was an item for 'turnips, carots and erbs' costing 1s. 3d.; 'Joe the porter' (no doubt a picture in his 'English hatt') received a sixpence Christmas bonus; in preparation for the big clean-up, a 'dust baskit' (1s. 6d), four pounds of 'sope' (1s.), and a mop (1s.) were bought; charges were also made for 'washing three paires of sheets' (1s. 6d.) and 'for baking a lofe' (2d.) Other items included:

	£	s.	d.
for a hundred pipens		3	0
for a pack of sault			7
for a bisket of nuts and apels			2
for tart and cheesecake			6
for tripe		4	0
for a quire of paper			4
for grinding a choping knife			3
for the Cooper for 5 garths		1	5
for a newse booke			6
for the char woman		1	6
for 3p[ound] + a halfe of backon		2	4

Nelly had presumably also been Christmas shopping with her sister, Rose Cassells, as the accounts also include 4d. being given to 'a porter that cared mis Casels things'.

Over the New Year period, other items of interest included a barill of oysters (3s.); a quart of white wine (1s.); a quarter of brandy (2d.); 'ote cakes' (2d.); a pound of sugar (1s.); 'apels and a bisket' (2d.) and 'a packe of cardes' (3d.). The butcher also provided '6 stone of beefe' for 14s.7d. and 'a legge of mutton 8 pound and a ha' for 2s.10d.

While great hunks of meat provided the staple diet of the day it all needed to be eased down and this is where the alcohol came in. To be honest, it came in whether food was there or not. Restoration Londoners were talented drinkers and Pall Mall was not the place to cultivate a dry throat. One of Nelly's bills for ale and beer alone in one month came to £14.3s. This is all the more remarkable when you consider that her entire food bill (which also included some alcohol) over Christmas 1675 came to about £8. A bill for ale and beer from 27 January to 4 August 1675 showed the championship standard of consumption at Pall Mall. The staple drink seems to have been ale (the traditional English brew of malted grain and water) and beer (hops added). Deliveries were taken of three kilderkins (a cask holding 18 gallons) of 'strong ale', six kilderkins of ordinary ale, and 23½ barrels (36 gallons each) of 'eights' (eight shillings beer). This meant that in just over six months no less than 1,008 gallons of ale and beer (or 8,064 pints) had been ordered and delivered. This equates to about 5¼ gallons a day, or 42 pints. This is serious supping. This was a society that began each day with a heartening drink of ale (children included), supported by a stiffener at mid-morning and the unrestricted free-for-all at lunch – the main meal of the day. Supper parties would often run into the small hours, while the steward would run into the cellar for another bottle or barrel depending on the company. Lord Conway told the earl of Essex that he had attended a party at Lady Shrewsbury's house in King Street, Westminster. He and the other guests, Nelly, Buckingham and Mr Speaker Seymour, all 'drank smartly' until 3 am.[39]

The limited medical knowledge of the time did not mean that the health industry's entrepreneurial prowess was left simpering and bedridden. Ill health was, is and always will be, big business. Physicians and chirurgeons (surgeons) were expensive. Most people relied on apothecaries, who were basically retail chemists who acted as community GPs. People were prepared to try anything in seeking cures. And although apothecaries were regulated (after a fashion) by the Royal College of Physicians, the level of expertise, knowledge and effectiveness between them and quack doctors was too slender to call. Physicians believed manfully in the healing power of bleeding. Apothecaries were not fond of blood, so they relied on something just as, if not more, painful: evacuation. Any illness of the body is best cleared out. 'If it's gone in, the quicker it comes out the better' was the shop counter-spun theory. And with a diet reliant on beer and meat, perhaps, it was advice worthy of note. Emetics was supplemented by a multifarious concoctions of herbs, spices, comfits, preserves and the like.

A preserved (just) apothecary bill, running to an extraordinary seven pages, delivered to Nelly on 15 January 1676, shows the variety available. Fragrant waters of juniper, rose, or mint were popular. As were plague water, the curiously titled Queen of Hungary water (a cosmetic toilet water) and Sir Walter Raleigh's water. Other items included 'plasters against the toothake', hartshorn, marigold flowers, syrup of violets, juice of liquorice, syrup of (the clove scented) gillyflower, balsamic pills, sugar candy, ounces of rhubarb and 'oil of nutmeggs'. However, it is the regularity of the emetic-related items that cause most cringing: the glysters and clysters (syringes), the ivory pipes and bladders, the bowls, the purging pills and the 'glystering plaisters'. Interestingly, occasionally the apothecary assigns the patient to the prescription. So we have Nelly's mother, 'old Mrs Gwin', being prescribed 'a plaistor', a quart of plague water, an ounce and a half of rhubarb, 'a cordial mixture', a large strengthening plaster, spirit of wine (that would have perked the old girl up) and a 'glyster'. Master Charles's 'codiall julep with pearls' was a rose-scented liquid sweetened with syrup or sugar and reduced down to the shape of small round pearls. He also needed 'two ounces of diascordium' – a medicine made of dried leaves. None the less, Charles was clearly in a healthier frame than his younger brother. Master James required an ointment, water for his face, 'five ounces of pectorall syrup' (for his chest), three doses of purging powder and to catch it all – 'a bole'.

Nelly's bill dated July–December 1675, which also included cordials and a glyster for her coachman, John Cooke, came to at least £75 (the shillings and pence section is lost). This bill would equate to over £5,700 today. For this and other bills, which were rather a lot to take care of in one payment, or simply when cash was a bit short, Thomas Grounds would offer an amount on account. This particular bill also noted that a former bill for £81 (so the amount is by no means unusual), which had been delivered to Mr Chiffinch, had yet to be honoured. One can imagine Nelly moaning to the king about the cost of medicines and him telling her to send them to William Chiffinch to pay – he'd sort it out. Which he would do. Eventually.

Given Nelly's income and splendid spending habits, the mundanity of taxation was equalled only by its relative inconsequence. An original receipt shows that one David Lloyd had collected £6.14s. ground rent for her house in Pall Mall. Ed Snelling was her collector of the scavenger tax – £1 a year. A receipt signed by 'George Taylor, collector' showed that 17s. had been received from Madam Gwynne 'for one half year's duty on seventeen fire hearths in her house in yᵉ Pall Mall' on 16 April 1675. This, of course, also meant that all these hearths needed cleaning. The household accounts that Christmas included a payment of 5s.6d. 'for yᵉ man that swept yᵉ chimnes'. And, once swept they needed filling up again. Between 5 and 7 August 1675, the house took delivery of 21 'loades of coales' at 13s. a load.

Nelly, proud to show off her house, entertained royally and royalty: the king and his brother being frequent visitors. She enjoyed organising candlelit musical soirées. Colly Cibber recalls an anecdote told him by Henry Bowman (1651–1739), one of the finest male singers of his day, which bears a striking resemblance to the story of the king and Nelly in a tavern, but is undoubtedly more authentic:

> Old solemn Boman, then a youth and fam'd for his voice was appointed to sing some part in a concert of musick at the private lodgings of Mrs Gwin; at which were only present the King, the Duke of York and one, or two more, who were usually admitted upon those detached parties of pleasure. When the performance was ended, the King express'd himself highly pleased, and gave it extraordinary commendations: Then, Sir, said the Lady, to shew you don't speak like a courtier, I hope you will make the performers a handsome present: The King said, he had no money about him, and ask'd the Duke of York if he had any? To which the Duke reply'd, I believe, Sir, not above a Guinea, or two. Upon which the laughing lady, turning to the people about her, and making bold with the King's common expression, cry'd, Od's Fish! what company am I got into![40]

Apart from being a delightful story, it also illustrates just how comfortable Nelly was with Charles: that she would laugh at him, gently mock him, and do as much using Charles's favourite expression. It's also fitting to end the chapter on money and the extravagance of the mistresses with the king himself out of pocket.

— 17 —

My Mistress, Politics

Hard by Pall Mall, lived a wench called Nell;
King Charles the Second, he kept her.
She hath a trick to handle his prick,
But never lays hands on his sceptre.
All affairs of the State, from her soul doth she hate,
And leave to the politic bitches.
The whore's in the right, for 'tis her delight
To be scratching just where it itches.

Anonymous, c.1680

As the above ballad demonstrates, one of the reasons Nelly was so popular was that she never meddled in politics, unlike the other mistresses who thrived on and thrilled at the intrigue. No, Nelly hated politics but loved the king. Well, as with the notion that she wasn't as extravagant as the other mistresses, the assertion that she wasn't involved in politics is part true, part fancy. She was no politician and politics (on the grand scale) was afforded little affection. But, make no mistake, she got involved. Or rather she got involved when her friends were involved: she valued her friends and helped when she could. She loved company and if that company dredged up terminable debates on politics, as long as they were happy so was she. She wanted to please and so would feign interest. She would cleverly call herself 'the sleeping partner in the ship of state', but would undoubtedly throw in her farthing's worth, when required.

Pall Mall was a hotbed of politics. Nelly may have played the hostess rather than the chair, but the king would regularly hold meetings there and it was the headquarters of what Andrew Marvell called 'the merry gang'. The merry gang included Harry 'Lying' Killigrew, Henry Savile (groom to the duke of York), Henry Guy (cup bearer to the queen), Baptist May (keeper of the privy purse), ex-lover Lord Buckhurst, Fleetwood Shepherd (a sometime poet who would become Nelly's steward), earl of Rochester, John Sheffield (earl of Mulgrave), and the duke of Buckingham (the last three were all gentlemen of the king's bedchamber).

The affection the merry gang had for Nelly is no better illustrated than through the correspondence between Henry Savile and Rochester. Savile, in exile, wrote to Rochester, who was convalescing at his country seat:

> Your friend and sometimes (especially now) mine, has a part in it that makes her now laughed att and may one day turne to her infinite disadvantage. The case stands thus if I am rightly informed: My Lady Hervey [Harvey] who allwayes loves one civil plott more, is working body and soule to bring Mrs Jenny Middleton into play. How dangerous a new one is to all old ones I need not tell you, but her Ladyship, having little opportunity of seeing Charlemayne [a nickname for Charles II] upon her owne account, wheadles poor Mrs Nelly into supping twice or thrice a week at W C[hiffinch]'s and carryeing her with her; soe that in good earnest this poor creature is betrayed by her Ladyship to pimp against herselfe, for there her Ladyship whispers and contrives all matters to her owne ends, as the other might easily perceive if shee were not too giddy to mistrust a false friend. This I thought it good for you to know, for though your Lordship and I have different friends at court, yet the friendship betwixt us ought to make mee have an observing eye upon any accident that wound any friend of yours as this may in the end possibly doe her, who is so much your friend and who speakes obliging and charitable things of mee in my present disgrace. When all this is done I doe not see in my present condition how you can make her sensible of this, for to write to her were vain; but I fancy my Lady Southaske has soe much witt and cunning that you might give her some directions in this matter that might prevent any future ill accident. I leave all to your Lordship to whom alone of all men living I would write with this freedome, where prudence would have advised silence, but my zeale for your service and my trust in your secrecy overcome all other thoughts or considerations.[1]

That Nelly was being duped by Lady Harvey is evident also from a letter written for her to Laurence Hyde, in 1678, saying 'We are goeing to supe with the King at whithall & my lady Harvie.' As Nelly never wrote her own letters, this may explain Savile's point 'that to write to her were vain'. It also sheds light on her innocent trusting nature being, as she was, 'too giddy' to realise that she was being used, which in turn, illuminates her limitations as a serious political contender. Her natural warmth was exposed starkly in a very cold light: her heart too soft to repel the cut and thrust of court politics. Undoubtedly, Jane Middleton, the puppet of Lady Harvey, was a beauty. However, she only succeeded in becoming a minor mistress and never seriously challenged Nelly, Louise or Barbara.

In June 1678, Rochester replied to 'the Honourable Mr Henry Savile' with the following advice for Nelly:

> But to confess the Truth, my Advice to the Lady you wot of, has ever been this, Take your measures just contrary to your Rivals, live in peace with All the World, and easily with the King: Never be so Ill-natur'd to stir up his Anger against others, but let him forget the use of a Passion, which is never to do you good: Cherish his Love where ever it inclines, and be assur'd you can't commit greater Folly than pretending to be jealous; but, on the contrary, with Hand, Body, Head and Heart and all the Faculties you have, contribute to his Pleasure all you can, and comply with his Desires throughout: Make Sport when you can, at other times help it. Thus, I have giv'n you an account how unfit I am to give you the Advice you propos'd: Besides this, you may judge, whether I was a good Pimp, or no.

Nelly's direct involvement in politics differed from Louise's and Barbara's in that her interest was altruistic rather than for self-aggrandisement, the thrill of power or personal profit. She was certainly not as politically ambitious as her rivals and had none of their 'king-making' pretensions. She did what she could, when she could. She became a sort of cooling agent for the hot water her friends occasionally found themselves in. Barbara and Louise, on the other hand, were bellows at the furnace.

Barbara's greatest triumph was persuading Charles to dismiss Edward Hyde, the earl of Clarendon. On doing so, Baptist May threw himself at the feet of Charles claiming that for the first time he could truly call him king. Gout-ridden and still mourning the loss of his wife, Clarendon heard of his dismissal from Charles's own mouth. Barbara, Baptist May and Lord Babington jeered him from an open window as he left court for the last time.

Louise, counselled by a succession of politically astute French ambassadors (de Croissy, Ruvigny, Courtin and Barrillon), was able to influence the king from the start. Early on, de Croissy wrote that he believed Louise 'has so got round King Charles as to be the greatest service to our sovereign and master...' He added that 'Milord Arlington' had informed him that it 'was better to have dealings with her than with lewd and bouncing orange girls and actresses, of whom no man of quality could take the measure.'[2]

Charles certainly discussed matters of import with Louise. De Croissy wrote, on 9 March 1673, that Charles 'told her yesterday that there was no course open to him but to dissolve parliament'. De Croissy could not yet trust the eager-to-please Louise at her word, and said that he would need to confirm this with Arlington. But the seeds were sown and bearing the promptest and plumpest of fruit.

Louise, who had taken to bedecking her child-like face with doll-like white make-up, was furiously tearful about an anonymous libel that was doing the rounds, entitled *Essay on Satire*. It lampooned her and Barbara:

> Yet sauntering Charles, between his beastly brace
> Meets with dissembling still in either place,
> Affected humour, or a painted face.
> In loyal libels we have often told him
> How one has jilted him, the other sold him,
> How that affects to laugh, how this to weep,
> But who can rail so long as he can sleep?
>
> Nor shall the royal mistresses be named.
> Too ugly, or too easy to be blamed...
> Was ever prince by two at once misled
> False; foolish; old; ill-natured and ill bred?

That Nelly was conspicuous by her absence only helped confirm in Louise's damp but avenging eyes that, as the rumours suggested, the author was poet laureate John Dryden. Louise decided this war of words should get physical. Narcissus Luttrell wrote that 'Mr John Dryden was sett on in Covent Garden by three fellowes, who beat him severely, and on peoples coming in, they run away: 'tis thought to be done by order of the Duchess of Portsmouth, she being abused in a late libell called an Essay upon Satyr, of which Mr Dryden is supposed to be the author.'[3] Whether Dryden was or not is unclear; John Sheffield, for example, has also been put forward as a possibility. The likelihood is that a number of hands were responsible.

The countess of Sunderland evidently sympathised with the character study of Louise in the satire. She wrote to Henry Sidney '...but truly I fear there will be some scurvy patching, for the Duchess of Portsmouth is so damned a Jade...for she certainly sell us whenever she can for £500.'[4] However, Sidney valued Louise's contribution to their cause: 'The Duchess of Portsmouth [is] a great support to our party,' he wrote on 21 June 1679. Five days later he records that she tells him to make great use of her if he wants to succeed: 'she hath more power over [the king] than can be imagined.'

Louise got her own way remorselessly. Appointment after appointment, decision after decision began to smack of her influence. Sir John Reresby noted in January 1674 that Buckingham 'was now in disgrace for which he was indebted to the Duchess of Portsmouth, a French lady, and now the most absolute of the King's mistresses, a very fine woman she was, but most think that she was sent on purpose to ensnare the king, who most readily ran into toils of that sort.' Luttrell affirms that it was at Louise's request that the king replaced the lord chief justice of Chester, Sir Job Charleton, with Sir George Jeffreys. She made Charles appoint Ralph Bridoake (the dean of Sarum) bishop of Chester during 1675. And yet while Charles listened to her demands for the replacing of ministers, judges and bishops, her demand that he dispose of Nelly fell on the deafest ears.

Charles did not succumb to 'petticoat influence' alone; a man of kind words and vague promises, he listened to everybody. He was driven by the need to be liked and as such simply agreed with the last thing he heard. The diplomat Sir William Temple (another Pall Mall resident) commented that 'he was very easy to change hands'. Charles's reign was certainly not one to be tarnished with anything approaching consistent, long-term or worthy policy. What policies there were reflected the man himself: 'wary, cynical and unprincipled'.[5] Burnet said the king 'hated business, and could not bear the engaging in anything that gave him much trouble, or put him under any restraint'. Rochester mocked that the 'government begins to thrive marvellous well, for it eats and sleeps heartily as I have known it, nor does it vex or disquiet itself with that foolish, idle, impertinent thing called business'; that ministers 'languish all day in the tediousness of doing nothing'; and that 'a committee of those able statesmen assemble daily to talk of nothing but fighting and fucking'. Grammont believed that Charles 'had an agreeable wit, he was affable and easy by temperament in mind . . . he was in turn compassionate to the unhappy, inflexible towards the wicked, and tender almost to excess.'

His political will is amply illustrated by his treatment of the regicides and his handling of Colonel Blood. On Restoration he wanted all regicides executed. After ten were put to death – eight at Charing Cross, two hanged at Tyburn – Charles decided that was enough. He had wanted to feast on revenge but his conscience bloated quickly: revenge left a bitter taste. He considered the point made.

Following the arrest of Colonel Blood in 1671 the town traded in gossip. Why did he try to snatch the crown? Was it part of a plot to remove Charles and hand the jewels to a new king? This theory gathered apace when it was also discovered that the Great Seal had been stolen from the Lord Chancellor's house. There could be no other sentence but death. Found guilty of high treason Blood could expect to be hanged but cut down before dead. He would then be castrated and have his entrails taken out – all of which would be burnt before his eyes. His head would then be cut off and his body cut up into quarters. His bits ending up wherever his majesty's pleasure directed. Usually this meant being displayed at separate and prominent parts of town as part of a learning process for would-be dissidents. London Bridge would have the heads, and Westminster Hall or one of the city's gates would have the limbs and their attached pieces of torso. Women were spared such an appalling end as it was thought inappropriate to hack up a female body in public. Spared the mutilation, women could breathe a sigh of relief and look forward to being buried alive instead.

As for Blood's death the only doubt was when it should take place. The provost marshal, Sir Gilbert Talbot, interrogated Blood. Three days later, Blood found himself being questioned personally by the king and the duke of York behind closed doors at Whitehall. Blood was remanded to the Tower. Amazingly, two months later, warrants were signed for his release and pardon, along with his son-in-law and their two companions. Blood also had his confiscated lands restored, and had even earned himself a place at court with an annual pension of £500.

Even by Charles II's standards, forgiveness was never this good. In all probability, Blood earned his freedom, plus expenses, by becoming a Restoration version of a supergrass. Shortly after his release, three of Cromwell's old captains were arrested and over time more than 20 other republicans were given up. However, it would be more in keeping with Charles's character if it was Blood's wit that saved him. And perhaps it played no small part. Charles, during Blood's interrogation, had asked him: 'What if I was to give you your life?' To which, the contrite Blood replied: 'Well then, Sire, I shall endeavour to deserve it.' Such a remark would almost certainly have brought a smile to Charles's face: and, once you had won that smile, tolerance, if not admiration, was but a soft old heartbeat away.

Such was Charles: as much man as king. The delicious ode, usually attributed to Rochester, and apparently pinned to Charles's bedchamber door ran:

> Here lies Charles, our Sovereign King
> Upon whose word no man relies on;
> Who never said a foolish thing,
> Nor ever did a wise one.

The easy-going Charles enjoyed humour – even at his own expense. However, on this occasion his mirth was increased with his own riposte that he agreed with the statement, for his words were his own and his actions were those of his ministers. But, of course, often they weren't: they were Charles's all right. Or those of his mistresses. Treated to public offices, all three main mistresses became ladies-in-waiting to the Queen. Nelly was appointed during 1675. However, it's uncertain that she actually did any waiting on the Queen, perhaps rightly feeling the awkwardness and inappropriateness of it all.

However, considering the potential antagonism that could exist between them, Nelly and the queen appear to have experienced a cordial relationship. Perhaps Catherine appreciated Nelly's ability to embarrass and ridicule the gruesome twosome. The appointment was prestigious, even if in name only and would have entitled her to an apartment at Whitehall, but it seems she was content with Pall Mall. Perhaps this also endeared her to the Queen, even though she herself spent most of her time in Somerset House rather than Whitehall. Certainly the symbolism of such a gesture would not be lost on Catherine.

However, Nelly's political involvement is best demonstrated by her efforts with Buckingham and Monmouth, her role in the downfall of Danby, and her facilitation of the merry gang.

The first duke of Buckingham, our Buckingham's father, was a great favourite of James I (who called him 'Steenie'). He remained influential with James's son, Charles I. Indeed, after the duke's assassination, Charles met his widow and told her that he would care for her as a husband and her children as a father. So the young George Villiers grew up virtually a brother of the future Charles II, who would call him 'Alderman George'. It was this long-standing relationship that founded Buckingham's rise to the top and became the safety net that would catch him in his frequent falls from grace and favour: he would end up in the Tower at least four times.

He had tried during the Commonwealth, unsuccessfully, to marry Charles's sister Henriette-Anne (Minette), and even put himself forward as a suitor to Cromwell's daughters – perhaps hoping that this might lead to the return of his confiscated lands and property. Although regarded as the 'most graceful and beautiful person that any court in Europe ever saw' and for someone who the 'trouble in wooing was, he came, and saw, and conquered', his wife was everything the dynamic Buck never looked for in a woman.[6] Mary Fairfax was remarkably plain, pious and virtuous. She would need all the piety she could muster to help lighten the misery that Buckingham would heap on her.

Perhaps her forbearance was given its sternest test with Buckingham's most notorious mistress. Anna Maria Brudenell, countess of Shrews-bury, was too scandalous even for this scandalous age: not a woman to upset was my lady Shrewsbury. She had high profile affairs with Thomas Howard, Henry Jermyn and Harry Killigrew. Her meek husband had not even twitched in defiance of the sensation she caused. That is until she was openly paraded by Buckingham, when he felt compelled to issue a challenge for satisfaction. It was accepted.

On 16 January 1668, the duel took place in a close at Barn Elms, a manor house with fashionable gardens (much frequented by Pepys) in south-west London. Pepys recorded 'the much discourse' in the town that the duel had caused. He says that 'my Lord Shrewsbury is run through the body from the right breast through the shoulder'.

Shrewsbury was mortally wounded and died two months later. One of Buckingham's seconds, Captain William Jenkins, was 'killed upon the place'. Pepys shook his head at what the world might think about the king and his councillors when Buckingham 'the greatest man about him, is a fellow of no more sobriety than to fight about a mistress'.

Lord Peterborough also alleged that the countess disguised herself as a page and watched the carnage while holding Buckingham's horse. And even went to his bed that night wearing the very shirt soiled with her husband's blood. St Evrèmond in a letter to Waller also said that she had hidden about her person pistols that should the result not be the desired one, she would not only shoot her husband, but herself as well.

Buckingham brought Lady Shrewsbury back to his house to stay. Understandably, the duchess was unhappy about this arrangement and told her husband that she would not share a roof with such a notoriously, disreputable woman. 'I thought so much, my lady,' replied Buckingham, 'that is why I have ordered a coach to take you to your mother's.' Such was the notoriety of Buckingham's affair that the court wits would refer to his wife as 'the dowager duchess'. Anna Maria had a child in 1671 and there was no doubting the father. The king even agreed to be godfather. Unfortunately the child – declared the earl of Coventry – died a few days later and, causing much sensation, was buried with pomp and ceremony at Westminster Abbey.

Buckingham, who according to Grammont was 'seduced by too good an opinion of his own merit', crafted his policies out of whim, and was as unpredictable as he was eccentric. His protégé, Sir Thomas Osborne, first Earl of Danby (1632–1712) had emerged in 1673 politicking successfully less through persuasion and argument than through nods, winks and bags of gold. From Kiveton, Yorkshire, his sound understanding of finance and business stood him in good stead and he became lord treasurer later that year. Called 'the white marquis' because of his deathly pallor, he was arrogantly smooth and never really popular. Danby led the court party which, committed to the rule of the king, was strong in the towns, but was branded 'Tory' by their enemies: a 'Tory' being an Irish thief and rebel; somehow it seemed apt. The court party was the natural home of Buckingham.

The opposition was led by Anthony Ashley Cooper, earl of Shaftesbury (1621–83). At about the same time as the emergence of Danby, 'Little Sincerity', as Charles called Shaftesbury, grew ever more hostile towards what he regarded as the king's pro-French and pro-Catholic policies, and his absolutist pretensions. Shaftesbury's country party were thus opposed to all things papist: the queen, the French, the duke of York and the court, all of whom they saw as puppets of popery. The opposition were also pro-Dutch, seeing a natural alliance with a protestant nation to form a front against the expanding French under Louis XIV. The country party were branded 'Whigs' by their enemies: a 'Whig' being a Scottish outlaw; somehow that too seemed apt. And yet it was with the country party and Shaftesbury that Buckingham formed an alliance – much to Charles's despair. The duke being the duke would speak out against the French, while simultaneously pocketing huge bribes from them.

Buckingham argued, in 1677, that Parliament should be dissolved because Charles had prorogued it for over a year, and by doing so had, in effect, already dissolved it. Charles disagreed. Quoting from a law passed over 300 years before, Buckingham commented knowingly that unlike women, acts of Parliament were not the worse for growing old. He argued that Parliament must meet at least once a month. He added that an accidental meeting can no more make a Parliament than an 'accidental clapping a crown on man's head can make a king.' It proved an unsuccessful argument. Defeated, he and three other peers (Shaftesbury, Salisbury and Wharton) were committed to the Tower of London for refusing to apologise for their comments. Characteristically, Buckingham asked if he could take his cook with him. Characteristically, not only was the cook permitted but his footmen as well.

Irrespective of the comfort Buckingham clearly had to suffer as part of his imprisonment, he was still imprisoned. Enter Nelly. She visited her friend in the tower and delivered him a letter of advice from Charles Buckhurst. It read:

> The best woman in the world brings you this paper, and, at this time, the discreetest. Pray, my Lord, resign your understanding and your interest wholly to her conduct. Mankind is to be redeemed by Eve, with as much honour as the thing will admit of. Separate your concern from your fellow-prisoner [Shaftesbury], then an expedient handsome enough, and secret enough to disengage yourself: obey, and you are certainly happy.[7]

Heeding the written advice and doubtless that offered verbally by Nelly, Buckingham wrote to the king:

I am so surprised with what Mrs Nelly has told me, that I know not in the world what to say... What you have been pleased to say to Mrs Nelly is ten thousand times more than ever I can deserve. What has made this inclination more violent in mee, than perhaps it is in other people, is the honour I had of being bred up with your Majesty from a childe, for those affections are strongest in men, which begin in theyre youngest yeares. And therefore I beseech your Mjesty to believe me when I say that I have ever loved you more than all the rest of mankind... I wish that all the curses imaginable may fall upon mee, if I tell a lye to free my life...[8]

Once again, this appeal to their past worked. Buckingham was released within days. But as Andrew Marvell reported in a letter to Edward Harlay on 7 August 1677, the release was only temporary in order to allow Buckingham time to recover his health. But, once out, the 'merry gang' would petition the king to make it permanent. He wrote:

The D: of Buckingham petition'd only that he had layd so long, had contacted severall indispositions and desired a moneth's aire. This was by Nelly, Middlesex [Buckhurst], Rochester, and the merry gang easily procured with presumption to make it an intire liberty. Hereupon he layd constantly at Whitehall at my L: Rochester's lodgings leeding the usuall life.

Danby and his supporters were shocked not only at Buckingham's release (given his comments about the king) but that he was permitted to stay at Whitehall. Charles did what he did best and compromised. Buckingham could keep his liberty provided he went to his country seat at Cliveden. He left Whitehall but soon returned to London, taking up the offer of lodgings at Pall Mall. Such an offer shows the strength of Nelly's position in the court and with the king. It did not go unnoticed by those in the court party. Lord Chancellor Boyle wrote: 'But I understand by some letters that the absence of the Duke of Buckingham at that juncture of time, and his present favour, and allowance to have his lodgings in Madam Nelly's house, doth not a little contribute to the jealousies and dissatisfaction of the people.'

Interestingly, on 22 September 1677, Sir Robert Southwell wrote to the duke of Ormonde claiming that because Danby refused to sanction Nelly being created a countess, this was why she was throwing her weight against him: ''Tis certain that Buckingham passes a great part of his time with Nelly, who because the Lord Treasurer [Danby] would not strive to make her a countess, she is at perfect defiance with him, so that the treasurer's lady is there acted, and the King looks on with great delight, which has a fatal prognostic unto some.' The comment that Nelly was 'in perfect defiance with him' suggests a real or imagined fear that she had direct influence over Charles. But, typically, she takes her revenge by hilariously imitating Danby's wife. Add to the mix, Buckingham's flawless impression of Danby and the comic duo had the king helpless with laughter. And with this king laughter led to influence.

And Danby knew it. He was concerned about the influence emanating from Pall Mall. He wrote to his wife from Newmarket on 28 September 1677, adding this postscript:

> Remember to send to see my Lord Burford without any message to Nelly, and when Mrs Turner [Nelly's clerk] is with you, bid her tell Nelly you wonder she should be your Lord's enemy that has always been so kind to her, but you wonder much more to find her supporting only those who are known to be the King's enemies, for in that you are sure she does very ill.

But Danby's hoped-for favour and support never arrived. The earl of Arran wrote to his father on 9 February 1678: 'Yesterday the Bishop of London told me with heavy heart [that] he looked on the Lord Treasurer as a lost man. That all this has been brewing since those entertainments at Nelly's upon which and the scenes of abuse there passing on Lord Treasurer.'

A letter dated 1 November 1677 from Henry Savile at Whitehall to Rochester shows the confidence with which Nelly moved among the noble and the great:

> Mrs Nelly, who is his [Buckingham's] great friend and faithfull councellor, advised him not to lay out all his stock upon the christning but to reserve a little to buy him new shoes that hee might not dirty her roomes, and a new periwigg that she might not smell him stinke two storeys high when hee knocks att the outward door.[10]

With Buckingham living in her house and the merry gang frequently supping there, politics was an established part of the menu. The factions sought to get their man appointed secretary of state. The ambassador in Paris, 'an almost indecently ambitious young man',[11] Ralph Montagu, had hoped to secure the appointment through the favour of lord treasurer

Danby's wife (the mistresses weren't the only women to be courted for preferment), who had great influence over Sir William Temple. But the merry gang were at work in favour of Nelly's friend Laurence Hyde.

Hyde (1641-1711) was the second son of Edward Hyde, earl of Clarendon, and thus sister to the first duchess of York. His eldest brother, Henry, inherited the earldom, although politically and intellectually he inherited little else from his father. It was Laurence who published his father's *History of the Rebellion and Civil Wars* in England through the Oxford University Press. Hyde, who was considered to be aloof, irritable and overbearing, hardly seems the type to engage Nelly. However, Roger North's description of him being a heavy drinker who 'swore like a cutler' lessens the surprise. And, anyway, Nelly usually brought the best out of those she liked.

In 1679 Hyde was appointed a commissioner to the treasury, soon rising to be first lord. Teamed with Sidney Goldolphin (whom Charles described as being never in the way nor out of it) and the early Sunderland, they became known as the 'Ministry of the Chits'. Hyde became the earl of Rochester in 1681 following the death of John Wilmot, Nelly's other great friend. Three years later, Hyde became lord president of the council, which was supposedly promotion but reduced his power and influence.

An appointment that moved Lord Halifax to coin the memorable phrase that Hyde had been 'kicked upstairs'.

Aware of Hyde's ascendancy, Montagu wrote from Paris to Charles Bertie on 29 March 1678:

> I know for certain there is a great caball to bring in Mr Hide and that Nelly and Duke of Buckingham are in it purposely that no friend of my Lord Treasurer may be in place, and they have engaged Mr Secretary Coventry by Henry Savell, whoe writt a letter last post to my Lady Cleaveland that his future depended on her coming over.

It's interesting, in this case, that it was thought worthwhile to seek the help of Barbara. Barbara had moved to Paris in 1676. A warrant from Danby on 26 February 1677 permitted '150 parcels of plate and goods belonging to the Duchess of Cleveland to be transported in the *John & Sarah* of London, to Rouen, Normandy for her Grace's use.'[12] During her time there she lived life the only way she knew how, and took a string of lovers: even the archbishop of Paris was suspected of an unholy alliance with our Barbara.

Another of her lovers was Ralph Montagu. However, she dumped him unceremoniously in favour of the marquis de Chatillon. His ego knocked out of joint, Montagu foolishly sought revenge by seducing Barbara's daughter Anne, who although only turned 17 was a wife and mother. Charles had acknowledged paternity of Anne (in 1673) but while Barbara's husband, Roger Palmer, genuinely assumed that he was the father, the child was generally believed to be that of the earl of Chesterfield who, according to Lord Dartmouth, resembled him in both face and person. Barbara's fury was unbridled. She wrote letters of complaint to Charles about Montagu's behaviour towards their daughter. In one of them she tries to play down her own behaviour, citing back at Charles what he had said to her: 'Madam, all that I ask of you, for your own sake, is, live so for the future as to make the least noise you can, and I care not who you love.' Barbara made plenty of noise about Montagu which only calmed once Charles had dismissed him from office. It was Barbara's last political triumph.

However, Montagu's dismissal had heavier consequences. He had been involved in the negotiations with Louis XIV over the continuance of the French subsidy. It was astonishingly unwise of Charles to act as he did. Montagu, armed with letters sent by Danby, got himself elected to Parliament (despite Danby's aggressive attempts to prevent it) and that December produced the documents to the House. Danby was impeached and later imprisoned in the Tower, where he remained until 1684. For his part, Ralph Montagu became the duke of Montagu, but ended up in marriage to the less than sane duchess of Albemarle, who believed herself to be the empress of China and as a consequence would make Montagu crawl on his hands and knees in front of her.

With Nelly on his side, Laurence Hyde's political career was assured. Indeed, Nelly's earliest surviving letter was sent to him around June 1678 while he was negotiating a peace treaty with the French (which was duly signed and delivered at Nijmegen on 10 August). She wrote:

Pray Deare Mr Hide forgive me for not writeing to you before now for the reasone is I have bin sick thre months & sinse I recoverd I have had nothinf to intertaine you withall nor have nothing now worth writing but that I can holde no longer to let you know I have never ben in any companie wethout drinking your health for I love you with all my soule. the pel mel is now to me a dismale plase sinse I have so uterly lost Sr Car Scrope never to be recooverd agane for he tould me he could not live allwayes at this rate & so begune to be a little uncivil, which I could not suffer from an ugly baux garscon. Ms Knights Lady mothers dead & she has put up a scutchin no beiger then my Lady grins scunchis. Mylord Rochester is gon in the cuntrei. Mr Savil has got a misfortune, but is upon recovery & is to marry an hairess who I thinke wont wont have an ill time ont if he holds up his thumb. My lord of Dorscit apiers wonse in thre munths, for he drinkes aile with Shadwell & Mr Haris at the Dukes house all day long. my Lord Burford remimbers his sarvis to you. my Lord Bauclaire is is goeing into france. we are goeing to supe with the king at whithall & my lady Harvie. the King remebers his sarvis to you. now lets talke of state affairs, for we never caried things so cunningly as now for we don't know whether we shall have pesce or war, but I am for war and for no other reason but that you may come home. I have a thousand merry conseets, but I cant make her write um & therefore you must take the will for the deed. god bye. your most loveing obededunt faithfull & humbel

       sarvant

       E.G.

Although written for her by her secretary, we still get a sense of Nelly out of this letter. We find out that the witty courtier and poet Sir Carr Scrope has been banished from Nelly's house because of his uncivil tongue. Scrope had fallen out with the earl of Rochester and Nelly had evidently sided with her 'E of R'. Interestingly, Nelly uses Rochester's phrase of 'ugly *beau-garçon*' to describe Scrope, who was noted for 'the ugliness of his squint, his conceit, and his rather squalid love affairs'.[13] In his attack on Scrope in 'On the Supposed Author of a Late Poem in Defence of Satire', Rochester writes:

> Who needs will be an ugly *beau-garçon*
> Spit at, and shun'd by ev'ry girl in town...
> While ev'ry coming maid, when you appear,
> Starts back for shame, and straight turns chaste for fear...

The tag obviously stuck and was appreciated by Nelly. Rochester himself, she tells Hyde, 'has gone in the country' – back to his house at Woodstock. Probably on one of his numerous enforced exiles from court.

The 'Mrs Knight' referred to is the singer Mary Knight. The 'scunchis' is an escutcheon, a hanging that is put up in the house in mourning showing the deceased's coat of arms. Mr Savil was Henry Savile, Rochester's constant friend and correspondent. The 'fat boy' of court would become envoy extraordinary in Paris. Indeed, he would be in Paris during the stay of Nelly's youngest son, James Beauclerk, 'my lord Bauclaire', whom she tells Hyde will be going into France. Henry Savile's supposed marriage to an heiress failed to happen. 'My lord Dorscit' was Nelly's ex-lover, Charles Sackville, Lord Buckhurst, now earl of Dorset. She lamented his poor attendance at Pall Mall because he spent all day drinking in the duke's House – Dorset Garden theatre – with playwright Thomas Shadwell and the actor Joseph Harris. The friendships were strong because it was Buckhurst who championed Shadwell as poet laureate, after Dryden had been sacked in 1688.

Finally, her comment on 'state affairs' illustrates Nelly's deep political thinking. She is for war with the Dutch, but only because that will mean her friend would be able to come home all the sooner. Politics was something that, at times, just got in the way.

The rise of Hyde and the disaffection of Montagu contributed to the downfall of Danby. This was exacerbated by the revelations being made amid the growing hysteria of the so-called 'Popish Plot'. Danby had seriously underestimated the potency of the plot. As indeed, at first, had the king. On 13 August 1678, Charles was informed by Christopher Kirby (a laboratory assistant with the Royal Society) of a plot to kill him. Unperturbed at the ludicrous prospect of Jesuit assassins, French-aided uprisings in the three kingdoms and the placement of his brother on the throne, he set out for Windsor and that evening 'his Majestie was at supper with Mrs Nelly'. However, the fear and hysteria whipped up by the plot's inventors, 'Dr' Titus Oates and Israel Tonge, was such that the very dawn cracked with paranoia. Danby's scepticism was well placed but badly managed. Shaftesbury and the Opposition quickly mapped the political mileage to be made and threw their lot in with Oates. Danby was doomed. His involvement with the hated popish French implicated him in the plot and paved the way for his five-year imprisonment.

Oates, meanwhile, was propelled to hero status as 'the saviour of the nation'. The whole episode caused Charles great unease. On 14 November 1679, Henry Sidney records that 'The King went to Hampton Court ... he is horribly vext, told me the story of the plot, and thinks we shall all be undone.' Against his better judgement, Charles was forced to lend credence to the plot by making Oates and his colleagues civil servants. Not only was Oates given lodgings at Whitehall and put on a salary of £10 a week plus '40 shillings p'week for dyett and expences' but informers, investigators and prosecutors were also on the royal payroll. For example, the exchequer records show, on 22 October 1679, that £40 was paid to Lawrence Mowbray and Robert Bolton (who later with his wife, Mary, would be on a retainer of 40s. a week) 'to defray their charges into Yorkshire, to give evidence on his Ma'ties behalf and to search for Popish priests'. Two other agents, a certain Peter Gill and Michael Sturtton, were rewarded with a bounty of £20 for 'apprehending Willm Marshall, popish priest'.[14] Dr Israel Tonge on 19 September 1679 received £50 'as of a free gift'. For perhaps the first time Charles himself realised what the term 'wasteful expenditure' meant. More alarmingly, the plot accounted for 35 executions.

The whole thing was, of course, poppycock. By March 1681, the plot was lost. It had been used as a backdrop to the Whig campaign to exclude the duke of York from the throne. When that collapsed so did the world around Oates's ears.

While the nation followed the scent of religious fear and fervour, Charles generally turned his nose up. The religion of his people interested him little: his experience of the fires of hell when at the mercy of the Scottish Covenanters before the battle of Worcester did it for him. He once asked: 'are hearts and minds not enough? Do I need to rule their souls as well?' As for his mistresses, he cared not which god they prayed to, if at all. He certainly wasn't interested in the souls of women. He twice tried and twice failed to bring in a Declaration of Indulgence which would grant freedom of worship to Catholics and other dissenters. The second failure (13 March 1672) was compounded by Parliament's hard-line introduction of the Test Act on 29 March 1673. This forbade Catholics from holding public office.

As Catholics were driven from court (Barbara's name was removed from the list of the ladies of the bedchamber), Charles had to seek special dispensation for certain of his staff: these included his barber, shoemaker and the queen's Portuguese ladies-in-waiting. Sir Thomas Clifford also resigned from government, putting his religion ahead of his career. He was to die a few months later, suicide being suspected. James, duke of York, resigned the post of lord high admiral confirming fears of a Catholic succession.

Despite the duke of York's haughtiness, aloofness, coldness and general all-round disdain for Charles's court, the moral, clean-spirited James was not averse to dirtying his toe in the mudbath of immorality: he was renowned as a great ogler and had more than his fair share of liaisons. His soul might be solid, his heart steel, but his flesh was as weak as the next adulterer's. John Wilmot, earl of Rochester, whose own death was popularly believed to have been caused by 'intensive drinking and whoring', had once complimented a courtier on having made more cuckolds than any other man alive. However, Charles was critical of James, not over his weakness for women, but rather over his choices. Charles said, 'My brother's mistresses are so ugly that I can only think his confessor imposes them on him as a penance. The last one squinted like a dragon.'

Perhaps James's most celebrated mistress was Catherine Sedley, daughter of the playwright, poet, wit and general all-round debaucher Sir Charles Sedley. The hapless Catherine famously commented about James's mistresses: 'We are none of us handsome, and if we had wit, he has not enough to discover it.'[15] On another occasion, James was embarrassingly caught mid-passion Lady Carnegie by the woman's unfortunate husband. To gain his revenge, Lord Carnegie visited carnally the 'foulest whore' his embittered money could buy so that he would catch the pox (which he did), so that he could give it to his wife (which he did), so that James would catch it also (which he did).

James's first wife was the plain and 'strong built' Anne Hyde, daughter of Edward Hyde, earl of Clarendon. They married in secret, after Anne had become pregnant. The marriage caused immediate distress for both Charles and Clarendon and, sadly, long-term distress for Anne. Pepys called her a plain woman 'like her mother' who was also 'of size': he records, with relish, kissing her 'most fine, white and fat hand'. The misery of her life and marriage meant she sought comfort and solace in food.

Clarendon sought to dissolve the marriage at once, but Charles, as ever his blustery anger calming into an inevitable acceptance, decreed that they should make the best of it. Clarendon was furious because he knew that his enemies would use the marriage against him. Already thought to be too powerful (mostly by those who were jealous of his power rather than fearful of it), and with James still the heir to the throne, this would be seen as a ploy to have his daughter become queen of England. Although Anne never became queen (she died of breast cancer in March 1671 at the age of 34) both her daughters did so: Mary II (1688–94) as co-regent with William III (who then reigned alone until 1702), and Anne (1702–14). Indeed, Anne ('Brandy Nan'), who inherited her mother's looks and build, was to be the last Stuart monarch to reign in Britain.

Following his wife's death and his enforced resignation under the Test Act, a nation's panicstricken eyes looked to see whom James might choose as his new wife. He stoked the anxiety by announcing with his usual bad timing – which was supreme even by his own exacting standards – his marriage to Marie d'Este from Modena, an Italian Catholic. He married her by proxy on 30 September 1673. Her arrival in England was delayed by illness for the best part of two months until 21 November. There was little celebration offered for the arrival of 'the eldest daughter of the pope' as she was generally known.

The French had intrigued for Madam de Guise to become James's wife. But James had received such a bad account of her from Charles's envoy – Henry, earl of Peterborough – the de la Guise's fate was sealed. Louise began to seek a preference for another Frenchwoman, Mlle d'Elboeuf. Louis XIV opposed the suggestion and asked his ambassador to 'adroitly apply yourself to cause hitches so that it will never take place'. It was a match which also angered Colbert and Arlington, but showed how important and influential Louise now thought herself. However, on this issue James was to prove his own man: he chose his own bride. The hapless d'Elboeuf became not a bride of a future king but rather a bride of Christ, as a Sister of the Visitation. However, Louise was to have more success as part of the negotiations for the marriage between James's daughter, the Princess Anne and Prince George of Denmark.

So with Queen Catherine childless and the duke of York embarking on a Catholic alliance, the people needed a Protestant champion. And who better than the handsome, dashing, athletic and Protestant eldest natural son of the king? James Crofts, duke of Monmouth, was the son of Charles's Welsh mistress Lucy Walter (who also called herself 'Mrs Barlow', taking the name from a maternal uncle). Evelyn described her as 'a browne, beautiful, bold but insipid creature'.[16] Monmouth was born in 1649 while Charles was in exile. Physically he was most definitely his father's son and, according to Buckingham in his *Memoirs*, inherited another royal trait as he 'was ever engaged in some amour'.

Charles doted on all his children but scarcely hid that his greatest pleasure was his firstborn. After Monmouth had killed a London beadle in 1671, such was his fatherly indulgence that Charles signed a warrant pardoning him from 'all Murders, Homicides and Felonies whatsoever at any time before 28th of February last past committed either by himself alone or together with any other person or persons'. However, this ceased the moment Monmouth accepted the Protestant mantle and became the willing tool of Charles's opponent Shaftesbury. With the Popish Plot and the succession crisis fracturing the nation, Charles had little option but to banish the popular Monmouth.

All this popularity went to Monmouth's head – which was convenient as there was clearly very little else in there.[17] In a thunderously ill-advised display of political naïveté, he returned from exile almost immediately and without permission. Indeed, his popularity with the London mob ensured that his return in November 1679 was greeted by bells and fireworks despite his 5 am arrival. Monmouth had defied his father and was now in the same city. There was possibly only one place where he would be safe to work towards a reconciliation with his father: the home of another common, pretty and (possibly) Welsh royal mistress.

Nelly took Monmouth in and agreed to do what she could to help. She understood the complications, but all she could truly see was a father and son not talking. However, Nelly was all too aware of the king's anger and had to bide her time. At first when Charles called to dine, Monmouth had to make himself scarce. In his letter to Lady Sunderland, dated 16 December 1679, Henry Sidney notes that Monmouth 'makes great court to Nelly, and is shut up in her closet when the king comes, from which in time he expects great matters.'[18] Barrillon confirms the arrangement in his letter to Louis XIV in December 1679, saying that Monmouth 'every night sups with Nelly, the courtesan who has borne the king two children, and whom he visits daily'.

However, on this occasion, Nelly was unsuccessful. Charles would not hear of granting an audience to his son. A contemporary account records:

Nelly dus the Duck of Monmouth all the kindness shee can, but her interest is nothing. Nell Gwinn begg'd hard of his Maj^tie to see him, telling him he was grown pale, wan, lean and long-visag'd merely because he was in disfavour; but the King bid her be quiet for he w^d not see him.

Robert Southwell confirms Charles's refusals in a letter to the duke of Ormonde on 29 November 1679, saying that Monmouth 'supped the last night with Mrs Gwynne, who was this day at her utmost endeavours of reconciliation, but received a very flat and angry denial, and by all appearances His Majesty is incensed to a high degree.'

The satires of the time also chronicled the event and display once again Nelly's humour and confidence. She called Monmouth 'Prince Perkin', making a reference to the infamous Flemish-born impostor Perkin Warbeck who laid claim to the English crown of Henry VII. The satire *A Panegyric* comments:

> True to ye protestant interest and cause;
> True to th' established government and laws;
> The choice delight of the whole mobile,
> Scarce Monmouth's self is more belov'd than she.
> Was this the cause that did their quarrel move
> That both are rivals in the people's love?
> No; twas her matchless loyalty alone
> That bid Prince Perkin pack up and be gone.
> Ill-bred thou art, says Prince; Nell does reply
> Was Mrs Barlow better bred than I?

Charles reacted to his increasingly wayward, self-deluding and feckless son's outrageous defiance by depriving him of his offices and ordering him into exile again. Once again Monmouth defied his father and proceeded to tour the country promoting the story of the infamous black box in which it was said existed a marriage contract between Charles and Lucy Walter. This would, of course, legitimise Monmouth's claim to the throne. The supposed marriage was something that Lucy Walter had repeatedly claimed until her death in 1658. Charles would silence his son's claims, signing a statement in the presence of the privy council confirming Monmouth's illegitimacy. As far as Charles was concerned he was without a legitimate child and he would be succeeded by his brother.

Oddly, Louise supported the exclusion of the Catholic James. Sir John Reresby, for one, wasn't sure why. He considered that it might be just politicking 'artfully to insinuate herself into the good graces of the [Whig] party,' or 'in compliance with France whose tool she was'.[19]

Perhaps. However, Louise figured that if Parliament was to pass a bill that gave Charles the right to nominate his successor (as had happened with Henry VIII) then, given that 'she was so absolutely mistress of the king's spirit, she might reckon that if such an act be carried, the king would be prevailed upon to declare her son his successor.'

Louise's own version was somewhat different. She told Henry Sidney that people don't like her because she is 'too much in the interest of France' and added that while she supports France, 'when it comes between France and England – she is on England's side'. Unfortunately for Louise, England was rarely on hers. And it suddenly got worse. A brilliant and beautiful Roman woman had arrived in London and quickly became a huge thorn in Louise's side. Nelly, as expected, was beside herself.

— 18 —

The Roman Conquest

...One of those lofty Roman Beauties, no way like our Baby
visaged, and Puppet-like Faces of France.

The Picture and Character of the Duchess Mazarin, Cesar Vicard

(the self-styled Abbé de Saint Real)

When thro' the world fair Mazarine had run
Bright as her fellow traveller the sun;
Hither at length the Roman eagle flies,
As the last triumph of her conq'ring eyes.

'The Triple Combat', Edmund Waller

Giulio Mazarini was an Italian by birth who became a naturalised
Frenchman and, as Cardinal Mazarin, succeeded the powerful Cardinal
Richelieu as minister of France in 1642. By his death in 1661, Mazarin
had amassed an enormous fortune. The beneficiary of that fortune – said
to be around 28 million francs (the equivalent of about £150 million
today) – was to be his niece Hortense Mancini. Hortense was explosively
beautiful. She had long, curling jet black hair, a 'sombre yet wild' face,
big eyes which were 'neither blue nor grey nor black' and which changed
colour with the light. Although she was dubbed the 'queen of the
Amazons', she also had a brilliant mind: she was fluent in many
languages, hugely well read and intelligent. Quite a catch, then. Her

uncle had reviewed and dismissed many suitors, including a homeless Charles Stuart whose proposal for marriage was born of love (although being an heiress to a rather large amount of money probably didn't pass the notice of the cash-strapped king in exile). The cardinal who had done business with Cromwell believed that Charles had no prospects and rejected him out of hand.

Armand de la Porte, the marquis de la Meilleraye, fared better. He married his prize on 28 February 1661 and was subsequently created Duc Mazarin. Level-headedness was not his strongest characteristic. Saint-Simon wrote that 'piety poisoned all the talents that Nature bestowed upon him.' He mutilated statues and painted over pictures that had any naked forms. He prohibited women from milking cows in case it gave them impure thoughts. He wanted to pull his daughters' front teeth out to rid them of their inherited beauty and, as such, prevent them from flirting. His jealousy was about as maniacal as his religious zeal. In her best-selling *Memoirs*, Hortense described the extent of her husband's envy:

> I could not speak to a servant but he was dismissed the same day. I could not receive two visits but he was forbidden the house. If I showed any preference for one of my maids, she was at once taken from me. He would have liked me to see no one in the world except himself. Above all, he could not endure that I should see either his relations or my own – the latter because they had begun to take my part; his own, because they no more approved of his conduct than did mine.

It's little wonder that after five years of this torment she sought sanctuary at a convent and petitioned Louis XIV for a divorce. Unable to secure this, she deserted her husband, children, fortune and country and embarked on her remarkable travels, frequently disguised as a man, and vividly (if not entirely accurately) recounted her adventures in her *Memoirs*. All over Europe she left a lasting impression and an awful lot of broken hearts and lovers.

A chance meeting with Ralph Montagu signalled her decision to visit England – somewhere she had never been. It was to become somewhere she would never leave alive. She landed at Torbay and disguised as a cavalier rode to London. She made her way to St James's Palace, where Marie d'Este di Modena, the duchess of York, related to her through her Martinozzi cousins, was overjoyed to welcome her; if not just for the relief of being able to speak Italian to someone. French ambassador

Ruvigny commented that 'The Duke of York is taking particular care of the Duchess Mazarin. The Duchess of York has affection for her. She is always with her.' The attention poured over her by the duchess of York caused Louise to complain to Charles that she was not given the same treatment: the duke of York had not permitted his wife to call on Louise.

In the absence of money, Hortense had lived on her wits. The allowance she managed to receive from her estranged husband was never enough. It seemed that another woman was about to make demands of an already under-siege exchequer.

Hortense's ally and counsellor during her entire stay was the French writer Charles de Marquetel de Saint-Denis, Seigneur de Saint-Evrèmond, who although tapping 60 had fallen in love with her ('A man can never be ridiculous in loving you,' he wrote). He described that all 'the movements of her mouth have charm, and the queerest grimaces become her wonderfully when she is imitating those who make them. Her smile would soften the hardest heart and lighten the profoundest dejection of mind.'[1] Despite his murmuring heart, their close relationship was never anything but platonic. Although they would quarrel and make up regularly, they would disagree on little: save perhaps hygiene. Someone as obsessed with cleanliness as Hortense would be a peculiar match for someone of whom it was written:

> Old Evrèmond renowned for wit and dirt
> Would change his living rather than his shirt.

He was something of a character and was admired by Charles for his wit. So much so, that when Buckingham appealed on his behalf to Charles, the king granted the old Frenchman an income. Typically, when censured for such a donation, Charles replied that it was not a gift but a salary, claiming he had made Saint-Evrèmond 'Governor of the Ducks in St James's Park'. He took his notional job seriously allowing rare species of ducks the freedom of his apartments (chickens also ran amok in his bedchamber), believing that living creatures about him helped to reanimate his decaying body and soul. Saint Evrèmond was quite unmistakable: a tall man who preferred to wear a small cap (rather than the all-conquering periwig) over his long white hair, and whose face was disfigured by a large lump on his forehead between his eyes. Beauty had found her beast.

With the arrival of Hortense, during Christmas 1675, Charles was sparked out of his inertia by the call of the chase. He would agree with Ruvigny who described her as 'being more beautiful than ever' adding that 'she is to all appearances a finely developed young girl'. Charles said that she appeared to grow more beautiful each day. Undeterred by his failure to capture her hand while in exile, he set about his business with renewed charm and vigour. Above all, he claimed, to enjoy her intelligent company. The old flame was flickering well enough. Charles was once again hopelessly in love.

Characteristically, Nelly remained Nelly: calm, secure and unthreatened; whereas Louise saw her world crashing around her. After all, this Italian could have been queen. The very title that Louise craved (and felt she deserved) had been offered to this woman by Charles himself – and she had refused. The battles between Barbara and Nelly now began to look like mere skirmishes: the real enemy had arrived and Hortense, with all her well-loaded cannons blazing, was scoring victories almost hourly.

Shuddering from this challenge, Louise's early tactics were as distinctly shaky as she was. Already feeling ill and listless following a premature birth, she made a sad attempt to divert Charles's lustful attentions: she bashed her head on her bedstead to give herself a black eye, hoping it would provoke sympathy and attention from Charles. The court amused itself by saying it was the pasty-faced Frenchie's attempt to darken her skin to compete with the delicate olive of Hortense. Nelly, clearly aware of the discomfort and irritation that the arrival of Hortense had on Louise, started wearing black: 'I am mourning the loss of Louise's hopes,' she said with that famous mischief in her eyes.

Louise considered that, in the circumstances, the best thing she could do was to retreat and get away from it all. What she couldn't see, couldn't hurt her. She hoped that Charles would miss her and either send for her or come and join her. And, if Charles conquered Hortense, at least she would not have to witness it for herself. Towards the end of May she left for the waters at Bath which she took for six weeks. Even with Hortense capturing the king's eye, Nelly was still stealing a peak or two. Courtin reported that Nelly had joked to him that she had armed herself in every possible way to protect herself from the resentment Louise would throw at her because of all the visits she had received from Charles during her absence.

Above Charles's cabinet room at Whitehall were the apartments once used by Barbara, but which were now being used by their daughter, Anne, Lady Sussex. Anne idol-worshipped Hortense, seeing her as a romantic adventuress. Hortense visited Anne daily. Charles, who could enter the apartments from his backstairs, also visited daily. Charles and Hortense would retire to a room and nobody, according to the French ambassador Honoré Courtin (who had replaced Ruvigny), was permitted to enter, not even the king's French musicians who would follow him everywhere.

On her way back from Bath, Louise stopped at Windsor Castle to dine with the king, but was mortified at not being asked to stay over and had to continue on to London. Her health may have improved but her grief was still in need of care. On 8 July she hosted a grand party for the departing Ruvigny. Charles appeared for the final hour to appreciate the musical entertainment. Louise could not help herself. She requested a Spanish song *'Mate me con non mirar mas no mate me con celos'* ('Kill me by not looking at me, but do not kill me with jealousy'). The guests, Charles included, found that enormously amusing.

Meanwhile, Hortense had been set up in St James's Square by the duke of York which, given her financial constraints, was thankfully only charged at a peppercorn rent. It was here that her salon became the place to be. It was a centre of wit, learning, the finest music and uninhibited gambling. Evelyn commented on meeting Hortense – 'the famous beauty and errant Lady' – at a dinner at the lord chamberlain's house, adding that 'all the world knows her storie'.[2] As well as being a focus for such social and political animals as Buckingham and Grammont, her salon had its fair share of real ones: dogs (with names like Little, Rogue and Chop), cats (one was called Monsieur Poussy), monkeys and birds: including Boule the bullfinch, Loteret the parakeet, Pretty the parrot and Jacob the starling.

Courtin delighted in the machinations of the court's social world. He wrote that the 'arrival of the Duchesse Mazarin has caused a great stir in that court. The King of England appears to have been attracted by her beauty, and though the affair has so far been conducted with some secrecy, it is likely that this growing passion will take the first place in the heart of that prince.'[3] With Charles spending time away from her, Louise began to look and feel lost. She feared her decline. Courtin visited her in her apartment and found her crying. He wrote on 6 August:

Yesterday evening I saw something which aroused all my pity... I went to see Madame de Portsmouth. She opened her heart to me in the presence of two of her maids... [She] explained to me what grief the frequent visits of the King of England to Madame de Sussex cause her everyday. The two girls remained propped against the wall with downcast eyes; their mistress let loose a torrent of tears. Sobs and sighs interrupted her speech. Indeed, I have never beheld a sadder or more touching sight.

Courtin advised her to dry her tears, accept the situation and display indifference. This she tried, but her eclipse continued. On 12 November 1676, Courtin wrote:

> The Duchess of Portsmouth has the king often at her rooms which are the place where he's seen most publicly. But I have ascertained beyond doubt that he passes nights much less often with her than with Nell Gwynne; and, if I can believe those who are most about him, his relations with the Duchess of Portsmouth have subsided into a virtuous friendship. As to the Duchess Mazarin, I know he thinks her the finest woman that he ever saw in his life.[4]

Louise's luck could hardly be more down and out – in a three-horse race for Charles's affections she trailed the tails of Nelly and Hortense. If losing face wasn't enough, she also had to face losing money and valuables when her steward disappeared with about £12,000. He had also pawned her jewels for another large sum of money. In the autumn, the court set out for its traditional decamping to Newmarket for the races. Upon arriving at the town, Louise suffered the ignominy of discovering that no lodgings had been booked for her. She had to carry on to another village. The mighty was falling. And fast.

On 17 December, Courtin wrote that he pitied Charles II who only really wanted to be liked but found himself surrounded by jealous women: 'He had to face the anger of the Duchess of Portsmouth for drinking twice in twenty four hours to the health of Nell Gwynne, with whom he often supped, and who still made the Duchess of Portsmouth the butt of her tickling sarcasms.'[5] Hortense, however, was still clearly in the ascendant. Charles regularly would go through the charade of retiring to bed, only to re-dress and sneak out joining Hortense after her card parties had finished, and return to his own bed at 5 am.

The new battle of the mistresses was the talk of the town. The MP and poet about court Edmund Waller (1606–87) wrote 'The Triple Combat' about the rivalry between Nelly ('the lovely Chloris'), Louise ('Little Britain') and Hortense ('The Amazon'). Nelly is thus described:

> The lovely Chloris well attended came
> A thousand graces waited on the dame:
> Her matchless form made all the English glad
> And foreign beauties less assurances had.

Although banished for his part in a Royalist plot, Waller was permitted to return to England by Cromwell in 1652 and repaid the favour by penning a gushing, celebratory poem on the lord protector. On the Restoration, he wrote a gushing, celebratory poem on Charles II, who complained that Waller's poem on Cromwell was superior to the one on himself. Waller replied smartly 'Poets, Sire,' he said, 'succeed better in fiction than in truth.'

The less sophisticated also marked the fortunes of the royal mistresses. For example:

> Since Cleveland is fled till she is brought to bed,
> And Nelly is quite forgotten,
> And Mazarine is as old as the Queen,
> And Portsmouth, the young whore, is rotten.

Hortense was actually nine years younger than the queen, but this may have been a reference to her looking a lot younger than she actually was. But, interestingly, this short verse once again gives us a clue to the age of Nelly. If we accept the 1650 birthdate, Nelly would be the youngest of all four of Charles's long-standing (or long-lying) mistresses. So, why would the balladeer make a clear reference to Louise as 'the young whore'? Once again the evidence points to Nelly being older than Louise and casts more doubt on the 1650 birthdate.

Courtin recounts an occasion at Hortense's apartments when Louise turned up to conduct a ceremonial visit (part of her strategy of indifference). However, she was followed almost immediately by Nelly and Lady Harvey (the woman that Henry Savile had warned was a 'false friend'). Nelly had arrived to thank Hortense formally for the compliments she had made following Nelly's son elevation to the earl of Burford. The three rivals, although finding themselves together by accident, and with Lady Harvey, whose hatred of Louise was well known (her brother Ralph Montagu blamed Louise for his disgrace), endured the awkward time cordially enough.

Courtin commented that everything 'passed off quite gaily and with many civilities from one to the other, but I do not suppose that in all England it would be possible to get together three people more obnoxious to one another.'[6] Louise, pushing her indifference past all known limits, buckled first and withdrew. At this point, according to Courtin, the bold, laughing Nelly asked him why the king of France didn't send presents to her rather than the weeping willow who had just gone out? She said he would profit the more for doing so, because the king of England was her constant night-time companion and was 'a thousand times fonder of me than her.'

It got even better for Courtin who enjoyed Nelly's joke. The others changed the conversation to Nelly's notorious undergarments, asking if they could judge the renowned quality themselves. Nelly was nothing if not immodest and happily and proudly lifted her dress, and lifted each petticoat (she wore many), permitting a thorough examination of each one by everyone – Courtin included. 'I never in my life,' he wrote to Pomponne, 'saw such thorough cleanliness, neatness and sumptu-ousness. I should speak of other things that we were shown if M. de Lionne were still Foreign Secretary. But with you, I must be grave and proper; and so, Monsieur, I end my letter.'[7] However, even Pomponne enjoyed the tale. He wrote to Courtin: 'I am sure you forgot all your troubles when you were making Mistris Nesle raise those neat and magnificent petticoats of hers...'[8]

Courtin also sought to improve relations between Hortense and Louise. He invited them both to a dinner party and hit on the idea of locking them in a room together. When he later opened it, he was pleased to see them skipping out together arm-in-arm. It may well have been an uneasy one but it was, at least, a truce. Hortense's reign as *maîtresse du titre* held firm into 1677. At the spring opening of Parliament, Hortense was seated more prominently behind Charles than the other mistresses. Whether or not Hortense wielded any political influence over Charles is unclear. She probably cared little about politics, much preferring amusement and the arts. However, not everyone was so sure. Courtin wrote on 12 March 1676: 'I have just learned that there is a definite and secret understanding between the King of England and the Duchess

Mazarin. She manages her intrigues with him very quietly: and those who had hoped to share in her triumph have not yet been able to do so.'

Unfortunately, not everything went her way as her great friendship with Anne Fitzroy was effectively terminated when Anne's husband, Lord Sussex, ordered her back to the family's country seat, Hurstmonceaux Castle. John Verney wrote that 'Lady Sussex is at last tho' unwillingly, gone with her lord into the country.'⁹ Barbara, presumably hopelessly unaware of the laden hypocrisy in her words, had also been advocating her daughter's removal from the unhealthy relationship she was conducting with the bisexual Roman beauty. Louise would also be happier without her interfering ladyship around to facilitate the liaison between Charles and Hortense.

However, by the summer Hortense's untroubled ascendancy was in decline. One part-time lover was clearly insufficient for her Roman blood. Never short of men declaring their undying love for her (she had rejected advances from the earls of Devonshire, Derwentwater and Arran), she finally honoured one of their number, the prince of Monaco. Charles was furious and even stopped her £4,000 a year pension. But, as ever, he soon softened and restored it. But though she remained a mistress, the damage was done: the Roman conquest was over.

— 19 —

The Business of Pleasure

And virgins smiled at what they blushed before.

Alexander Pope

Why dost thou abuse the age so? Methinks it's as pretty
an honest, drinking, whoring age as a man would wish
to live in.

John Wilmot, earl of Rochester

A hound and a hawk no longer
Shall be tokens of disaffection
A cock-fight shall cease
To be a breach of the peace
And a horse race – an insurrection.

A popular drinking song at the time of the Restoration

Charles II has been much criticised; his lifestyle in particular had come
under attack by both his contemporaries and historians. There was no pleasure to be had in business so he gave himself over to the business of
pleasure. On the Restoration, the country emerged out of a largely oppres-
sive and puritanical darkness to the light of social liberty. You could hear
England smiling again. There was such delirious need to make up for lost
time that the week after Charles's Restoration the very land was hungover.

The king's lifestyle was not lost on his people and only incited resentment in people like Andrew Marvell, who scowled in his *Upon his Majesties being made free of the City*:

> He spends all his days
> In running to plays,
> When in the shop he shou'd be poreing
> And wasts all his nights
> In constant delights
> Of Revelling, Drinking and Whoreing.

> Tho' oft bound to the peace,
> He wou'd never cease
> But molested the neighbours with Quarrells
> And when he was beate
> He still made a retreat
> To his Cleavelands, his Nells and his Carwells.

And John Lacy in his *Satyr* scorned:

> Thy base example ruins the whole town;
> For all keep whores, from gentleman to clown.

> An honest lawfull wife's turn'd out of doors,
> And he most honour has that keeps most whores.

Pepys said that the king 'did doat on his women, even beyond all shame'. The English court was drenched in handsome women and beautiful men. As Grammont said: 'As for the beauties, you could not look anywhere without seeing them.' However, it wasn't exclusively so. Grammont continues: 'The new queen gave but little additional brilliancy to the court, either in her person or in her retinue which was then composed of...six frights, who called themselves maids of honour.'[1]

It could be argued that Charles saved the monarchy. At that point in its history, following Charles I and the Cromwells (Oliver and Richard), an affable, easy-going, popular ruler was essential. He was a striking and recognisable figure: tall, dark, slim, graceful, and while not blessed with the prettiest of faces he was certainly not unattractive. He was intelligent, charming and self-deprecating: he was amused by jokes about his laziness, untrustworthiness and lack of money.

He may well have had absolutist desires but he knew his tactics had to fit with the mood of the times and people. For the time being he was at the centre of an open monarchy. He was a people's king: the people could see him and he could see the people. Each day he dined at Whitehall in the hall where his father had walked out on to the scaffold to his execution. Now the son had replaced his father and trust was once more among the people. People would fill the galleries to watch their monarch eat. At Newmarket he delighted in spending time with jockeys talking horses and being just another punter.

Charles first visited Newmarket in 1666. By 1669 he would decamp the court there twice a year without fail – in spring and autumn, staying for up to a month each time. The openness of Newmarket Heath freed him from the shackles of his duty. No more battling against the tide, he upped the anchor of kingship and floated downstream, freely and happily. This was the England he craved the most: green, open, sweet-aired. He would surround himself with wine, women, jockeys, horses and England's green and pleasant, and be a man and not a king.

At Newmarket Charles Stuart could be himself. He liked to, as he called it, 'put off majesty'. Such informality punctuated his reign. He once caused a sensation when one hot day he visited the fleet (his true passion it has to be said was more likely to be ships than women or horses) and took off his pourpoint (a quilted waistcoat) and periwig to cool down. He would answer his critics by saying should he be more like the king of Spain 'who would do nothing unless under some ridiculous form and would not even piss unless someone else held the chamber pot?' However, informality is also relative. Deciding to travel to Newmarket, Charles declared that that he would travel with just his night bag. His steward, taken aback, ventured that surely his majesty would not travel without forty or fifty horse; to which Charles replied: 'But that is my night bag!'

Newmarket was his bi-annual escape from Whitehall. Ministers and ambassadors would travel there also but would find business hard to come by. Nothing could block his road there. One year a committee meeting set for 2 October to 'receive proposals for farming on the whole excise for three years' was adjourned until the end of the month 'in the fore-noon' because 'his Majesty now intends to be at Newmarket'. A contemporary satire noted the trend:

So at the next Newmarket meeting
(when thy senate should be sitting)
Where knaves & fools & courtiers do resort
And players come from far to make their sport.[2]

Charles simply preferred talking horses with jockeys. It was Charles II's involvement with horse racing that led to its being called 'the sport of kings'. One of Charles's favourite old stud horses was called Old Rowley. It amused him greatly that, for all too obvious reasons, it became one of his own nicknames. Indeed, one story has it that a maid of honour was singing a popular song about 'Old Rowley' when the passing Charles overheard. He knocked at the lady's door and replied, when asked who was there, 'Why, Old Rowley himself!' To this day, part of the Newmarket course is called the Rowley Mile.

The informality even extended to his palace at Newmarket which lacked grandeur. Evelyn called it 'meane enough, & hardly capable for a hunting house'.[3] It was designed by Sir Christopher Wren. On inspecting it with him, Charles commented the ceiling seemed low. Wren replied that it was high enough. Charles then squatted his six-foot two-inch frame down to that of the five foot tall Wren and said, 'Aye, Sir Christopher, they're high enough.' Nelly had her own house across the way from the palace (as ever with the statutory secret passage). Nelly nearly always accompanied Charles to Newmarket. Indeed, she is the only mistress to have an annual Newmarket race named after her: the Nell Gwyn Stakes which is a trial race for fillies (appropriately) aimed at the season's first classic – the 1,000 Guineas. However, she missed the autumn meeting in 1679. A letter from Lady Diana Verney to her brother on 2 October that year explains the good reason why: 'Mrs Nelle could not come this time to Newmarket by reason her son my Lord Burford is very ill of this new distemper.'[4]

In 1675, Charles won the prestigious 'Twelve Stone Plate' for the second time. He remains the only British monarch ever to win a competitive horse race. On 24 March 1675, Sir Robert Carr dispatched the following commentary to those left behind at Whitehall:

> Yesterday his Majestie Rode him three heats and a course and won the Plate, all fower were hard and nere run, and I do assure you the King won by guid Horseman ship. Last a night a match was maid between Blew Capp [the king's

horse] and a consealed horse of Mr Mayes' called Thumper, to run the six mile course twelve stone wait upon Tuesday in Easter week for 1000 guineas.

The names of horses sometimes echoed the salacious times: Jack-come-tickle-me, Kiss-in-a-corner and Sweetness-when-naked.

Evelyn, who first mentions Newmarket on 22 July 1670 when he visited to 'see the Stables and fine horses, of which many were here kept, at vast expense, with all the art & tendernesse Imaginable', was impressed with a race he saw the following year. After his dinner, he 'went on the heath, where I saw the greate match run betweene Woodcock & Flatfoot the Kings & Mr Eliots of the Bedchamber, many thousands being spectators, a more signal race had not ben run of many yeares.'[5] Although Evelyn doesn't say so, the king rode his own horse but lost. J B Muir's *Ye olde New Markitt Calendar* confirms, however, that three days later Charles won the Plate for the first time.

However, impressed as he was with the racing, Evelyn was less enamoured with the whole social occasion, finding 'jolly blades, Racing, Dauncing, feasting & revelling, more resembling a luxurious & abandon'd rout, than a Christian Court: The Duke of Buckingham... had with him that impudent woman, the Countesse of Shrewsbery, with his band of fidlars.'[6] That obviously did it for Evelyn, as he never returned.

The life of the king at Newmarket was ably drawn out by Sir John Reresby:

> The manner of the king's dividing his time at this place was this he walked in the morning till ten of the clock; then he went to the Cock Pit till dinner time; about three he went to the horse races; at six he returned to the Cock Pit, for an hour only; then he went to the play, though the actors were but of a terrible sort; from thence to supper; then to the Duchess of Portsmouth's till bedtime; and so to his own apartment to take his rest.

Always up at five, this notoriously lazy monarch was remarkably physical. He hated formal occasions and council meetings. He worked best when at play and preferred to carry out the business of state socially: playing tennis, at dinner and during walks where politicians, courtiers and even the public would walk with him and try to keep up long enough to conclude their matters with him. For the devilishly fast pace of his 'saunterings' – as Charles called them – was legendary; what the naval chaplain Henry Teong in his diary called 'his wonted large pace'. Burnet affirmed the king's liking for walks 'which he commonly did so fast, that, as it was really an exercise to himself, so it was a trouble to all about him to keep up with him'.

Such was the distance he preferred to cover, Charles would conduct his 'saunterings' in parks – mostly St James's where he could view the ducks and admire the aviary (which gave its name to Birdcage Walk). But he also walked beyond the park. Indeed, it is believed that Constitution Hill is so called because this was the route Charles's morning walks would often take. He enjoyed his public walks. The duke of York was less sure. He questioned his brother over the safety of such public walking. Charles replied that he shouldn't worry as he was sure no one in England would kill him so that James could be king.

Charles also loved dogs and had a pack of spaniels (the breed that now takes his name) that followed him on his walks and to most other places as well: even into bed; specially into bed. Charles's bedroom was not the most perfumed and it's little wonder that he conducted his mostly horizontal business elsewhere. Evelyn remarked that Charles 'tooke delight to have a number of little spaniels follow him, & lie in his bedchamber, where often times he suffered the bitches to puppy and give suck, which rendred it very offensive, & indeede made the whole Court nasty & stinking.' But his beloved dogs, who even got sumptuous cushions to rest on, could do no wrong in his eyes. One unfortunate cavalier looking to keep the king's favour, attempted to stroke one of the spaniels, but was repaid with a sharp nip. In pain, he reacted sharply by saying, 'God bless his majesty, but God damn his dogs'. Charles's very human love of his pets is reflected in this advert which ran in *The London Gazette* in the 16–19 July 1673 edition:

> A small liver coloured Spanish Bitch lost from the King's lodgings, on the 14th instant, with a little white on her breast and a little white on the top of her hind feet. Whoever brings her to Mr Chiffinch's lodgings at the King's Back-Stairs, or to the King's Dog-Keepers in St James's Park shall be well rewarded for their pains.

Charles enjoyed tennis although the fact that he wasn't exceptional (unlike his riding or walking) didn't prevent royal plaudits, as Pepys records: 'Thence to the Tennis Court, and there saw the King play at tennis, and others: but to see how the King's play was extolled without any cause at all was a loathsome sight, though sometimes, indeed, he did play very well and deserved to be commended; but such open flattery is beastly.'[7] His other sporting interests included hawking, skating, pell-mell, yachting, fishing, sailing and swimming. Courtin reported that during the summer of 1676 Charles bathed in the Thames every night 'in four or five little boats with three or four persons. The ladies do not go with the men. It is the only decency which they observe in this country.' Although he also hunted and played golf he wasn't as enthusiastic about those sports as his brother.

Henry Sidney was with the king at Windsor in the summer of 1679. He records on 30 June that the day had 'passed in walking about'. The next day 'little was done all day but going a-fishing'. However, this favoured sedate activity would be followed by more energetic ones: 'At night the Duchess of Portsmouth come. In the morning I was with the king at Mrs Nell's.'[8] Such was the king's love of fishing that satirists would cast a few lines of their own at his expense. As the 1680 _Flat-foot ye Gudgeon taker_ shows:

> Fine representative indeed of God
> Whose scepter's dwindled to a fishing rod.
>
> To well, alas, the fatal bayt is known
> Which Rowley does so greedily take down;
> And how e'er weak & slender be the string,
> Bayt it with whore, & it will hold a king.

Nelly brilliantly exploited Charles's passion for fishing with one of her scams. During the long, hot summer of 1675, Charles was hosting a visit from Philip William, the count of Neuberg, whose father, Wolfgang Wilhelm, had received the exiled Charles to his court in Dusseldorf. He decided to take the prince on a river trip up the Thames to Hampton Court.

A Frenchwoman, Marie Catherine Le Jumelle de Berneville, Baronne d'Aulnoy, who was part of the entourage, recorded the trip in her memoirs:

One of her schemes which was previously arranged, proved very amusing. She suggested to the King that they might stop awhile, the better to enjoy the beauty of the evening & music; this done she had some fishing tackle produced; it was all painted and gilded, the Nets were silk, the Hooks gold. Every one commenced to fish, & the king was one of the most eager. He had already thrown his line many times & was surprised at not catching anything. The Ladies rallied him, but calling out that they must not tease, he triumphantly showed his line to the end of which half a dozen fried Sprats were attached by a piece of silk! They burst into laughter in which all the Court joined, but Nelly said it was only right that a great king should have unusual Privileges! A poor Fisherman could only take Fish alive but his Majesty caught them ready to eat!'[9]

The Prince de Neuberg said that six sprats would not be enough to go around and cast his line to try and catch some more. The prince reeled in his line only to find a little purse on the end. Inside he discovered a small gold box, inside which he found a portrait of one of the court ladies that he had taken quite a fancy to. The prince 'gave a cry of joy' while the king was hugely amused. Nelly had arranged for some divers to be in the river to attach the prizes, recalling the story of how Cleopatra had likewise fastened a sardine to the hook of Mark Antony. In gratitude, once the prince had returned to Germany he sent Nelly a gift of fine lace.

Baronne d'Aulnoy also relates a story of a masque the previous night where she witnessed 'the arrival of Nelly Gwynne' dressed as a shepherdess:

> As soon as she entered & had danced the *contre danse* (which she did very well, although her manners were as singular in dancing as they were in everything else that she did) she cried out: that the heat of the room was unbearable, and that they must have some air, that of a truth the season was unsuitable for such amusements, & it was most uncomfortable to stay shut up with so many people, & so many candles.

Nelly's solution was to take the party outside into the cool night. So everyone adjourned to St James's Park and arranged themselves around the bowling green, dancing to music by moonlight ('the night was vivid, they needed no lights') until dawn. Nelly's wit and antics ensured that everyone had a good time: 'her spirits were such that it was difficult to remain long in her company without sharing the gaeity.'[10]

For Nelly the stars were there to dance under, but for others they were there to read, and heavenly bodies entranced people as much as their earthly counterparts. Such was the preoccupation with astrology that Louis XIV saw an opening. He sent to Charles's court an Italian Theatine monk, Abbé Pregnani, for the Royal Society to study (or so he claimed). In reality Pregnani was in the pay of Louis and was sent over to persuade Charles of the benefits of continued alliance with France by making predictions to that effect. Charles, ever the pragmatist with a cynical streak, asked him to predict the winners of three races at Newmarket. The Abbé went to work, seeking solar inspiration and so on, but as all three races were match races he had a 50 per cent chance of success anyway. He failed to predict a single winner. Following this dismal performance he was sent packing back to France. Many people, including Monmouth (who knew of him in Paris and talked up his skills) and Buckingham, backed the monk's judgement and lost vast amounts of money. Pregnani's departure was rather hurried.

This gullibility of people was heartlessly exploited by Rochester. He set himself up as an Italian astrologer, Alessandro Bendo, sporting a flowing black cloak patterned with the signs of the zodiac. Nelly helped distribute his advertising posters. People flocked from all over for his one month residency. Even distinguished astrologers called for advice, which Rochester expertly but fraudulently gave.

However, if astrology was a minor infection then gambling was the plague. In the late seventeenth century, gambling enjoyed a greater boom than probably at any other time in British history. The passion and fervour were relentless. Gambling was *the* social drug. Charles wasn't as addicted as most, treating it as a small leisure. He would set his limit which was usually quite low, but sometimes as high as £100, and stick to it. He despaired of the amounts piled in by his mistresses. John Sheffield (later created duke of Buckingham following the death of George Villiers, and who built the palace that takes his name) wrote that while Charles 'sacrificed all things to his mistresses, he would use to grudge, and be uneasy at their losing a little of it again at play, tho' never so necessary for their diversion.'[11]

Theophilius Lucas wrote that gambling was 'an enchanting witchcraft' inspiring the highest highs and the lowest lows: 'if he wins, the success so elevates him, that his mad joys carry him to the height of all excesses, but if he loses, his misfortune plunges him into the lowest abyss of despair...He that is worth 4 or 5000 pounds at noon, shall not be worth a farthing by night.' The stakes, it seems, were fashionably high. Grammont bragged that he 'played high but seldom lost'.

The mistresses also played high but, with the exception of Hortense, seldom won. Hortense was 'as great a proficient as any at that time;

witness her winning at Basset of Nell Gwin 1400 guineas in one night [over £100,000 at today's tables], and of the Duchess of Portsmouth above £8,000, in doing of which she exerted her most cunning.' There was another account of Nelly losing £5,000 to Hortense in one very expensive night. Hortense would also entice a reluctant Charles to play with her (and he keen for her favours granted her this favour) and would trounce him. Lucas said that she mostly played fair, but if confronted by a fellow gamester she 'would play altogether upon the sharp as any game upon cards; and generally come off a winner.'[12] Hortense was head girl at the bet-on-two-raindrops-rolling-down-a-window school of gambling. She would organise women to ride each other on the back with the courtiers betting on the outcome. Hortense's salon established itself at the epicentre of gaming, eclipsing even the Groom-Porter's lodge at Whitehall, where Evelyn had earlier witnessed 'deepe and prodigious gaming' that saw 'vast heapes of Gold squandered away'.[13]

There were other forms of gambling. Evelyn bought tickets in a 'loterey' organised by Arthur Slingsby as early as July 1664 which was grandly drawn at the Banqueting House at Whitehall. However, he suspected Slingsby of fixing the draw and thought him 'in truth a meer shark'.[14]

Out of the momentum of gambling inevitably evolved the deadliest of such sharks: the gamester, the professional gambler who would rarely rely on just skill and good fortune. A gamester was, according to a contemporary description, someone who had 'happily lost shame'. One of its exponents was Major-General 'Handsom', or 'Beau' Fielding, who was so desirous of an extravagant lifestyle that he 'was obliged to support his ambitious grandeur by horse racing at Newmarket-Heath, and other places, and herein was successful, by bribing jockeys to ride foul matches.'[15] Professional gambling was a science, but cheating was an art. However, some sharp tactics cut the wrong way.

One gamester, Colonel Panton (whose name is recalled in central London's Panton Street) had won vast sums at cards (usually L'Ombre, Basset and Picquet) from the likes of Monmouth, Buckingham and Lauderdale. However, he was unceremoniously, if somewhat innocently, turned over by the king's forgotten mistress Moll Davis. Moll had approached the table saying that she had gotten lucky at her first game of cards and would like a second go. Panton smelt blood. Armed with a bag of 1,500 guineas he took out 150 as a loss-leader: he would let her win this amount in order to sucker her into losing all her money back to him. To his shock after this first game, Moll picked up her winnings saying she only ever played one game at a time and walked off with Panton's money: 'he was much vex'd to see how he was taken in by a woman for 150 guineas'.[16]

However, he inevitably gained his revenge. The next time he played her at basset, he set her in front of a mirror so that he could see her cards (a tactic frequently employed by sharpers on the uninitiated). He won £1,100 from her and 'then laughed at her folly'.

Undoubtedly, card games were king at the tables. The French game, basset (where you bet on the identity of the card next to be dealt off the pack) was enormously popular. It was deemed to be the most 'courtly' game, practised as it was by royalty and nobility all over Europe. The card mania is no better illustrated than by the story of Sir John Denham. His sudden realisation and disgust at how much time and money he had wasted at the gaming tables caused him to become born again: he stopped gambling and became a fierce critic, publishing an anti-gaming discourse. His father was so pleased with his son's honourable repentance and complete character change that he reversed his earlier decision to disinherit him, leaving him an immense fortune. Sir John then proceeded to lose the lot at cards.

Gambling, like most fashionable things in Restoration England, had travelled across the Channel from France. The character Mr Frenchlove in James Howard's play *The English Monsieur* sums up the high taste for things French when proclaiming, 'Twould vex me plaguly were I not a Frenchman in my second nature in my fashion, discourse and cloathes.' Charles, ever the Francophile, particularly admired French fashions. His tailor, Claude Sourceau, as you might suspect, was French and was persuaded by Charles to settle in London. He also employed a French barber and shoemaker. Shoes were an obsession for Charles. This may well be linked to his escape from the battle of Worcester: Disguised as a wood-man he had to use the boots of one of the people helping him to escape. Unfortunately, they were too small and had to be cut to enable Charles to get into them. So painfully uncomfortable were they that he never forgot them and had ever since treated himself to the best, most comfortable shoes he could buy. And these were usually French. Perhaps he felt some way obligated to spend some of his French money in this way.

His French money was administered by William Chiffinch who succeeded his brother Thomas as page of His Majesty's bedchamber and keeper of the king's private closet. Charles could not have hoped to have found anyone more loyal, trustworthy, useful or discreet as Chiffinch. The old faithful would invite people for supper and ply them with drink in order to coax out of them their true feelings towards the king. Unsurprisingly, the distrustful and rapacious Louise and Barbara disliked him; but Nell counted him a friend and often supped with him. His wife, it was said, kept a list of approved women who could be procured to satisfy a monarch's fancy. They were shepherded in by Chiffinch and taken up the infamous backstairs – as Nelly would have been at first. As David Ogg's oft-quoted (and deservedly so) comment has it Chiffinch 'performed a great and honourable service to the Stuarts by *not* writing his memoirs'.[17]

Charles, of course, continued to patronise the theatre. And, although off the stage, Nelly kept her association with it also. Sadly, a tragedy struck the King's House in January 1672: a fire destroyed the theatre and a young actor, Richard Bell, was killed. A letter dated 25 January 1672 related the events:

> A fire at the King's play house between 7–8 on Thursday evening last, which half burned down the house and all their scenes and wardrobe; and all the houses from the Rose Tavern on Russell Street on that side of the way to Drury Lane are burned and blown up, with many in Vinegar Yard; £20,000 damage. The fire began under the stairs where Orange Moll keeps her fruit. Bell the Player was blown up.[18]

A contemporary balladeer (or their printer) took the opportunity to pun on the name of both the dead actor and the theatre's most famous daughter:

> He cries just judgement, and wishes when poor Bell
> Rung out his last, had been the stage's kNell.

As the company sought the backing to rebuild their theatre, they went back to the old Lincolns Inn Field theatre and opened there on 26 February 1672. In dire financial straits and seemingly tired of trying to reclaim bad debts, on 6 November 1672 the theatre management persuaded Charles to order 'that no person of what degree or quality soever do enter into Our Play-house [before or during a perfomance] without having first paid the price usually demanded & taken for such place.'[19] However, clearly this did not affect those who were permitted to use the royal box. Of course, this included Nelly, who characteristically made sure that the bill was sent for royal payment. One such bill for the rival Duke's Company, now part of the Harvard Theatre Collection, shows that, between September 1674 and 9 June 1676, Nelly and her guests attended Dorset Gardens 55 times, watching at least 42 plays. She particularly enjoyed Thomas Shadwell's operatic *Psyche* and a new operatic version of *The Tempest* seeing them six times and four times respectively. She also saw *Macbeth* twice. It is safe to assume that she would have attended a similar amount at her old stomping ground the King's Theatre (which, designed by Christopher Wren, re-opened on 26 March 1674). This would make Nelly, not unsurprisingly for an ex-actress, a prolific theatre-goer. Interestingly, it appears that on ten occasions covered by the bill the king was also present, but only once did Nelly sit with him in the royal box.[20]

Undoubtedly Henry Savile had Nelly in mind when, in December 1677, he wrote to Rochester that he had the fortune to see an itinerant French company of actors who were briefly in England. He wished that they could stay longer 'especially a young wench of fifteen who has more beauty and sweetnesse than ever was seen upon the stage since a friend of ours left it'.

Nelly's presence at Dorset Gardens provoked an outrageous attack on her character and her defence came from what at first seems an unlikely source. On 26 January 1680, Luttrell records that 'Mrs Ellen Gwyn being at the duke's playhouse, was affronted by a person who came into the pitt and called her whore, whom Mr [George] Herbert, the Earl of Pembroke's brother, vindicating, there were many swords drawn and a great hubbub in the house.'[21] The earl of Pembroke, Philip Herbert, had married Henriette de Keroualle, Louise's sister (the actual marriage was delayed giving Pembroke time to get over his pox). Pembroke was an infamous drunkard noted for his brawling. However, despite the Pembroke connection with Louise, Nelly was friendly with George. He would inherit his brother's title and would become a trustee for Nelly's will.

Henriette de Keroualle had come across to join her sister and was immediately set up with a £600 pension and had her portrait painted by Peter Lely. Pieter van des Faes, German by birth but Dutch by upbringing, took his name from his house in the Hague 'which bore the device of a lily on its gable'.[22] He succeeded Van Dyck as the court painter (on a £200 per year pension) and developed that artist's elegant and grand portraiture style. Lely was in such demand that he mastered the factory output – he himself would only 'finish' paintings, that is, paint the face and sometimes the hands, leaving the background, dress and so on to his assistants. Sitters had a choice of standardised backgrounds to choose from. His fees rose with his popularity: a £5 per head in 1647 became £20 by 1671. He played to the crowd and gave them what they wanted. Hence so many of his portraits are almost indistinguishable. This has meant, inevitably, that any unidentified female has often been labelled Nell Gwynne, making it difficult today to identify the genuine article.

One authenticated portrait is the Lely showing Nelly nude, as Venus, with her son Charles as Cupid. In 1721, George Vertue wrote of the portrait:

> At the Duke of Buckingham's...Nell Guin naked leaning on a bed, with her child. by S' Peter Lilly. this picture was painted at the express command of King Charles 2ᵈ. Nay he came to Sr Peter Lillys house to see it painted. when she was naked on purpose. Afterwards this picture was at Court. Where the Duke of Buckingham took it from (when K James went away) as many others did like.[23]

Lely's preferred 'look' – the heavy-eyed, sensuous beauty (Pope wrote that the artist 'on animated canvas stole/the sleepy eye that spoke the melting soul') – was how all fashionable women wanted to be portrayed. This sameness undermined any portraiture realism. Pepys said Lely's paintings of the court beauties were 'good but not like'.[24] This is in stark contrast to the famous instruction, according to Vertue, given to Lely by Cromwell: 'Mr Lely, I desire that you would use all your skill to paint my picture truly like me, and not flatter me at all; but remark all those roughnesses, pimples, warts, and everything as you see me, otherwise I will never pay a farthing for it.' However, it is more likely that Cromwell said this to Samuel Cooper, one of the greatest miniaturists. Certainly his portrait seems more realistic than Lely's. Louis XIV reputedly offered Cooper 3,750 francs for his miniature of Cromwell, but Cooper would not sell. However, not all of Charles II's portraits were flattering. On seeing his portrait by Riley, Charles famously said: 'Is that like me? Then, oddsfish, I am an ugly fellow.'

However, not everybody thought Lely's output repetitive. Grammont commented that 'every picture appeared a masterpiece; and that of Miss Hamilton appeared to be the highest finished'. So much so that the duke of York 'began again to ogle the original'. All studios knocked out copy portraits. Pepys was determined to have one of Barbara that had roused his desires. An original receipt, dated 24 April 1675, exists for Nelly's purchase of three pictures: 'one of the king and two being copies after Cooper of Madam Gwin . . .' She paid 'Peeter Crosse, picture drawer' £34 for the three. Peter Cross (1630–1716) was a miniaturist who did a brisk trade in copy portraits. The Cooper portrait, thought to have been painted around 1670, is sadly lost.

Another receipt in the Crofton Croker collection, dated 7 May 1675, reads as follows:

Mr Grounds

I understand Mrs Guin ordered you to pay mee fifty shillings for a picture I sould her, pray pay it unto this bearer my servant and it will be the same thing as paid unto your friend – Nicholas Dixon.

The receipt was signed by Dixon's servant, Richard Weaver. Nicholas Dixon succeeded Samuel Cooper as the king's limner in 1672. As well as drawing for the king, Dixon would illuminate manuscripts, usually with the king's face. And that is one image we can be sure that looked out from many a wall at a certain Pall Mall home.

— 20 —

A Kind Heart Broken

Kind jealous doubts, tormenting fears,
And anxious cares, when past,
Prove our hearts' treasure fixed and dear,
And make us blest at last.

'The Mistress', earl of Rochester

If the sparkling seventies had seen Nelly centre stage performing her triumphant role as mother and mistress, the eighties were to be less kind. The decade would last longer than most of our main players as it became one of death and decline. For Nelly, who lost her mother the year before, 1680 was to be another tragic year. She was still reeling from the death in July of her good friend and merry gang member, John Wilmot earl of Rochester, when she heard in September that her youngest son, James, had died. He was just eight years old. Worst for Nelly was that she wasn't there at his death. James had for two years been tutored in Paris where education and deportment were considered the best in Europe.

So little is known that we are uncertain even when he died. In an undated letter to his father (but which is filed between 27 May and 21 June 1680) John Verney wrote to Sir Ralph Verney that 'Nell Gwynne's second son is dead in France.'[1] However, most of Nelly's biographers have recorded James's death in September. One manuscript states that James 'Beauclerck' died 'in France about Michaelmas [29 September] in the year 1680'.[2] The Laing Manuscripts include all we know about the cause of death: 'James Beauclarc...died in France of a sore leg, 1680.'[3]

It is quite extraordinary that so little is known of the fate of Master James. Henry Savile, the envoy in Paris, was a friend of Nelly's and a prolific letter writer. James was the son of the king (who loved his children) and the most famous woman in England. And yet I have been unable to unearth any further references to Lord James Beauclerk in either London or Paris. Savile's letters were not exclusively political in content, either. He enjoyed commenting on the social state of affairs in Paris, moaning about the tiring journeys as he followed Louis XIV and his court on royal progresses. He writes of the fears and concerns over the Dauphin's ill health. His letters to Sir Richard Bulstrode kept at the British Library mention nothing in the June or July dispatches and unfortunately show a gap between 24 August and 11 November 1680. It is not known on what date James died, the date of his funeral (and who attended) or where he was buried, although the likelihood is that the funeral took place in France.

Naturally, Nelly was a broken woman. The fact that there is very little mention of her for the rest of the year and the start of the next suggests that she went into deep mourning and shut herself off at Pall Mall and Windsor. The treasury records show that 'a brick wall for Madam Gwin's garden on the south side of her house at Windsor' was built in January and that a Monsieur Bodevin was paid for 'repairing Madam Gwin's house.'[4] It is unlikely that Nelly attended her son's funeral as there is no evidence that she ever left the country. It seems almost inconceivable to us today that she didn't visit James's grave.

The 1680s were to be a difficult time for Nelly: the bigger the heart the bigger the damage. And no one can doubt the size and kindness of her heart. Nelly's household Christmas accounts of 1675 show examples of her natural generosity. Entries include 6d. 'for a pore woman', 6d. 'for a pore man at yᵉ exchange', 6d. 'for pore woman in Fanches [?Fenchurch] Street', and the obligatory sixpence 'for a pore man in St James parke'. The New Year accounts show also 6d. for 'a pore woman at yᵉ dore'. However, there was double Christmas cheer for 'yᵉ mad wench at yᵉ dore' who scooped a whole shilling on 23 December 1675.

Nelly always looked kindly upon her friends and those she knew well. It has been suggested that she aided the release of Samuel Pepys in 1679 from the Tower where he had been imprisoned on the (wrongful) charge selling naval secrets to the French, although Pepys's biographers do not refer to this, it seems that Pepys maintained his admiration of Nelly, for he had the pleasure at times of providing her with a yacht for her use on the Thames.[5] He also kept among his prints an engraving of her naked except for a pair of angel's wings.[6] Later, after Charles's death when Nelly was being hounded by creditors, he did her the kindness of putting a yacht at her disposal free of charge.[7] All of this could well suggest that he was grateful for her kindness – and he was pleased to be able to repay it.

Actors were never too far away from her heart or door. Jo Haines's epistle to Nelly (possibly late spring 1682) asked her to 'Get the King to speak to my Lord Chamberlain/That in the Duke's House I may once act again.' She clearly did so because soon after the Lord Chamberlain issued a 'Notice to all persons that Joseph Haines is His Majesty's Servant and entitled to all rights and privileges belonging thereunto.'[8]

She often helped struggling artists out financially. Samuel Butler, the son of a farmer, had a literary career that peaked as sharply as it fell. His poem 'Hudibras' – a mock romance that satirised the fanaticism of the Puritans – was timely and hugely successful in the early years of the Restoration. Indeed, the poem was a favourite of Charles II, who carried a copy around with him and delighted in quoting from it. Pepys, who had been unimpressed with this 'new book of drollery' sold it (losing a shilling on the deal), but responded to the hype surrounding it and felt obliged to purchase another copy.[9] One-time secretary to the duke of Buckingham (upon whom he wrote a brilliant character sketch – '. . . he does nothing but advise with his pillow all day. . .'), Butler's world had collapsed into poverty. Despite Nelly's help and influence, Butler died poor and unemployed in 1680. He was, however, given a memorial in Westminster Abbey, although he probably would have preferred the money.

Nelly's generosity extended also to the playwrights Nathaniel Lee and Thomas Otway (who had both failed as actors owing to their nervousness), even appointing the latter tutor to Master Charles. This episode was duly satirised:

> Then for that cub, her son and heir,
> Let him remain in Otway's care.
> To make him (if that's possible to be)
> A viler Poet, and more dull than he.[10]

Otway had been so desperate he had even joined the army and fought at Flanders in 1678–9. He was also a witness to James Fraser taking power of attorney over Nelly's pension, who would advance her cash against it, for a fee, naturally. The document, which was signed on 1 June 1680, is part of the impressive collection held at the Pierpont Morgan Library, New York. As Otway's biographer noted: 'in his time of despondency, the hand of Ellen Gwyn reached down with aid and comfort.'[11] However, Otway proved to be too fond of punch (and apparently one of Nelly's maids) and had to be dismissed, although he was settled enough to be able to write his most famous work, the sentimental tragedy *Venice Preserv'd*. But, as with Butler, despite Nelly's influence and patronage, Otway died in penury in 1685. Lee's fate was similarly tragic as he went insane and spent five years in the Bethlehem Royal Hospital ('Bedlam') and died in 1692.

It was at this hospital that another act of Nelly's kindness is recorded. Throughout the seventeenth century, visitors had been allowed to observe, from viewing galleries, patients chained in cells. Indeed, it became one of London's most popular attractions. Pepys, for example, records that house guests of his went there while he went to work.[12] The story (for, after all, that is probably all it is) runs that on a visit Nelly took pity on one of the patients who was said to be Oliver Cromwell's porter. He was fearful of hell's fire and she gave him a gift of a Bible.

But it is her involvement with the grand scheme to build another hospital, this time in Chelsea, for old or disabled soldiers, that Nelly's generosity may most famously come into its own (although it may well be that she had nothing to do with it at all). Two fairly strong traditions link Nelly with the founding of the Royal Hospital Chelsea. One has her, in typically generous style, listening to the plight of a disabled soldier who was begging for money (the Vagrancy Act was amended to permit wounded or maimed ex-soldiers to beg). Dismayed at his tale and remembering the hardships faced by her own father after the Civil War, she appealed to Charles to provide something for them – the hospital being the result. The other tradition concerns Nelly walking in on Charles and Sir Christopher Wren as they were going over the plans for the hospital. Unimpressed at the proposed scale, she suggested that the plans should be at least the size of her handkerchief. Taking it out, she tore it into four strips and placed them around the edge of the plans, thereby doubling the size of the hospital. Both of these stories are of very doubtful authenticity, but they ring true because they sound just like Nelly.

T Horton, comedian, who wrote the 1828 play *Nell Gwynne: The City of The Wye; or, the Red Lands of Herefordshire – An historical play*, has clearly swallowed the legend whole. He beamed 'that Chelsea Hospital owes its foundation to her, will stamp the true value of her memory, on the heart of every lover of his country.' The last lines in his play are spoken by Charles II:

> ... and that famed native spot of thine, of which they are so fond of boasting, will not fail to reward thy memory. The Red Lands of Hereford will be proud of the Red Land favourite of Charles, and while there is a veteran in England's service, reclining under the shadow of thy bounty, beneath the roof of Chelsea Hospital, his grateful song shall be of the king that fostered thee! – and of the Lands that gave thee birth! – and, when their daily wholesome meal is o'er, each veteran soldier, in his cup of gratitude will toast NELL GWYNNE.

He claims that the toast 'is the case in Chelsea Hospital to this day'. However, the official history of the hospital refuses to co-operate with any such notion. The opening chapter of the official history of the hospital is called 'Fact and Fancy' and any involvement by Nelly is admitted only as fancy.[13] Tradition tends to draw strength from sentimentality but, in this case, how fanciful is it and who should receive the acclaim? Four names crop up regularly: Charles II, Nelly, the duke of Monmouth and Sir Stephen Fox.

The idea of a hospital for disabled soldiers was certainly not a new one – it was a logical advancement from almshouses. However, three similar ventures seem to have shaped the thinking around Chelsea: the Hotel Royal des Invalides at Paris; Kilmainham on the outskirts of Dublin; and the Coningsby Hospital, Hereford.

If Nelly was born in Hereford, she would most assuredly have known about the Coningsby Hospital and their pensioners – 'Coningsby's Company of Old Servitors'. The pensioners all wore a uniform, part of which was a 'seemly gown of red cloth reaching down to the ankle, lined with red baize', The hospital originally accommodated a chaplain and 11 old servitors who had been soldiers or mariners of at least three years' service in the wars, or old serving men of at least seven years' service to one family.

The duke of Monmouth, often in Paris, had been hugely impressed with Les Invalides, which was founded in 1670 by Louis XIV. He visited and inspected the hospital in 1672 and again in 1677, by which time over 2,000 soldiers had used its facilities. Monmouth even wrote and asked for the architect's plans, but they were apparently never sent. It is simply unfeasible to imagine that Monmouth and his father did not discuss the merits of Les Invalides and the possibility of something similar in England. A Francophile king like Charles would happily contemplate emulating the French.

In 1680, the duke of Ormonde set up a building committee to oversee the construction of a hospital for 300 soldiers in Ireland. In September of the following year, Charles had three long audiences with Lord Longford, master of the ordnance in Ireland, and part of the building committee. Following this meeting he instructed a treasury commissioner, Sir Stephen Fox, to plan and manage a similar scheme for London. Fox, 'whose employ' as the paymaster-general of the army (1661–76 and 1679) was 'valued at £10,000' a year, had made a substantial fortune from the post. Evelyn believed it to be around £200,000. Fox is credited with the founding of the hospital in its own official history.

However, one piece of evidence links the main players. In a letter to his father, John Verney wrote, on 1 December 1679: 'Sir Thomas Lee was on Saturday to visit Monmouth, but Nell Gwynne and Sir Stephen Fox being there before him, Sir Thomas could not see his grace.' This may be just a coincidence but here is evidence that a long meeting took place between the three and over 18 months before Evelyn records his first acquaintance with the scheme.

It was at this time that Nelly had taken Monmouth in, so they could have met together at any time. Clearly, they were meeting Sir Stephen Fox for a specific purpose. Monmouth knew about Les Invalides, Nelly about Coningsby Hospital (and even if she didn't she would most assuredly have warmed to the suggestion in hand). It is entirely plausible that as Monmouth and Nelly were working at getting Monmouth back into the king's favour, that they either came up with the scheme or, if it was already known, decided to push its merits further. Perhaps suggesting the idea of a royal hospital might take the king's imagination and soften his resolve against his eldest son. Of course, this can only be speculation and it still doesn't follow that one of them had the idea, but it surely suggests a possibility.

The role of Fox seems to have been that of the civil servant making the idea a reality and in that he was clearly influential. He donated the £1,300 needed to purchase Chelsea College from the Royal Society. Fox's memoirs make no founding claims on his behalf. He was involved at the express wish of the king, but was also rich and influential enough (particularly with bankers) to contribute most effectively. In his funeral oration in 1716, Richard Eyre said that Fox's motive had been expressed to him in his own words: '...he said, He could not bear to see the Common Souldiers, who had Spent their Strength in our Service to beg at our doors.' It can be suspected that he also wanted to give back to those what he had so gratefully (although openly and legally) taken. Although £1,300 was a substantial amount of money, it would hardly dent a treasure chest of £200,000. None the less, Fox lived out his years as a great benefactor, founding an almshouse and building a church at Farley, Wiltshire – the place of his birth – and a hospital at Redlinch, Somerset among other 'acts of piety and charity'.[14]

Eyre also called Fox the 'first Projector of the noble Design of Chelsea Hospital' which first planted the credit with him. The dismissal of Nelly's involvement rests with two pieces of evidence. First, Evelyn, who was well informed of the plans and progress, never mentions Nelly. This, however, is not surprising. It is most unlikely that the man who, when he deigns to mention her, is compelled by unconditional disgust to describe her as 'impudent', 'curse of our nation' and a 'prostitute creature', will issue Nelly with any credit she might be due. More convincing, though, is that she is not listed as a benefactor. It is hard to believe that if she really influenced the scheme that she would not have contributed to it, even if only with a token donation.

Although confounded by her own extravagance around this time, she responded in character to the news of the devastating fire at Wapping in November 1682. A letter from Joshua Bowes to Lord Preston on 11 December 1682 confirms Nelly's donation: 'His Majesty hath been pleased to give £2,000, a person of quality £500 and Madam Gwin £100 toward the relief of the dreadful fire which happened at Wapping.'[15] So money wasn't exactly an insurmountable problem. Perhaps she thought that her background work on the hospital was contribution enough. Or maybe she thought the scheme was already financed and needed no other contributions. Or perhaps her natural modesty declined any credit-seeking.

It would be only the coldest of hearts, however, that would fail to agree with Edward Walford when he says that 'we would like to believe this story'.[16] On balance, it is possible that Nelly knew of the scheme and, as such, would surely have approved and promoted it. But it is probably unlikely that she was actively involved beyond that. Perhaps, rightly, the hospital is considered an act of the benevolent king. Founders Day was originally celebrated on Oak Apple Day, 29 May – Charles's birthday. However, irrespective of the reality behind Nelly's involvement, it says it all that there has been not a breath wasted or a drop of ink spilt suggesting that any of the other mistresses would be in any way involved in such a grand, altruistic scheme. And maybe that is just the point. As a biographer of Charles II commented:

> Yet if Nelly is credited wrongly with establishing this excellent institution with which her name has long been connected, many acts of charity were performed by her which the world knows little or nothing. Few people attain a widespread reputation for either good or evil qualities without having done something to deserve it.[17]

Although the hospital was not finally completed until 1692, the first 'old, lame or infirm' soldiers – 476 of them – were admitted in 1689. Clearly they deserved it, too.

— *21* —

The Quiet Life

The Lady Allington brings up the rear;
Were't not for Nell she should in th'front appear;
But the contending Allington must own,
Illustrous Nelly equal'd is by none.

A satyr, 'Ignis Ignibus extinguitur', anonymous 1682

Now Nelly you must be content
Her Grace begins to reign;
For all your brat you may be sent
To Dorset back again.

A satyr, anonymous 1682

The curtain rose on 1680 with the king approaching his fiftieth year. It proved a significant time marking the muting of the noise of his earlier life. Charles may never have mastered acting his age but he was certainly beginning to feel it and his mood and character set the scene for everyone else.

It was the beginning of the last five years of his life and over this period, by and large, Louise would play the role of his wife: comfortable, assured and together – outside the bedchamber at least. Nelly would be more of the mistress – a diversion for him, fun and still sexy. Hortense and Barbara would be there but as far as Charles's affections were concerned they would be filling in the background along with the queen. There would still be beautiful young women to spark the rakish dash of his eye, but they were fewer and less regular than before. The wild winds that blew scandalously through the court would now be gentle, cool breezes with only an occasional gust of times past.

Louise, in her calculating and manipulative way, went about her business and consolidated her position. In a letter to Louise, Charles wrote: 'My dear Life, I will come tomorrow either to dine, or immediately after, and then will settle all, but certainly I shall not mind the Queen when you are in the case. Adieu, I am yours.' In another, probably from 1680, he wrote: '...all I will add is, that I should do myselfe wrong if I tould you that I love you better than all the world besides, for that were making a comparison where 'tis impossible to expresse the true passion and kindnesse I have for my dearest dearest Fubs.'[1] It was around this time that Charles bought a boat for Louise which he dubbed 'Fubbs' Yacht'.

Louise, it was felt, had a noose around Charles's neck and roped him along at will. Charles knew the anti-feeling against Louise but wished not to hear about it. The king had made his bed and he would lie in it – although, literally at least, not often with Louise. On one occasion, three of Charles's ministers were actively engaging the king on matters of policy. 'They had a conversation with the king,' wrote Henry Sidney, 'and had brought him to consent several things, but, when they began to speak of the Duchess of Portsmouth, he rose and went away.'[2] Similarly, if Louise felt slighted publicly, under pressure Charles would seek retribution unless, of course, Nelly was the perpetrator. On one occasion, the Dutch ambassador made a remark about the familiarity between Louise and the French ambassador Barrillon, who would visit her night and day. An outraged Louise demanded and received profuse apologies. We can imagine Nelly standing the apologetic ambassador a large drink.

Louise was still up to her pearl-strung neck in politics. Henry Sidney records that he witnessed her 'crying all day for fear that the Parliament should be dissolved'.[3] It must have been a performance to match her rival at her best on the stage. She dined at Windsor in September 1680 with the lord chief justice, the sinister Sir William Scroggs. That summer Scroggs had discharged the loaded Whig jury at Middlesex in the case brought by Shaftesbury accusing the duke of York of being a Catholic recusant and Louise of being a common prostitute (which could have seen her in the stocks). Scroggs also presided over the acquittal of the queen's physician during the Popish Plot trials.

In June 1681, Louise played a prominent role (she was one of 'severall witnesses') in the trial of Edward Fitzharris who was accused of high treason. Dr Hawkins ('who is a great creature of the Duchess of Portsmouth') had obtained a confession which was generally thought to be a sham. However, the king had made it clear that he wanted this petty informer executed. And Louise helped secure the verdict. Charles made his point, Fitzharris's neck felt a sharper one and history sees that even an easy and flexible king can be ruthless, if so pushed.

Louise claimed in a letter (although the authenticity can be doubted) to Monmouth that she was responsible for the appointment of Robert Spencer, earl of Sunderland, as secretary of state, replacing Sir Joseph Williamson. The king, she said, 'never had a good opinion of [Sunderland] till I recommended him.'[4]

She was also impressing the French king. Barrillon wrote to him in March 1682: 'The truth about her is, that she has shown great, constant and intelligent zeal for your Majesty's interests, and given me numberless useful hints and pieces of information.' On her arrival in France in March 1682, she was treated with the dignity reserved for a queen. Saint-Simon wrote:

> When on high holiday, she went to visit the Capucines in the Rue Saint-Honoré, the poor monks, who were previously told of her intention, came out to meet her in procession, bearing the cross, the holy-water, and the incense, as if she had been a Queen, which made her strangely embarrassed, since she did not expect so much honour.[5]

Her estates in Aubigny were elevated to a duchy by Louis XIV in a letters patent of January 1684. The following year, her son, the duke of Richmond, was naturalised French so that he was able to inherit his mother's estates there. To top it all, Louis XIV began referring to her as *ma cousine*.

Louise also made sure her son was well looked after. Narcissus Luttrell relates that, on 4 April 1681, there was 'a chapter held at Whitehall, where his Majestie was pleased to make the Duke of Richmond...one of the most noble order of the garter.'[6] He also succeeded Monmouth as master of the horse. Any assistance that the prodigious nine-year-old might need in such an office would be forthcoming from Major Oglethorp who was to act under him.

After Louise prevailed on Charles to make Lord Lumley an officer under their son, Sir John Reresby lamented the power she exercised over the king. 'The duchess,' he wrote, 'was certainly sometimes to blame, in things of this nature, for to display her power with the king, which indeed was great, and to express her friendship to some, she would often break his engagements with others, which was not for his honour.' He added that Charles's relationship with Louise had become platonic: 'And yet his majesty was not, at this time, thought to be charmed with her bed, it generally believed he had not lain with her, since he was at Newmarket, at least four months before.'[7]

Reresby recounts an incident that reflects the all-conquering mind of Louise and the callousness that bred there: '...the Duchess of Portsmouth,' he records on 11 May 1684, 'contrary to custom waiting upon the queen, at dinner, as lady of the bedchamber, her majesty was thereby thrown into such disorder, that the tears stood in her eyes, while the other laughed at it, and turned it into a jest'.

In April 1683, Francis Gwyn (no relation to our Nelly), the groom to the bedchamber, in a letter to the earl of Conway showed that while she tolerated the mistresses, the queen would still occasionally get upset about them. Gwyn described the queen to be in 'very ill humour at Windsor' complaining about the privileges of her servants, to which the king replied that she had the equal if not more of her predecessors. The queen 'replied very angrily that the Queen Mother did a great deal more, but that now the mistresses govern all'. Gwyn, without a slurp of irony, added that this 'nettled the king so much that he complained of it at the Duchess of Portsmouth's.'[8]

Such was Louise's status that when Nahed Hamet, the Moroccan ambassador, was received at court in January 1682 seeking a peace in Tangier, he was lavishly entertained at her sumptuous apartments rather than the queen's or the duchess of York's. Nelly was also a guest, one of 'the concubines and cattle of that sort' as Evelyn, another guest, so adoringly called her. He describes the evening:

I was at the Entertainement of the Morocco Ambassador at the Dut: of Portsmouths glorious Appartment at W.hall, where was a great banquet of Sweetmeates, & Musique &c but at which both the Ambassador & Retinue behaved themselves with extraordinary Moderation & modestie, though placed about a long Table a Lady betweene two Moores: viz: a Moore, then a Woman, then a Moore &c: and most of these were the Kings natural Children, viz: the Lady Lichfield, Sussex [both daughters of Barbara], DD of Portsmouth, Nelly &c: Concubines, & catell of that sort, as splendid as Jewels, and Excesse of bravery could make them.[9]

Evelyn goes on to say that the Moroccan delegation 'dranke a little Milk & Water, but not a drop of Wine, also they drank of a sorbett and Jacolatte: did not looke about nor stare on the Ladys'. The king did not arrive until the ambassador was about to leave. Reresby records that the ambassador's present 'to the king consisted of two lions, and thirty ostriches, at which his Majesty laughed, and said "he knew nothing more proper to send by way of return than a flock of geese!"'[10] Louise was no doubt overjoyed at the Moroccans' parting compliment that 'God would blesse the D: of P: and the Prince her sonn, meaning the little Duke of Richmond'. Her son a prince? It must have been a glorious mistake as far as Louise was concerned.

Despite a more relaxed attitude to the king's mistresses, they were still the regular targets of broadsides. On 12 February 1682, for example, Thomas Rundle, a schoolmaster of Tavistock, was bound over to the assizes for writing a libel *The humble Address of the Ladies of Honour to the King*. It names Louise and 'Madam Gwin' as the chiefs of 'the ladies of pleasure in the seraglios of Moorfields, Whetstone Park, Lukner's Lane, Dog and Bitch Yard . . .'[11]

For the public the rivalry that Nelly and Louise symbolised was as strong as ever. One libel dated 1681 called *A Pleasant Battle between two lap dogs of the utopia court – Tutty & Snap-short* imagined a fight between dogs owned by Nelly and Louise. The anonymous author called Nelly's dog 'Tutty', which may well have been taken from T Flatman's *Heraclitus Ridens, No. 39* published the same year which contained the lines: 'It is a little tutty-ros'd yappeting sprite; the Good old Cause's lap-dog.' The word 'tutty' can also mean, quite conversely, a posy of flowers or peevish, testy and irritable. One exchange runs:

Snap-short: Me-thinks 'tis strange, your open-arse Lady, who came lately from selling oranges and lemmons about the streets . . .

Tutty: . . . and being much more short of money than your lady.

Later Louise's dog confesses: 'Ha, good Tutty, rather than my Lady should be ruined, I will persuade her to turn protestant too, I am confident she will do anything to serve her own interests.' Unsurprisingly as far as this battle was concerned, 'Tutty wins the fight at the dog-pit.'

Published in the same year was a satire purporting to be a letter to Nelly from Louise on her landing in France and a reply from Nelly. Louise's 'letter' begins: 'To tell you I arriv'd safe at *Callis* wou'd bee too much trouble to you, that I had an ill Passage, or was Shipwrack'd by the way, wou'd give you occasion of too much joy.' But the passage was good, 'the Winds fair, the Sea smooth, and the Ship sound (not every Plank three inches assunder, as you wish'd at parting.') Nelly 'responded' to this note of a safe passage with: '... what says *Pluck* the more whore the better luck...'

Seemingly content with her queen-in-all-but-name status, Louise suddenly risked everything by falling in love. Phillipe de Vendôme, arrived in England in 1680. He was the grandson of Henri IV of France and his mistress, Gabrielle d'Estrees, and thus a cousin of Louis XIV, who would refer to him as *le grande prieur* (the grand prior). Vendôme was dashing, moneyed, handsome, supremely arrogant and irreparably addicted to wine, women and gambling. He boasted that he had never gone to bed sober, or without being carried there, all his adult life. Louise, alone mostly in her own bed, was clearly excited at the prospect of carrying some young noble French body there herself. Saint-Simon was not overly impressed, describing Vendôme as a 'liar, swindler, thief, frivoller, dishonest man, even to the marrow of his bones'. The court delighted in the affair, because they believed it would bring Louise down.

Charles was upset by the affair which bore depths of untapped jealousy. Barrillon was aware of the dangers and saw bouts of the king's displeasure but, as ever, 'his bad temper does not last long'. It lasted long enough, however, to see Vendôme removed from the kingdom. An officer of the guards, Lieutenant Griffin, gave Vendôme a couple of options: either he leave the country voluntarily within two days or be arrested and deported. By four o'clock the next day the luckless Frenchman was sailing home.

Luttrell notes in November 1683 that 'the grand prior of France having been in court for sometime past, is lately banished thence, for being (it is said) a little too free with the Duchess of Portsmouth.' Reresby confirms that the French aristocrat was 'observed to be very fond of the Duchess of Portsmouth, and she of him, the king conceived so great a jealousy threat, he sent him away; and it was shrewdly suspected the Duchess would not be long behind him, which few people seemed to be sorry for.'[12]

As far as Charles was concerned, there was always Newmarket. The earl of Conway kept secretary of state Sir Leoline Jenkins up to speed with the races. On 10 March 1681 he wrote:

> The king's horse, called Corke, had the ill-fortune to be beaten by Mr Rider's, called the French horse; and the crack this day is 6 to 4 on Sir Rob. Car's horse called Postboy against a gelding of his Majesty's called Mouse. Pray don't acquaint my Lord Halifax with this, for he will laugh at us secretarys for communicating such secrets, which I assure you is all the place affords.[13]

Unfortunately for Charles, after losing in the morning to the aptly named Mr Rider, his Mouse was beaten in the afternoon with Postboy stamping his authority. With the king's horses in such poor form, the following day an incredulous Conway wrote that 'there is no less than 3 to 1 generally offered against his horse that is to run this afternoon'. A sure sign that the king was slowing down is illustrated in a letter that Conway sent from Newmarket on 7 March 1681: 'I found his Majestie so much alone that for his diversion he was forced to play bassett; and as I am informed retires to his chamber every night at 9 o clock.'[14]

Nelly enjoyed her time at Newmarket. She wasn't a great rider – she fell badly once – but enjoyed the social side and horse talk. She would dress up as a male racehorse owner and see how long she could get away with it without being rumbled. One authentic anecdote from Newmarket illustrates her cheeky confidence. At the end of September 1681, enjoying a stroll in the Suffolk countryside, Charles was presented with a petition by a supercilious and republican alderman called Wright. 'The King walking in ye fields met Nell Gwynne and Nell cal'd to him "Charles, I hope I shall have your company at night, shall I not?"'[15] The alderman, shocked at such familiarity, told his friends that all those bad things he had heard about the king had now been confirmed in front of his own eyes.

During the spring meeting of 1683 Newmarket caught fire. On 23

March, Henry Savile wrote that the fire 'has consumed near half this town. The whole side in which the king's house stands is untouched... Clifford, the Duchess of Portsmouth, Mazarin, Clarendon all lost coaches.'[16] The fire meant that Charles returned to London a week ahead of schedule. As it transpired, the fire probably saved his life and that of his brother too. The public were about to discover the unravelling of the so-called Rye House Plot.

In Act III, Scene ii of his celebrated play *The Rehearsal*, Buckingham unleashes the masterly line: 'Ay, now the plot thickens very much upon us.' Given the number of intrigues brewing in the aftermath of the discredited Popish Plot, we could well take liberty with Buckingham's line to say that the plots thicken upon us. On 9 January 1683, Sir Leoline Jenkins received an anonymous letter warning him of a plot to assassinate the king. The letter ran:

> Today, as the King went through the Park in his sedan from Mistress Gween's to Whitehall, two men were observed In disguise, whispering near the garden wall between the Pall Mall and the garden wall and I heard them say, Damn him, we shall never have such an occasion again. Prevent any evil that may happen, if neglected, or we three, that were witnesses and are known in the world, will call you to an account.

Henry Sidney had written earlier in March 1680 that Monmouth 'resolves to take up arms in case the king dies, for he will conclude him murdered.'[17] Even in these plot-infested times the Rye House Plot shocked the nation. It took its name from the house belonging to Richard Rumbold at Hoddesdon, near Ware, Hertfordshire. Rumbold had been one of the guards at Charles I's execution. The house was on the London to Newmarket road and it was intended to block the road by the house with a hay cart and then assassinate the royal brothers when returning from Newmarket. The fire thwarted the plan. It was not until June that the details of the plot emerged. However, as investigations got under way, it became clear that there were two plots: the daring murder plot and one to overpower the guards, seize Whitehall and take the king into custody. The first was mooted by low-ranking old Cromwellians, three of whom were hanged, but the second, however, was hatched by leading Whigs, including Lord William Russell, Arthur Capel (the earl of Essex) and the self-proclaimed 'Commonwealthsman' Algernon Sydney.

Russell, who led the campaign to exclude James from the throne, was found guilty, on flimsy hearsay evidence, of high treason on Friday 13 July. His allies pleaded for his life: his pardon 'would lay an eternal obligation upon a very great and numerous family, and that the taking of life would never be forgotten.' Charles replied: 'All that is true; but it is as true that if I do not take his life, he will soon have mine.'[18] Russell was beheaded at Lincoln's Inn Fields and passed into Whig martyrdom. Rather than face a public trial, Arthur Capel cut his own throat. Charles admitted he would have pardoned him saying that he owed him a life, referring to the execution of Capel's Royalist father in 1649 after the fall of Colchester. The republican Sydney was tried before Judge Jeffreys in November and despite his competence in defending himself was found guilty. He was beheaded on Tower Hill and joined Russell as a celebrated martyr.

More worryingly for Charles, his son Monmouth was also implicated. However, despite his disfavour Charles decided his involvement, mirroring his personality, lacked any depth. He wasn't even arrested, but was banished from court. However, after a short reconciliation he fled to Holland. Charles would never see his eldest and once favourite son again. More pleasingly for Charles, he heard that his arch-enemy Shaftesbury had died. Shaftesbury had been sent to the Tower in 1681 on a charge of high treason. On his release he had fled to Holland where he died in Amsterdam in 1683. At last there was something for Charles to celebrate: 'Little Sincerity' was finally out of his periwig.

In the aftermath of the Rye House Plot, Charles's love affair with Newmarket understandably hit a rocky patch. He was also tiring of London and began to see the benefits of Louis XIV's preference to be out of the public eye. Charles devised his grand plans for a new palace to rival Versailles at Winchester, Hampshire, to be designed by Sir Christopher Wren. It was to have 160 rooms, a cupola, a staircase with marble columns and would sit in a park (also designed by Wren) and have a grand street to connect it to the cathedral. On 23 March 1683 the foundation stone was laid. Charles would visit regularly with his entourage, which included Nelly and Louise, to inspect progress.

On one such inspection in August of the same year, one of Charles's staff, the so-called 'harbinger', had the job of a organising lodgings for the king and his visitors. The bishop's palace and the houses of the dean and prebendaries were allocated to the most important visitors. Nelly was assigned to the house of the newly appointed court chaplain, the small, swarthy and principled Thomas Ken. However, Ken boldly refused to meet the king's wishes: 'Not for his kingdom,' he said, would he have his house adapted for Nelly. He explained his refusal by saying that 'a woman of ill-repute ought not to be endured in the house of a clergyman, least of all that of the King's chaplain.'[19]

Tradition also relates that to stop his hand being forced, Ken turned his house over to builders to remove the roof. Nelly would surely have found Ken's stance irresistible, particularly as the dean (Dr Meggot) found her alternative accommodation in his house. Indeed, he had a room built for her at the south end of the deanery, which became known locally as 'Nell Gwynne's room' until it was demolished by Dean Remmell in 1835, very possibly simply because of the connection. Charles certainly admired Ken's stand and piety. His preaching at court would lead Charles to say, 'I must go and hear little Ken tell me of my faults.' To defy a king, the defender of the faith, may not seem the best way to progress a career but, typically of Charles II, it did Ken more good than harm. When the bishopric of Bath and Wells became vacant, Charles is said to have declared 'Oddsfish! Who shall have Bath and Wells but the little black fellow who would not give poor Nelly a lodging?'[20] The story had some mileage. Much later, on 20 January 1747, Edward Young wrote to the duchess of Portland: ''Tis certain Nell Gwin made Dr Ken a bishop.'[21]

It was also en route to Winchester that Nelly found herself held up by a highwayman. Her coach was stopped on Bagshot Heath but even this potentially dangerous episode ended with Nelly laughing. The highwayman said, 'I hope, madam, you will give me something for myself after I have took all you have away?' This amused her and she laughed her famous laugh and handed over her money and jewellery. Whether she handed over a kiss remains speculative.

Louise was similarly held up although the outcome was somewhat different. Her small retinue was stopped, somewhat aptly on the old Portsmouth road, by the notorious highwayman 'Old Mobb'. Presented with a demand for money, Louise, in her furiously ruptured English, made her own demand: 'Do you know who you are addressing, you rascal?' But Old Mobb was an old hand. 'Yes, madam,' he replied, 'indeed, I do. I know you to be the greatest whore in the kingdom and that you are maintained at the public charge. I know that all the courtiers depend upon your smiles and that the king himself is your slave. But what of that? A gentleman collector is a greater man on the road and much more absolute than His Majesty is at court.' Louise's anger blurted out to warn him what to expect for this outrage upon her very noble person. 'Madam, that haughty French spirit will do you no good here,' replied Old Mobb. 'Your money is English and proof of English folly. I would have you know that I am king here. And I have also a whore of my own to keep on the public's contributions, just the same as King Charles has...'[22]

Back on the home front, it was proposed in 1682 that Nelly's son should be sent to France to live with Sir Richard Graham, Viscount Preston, the envoy extraordinary to Paris, who had replaced Sir Henry Savile.[23] Charles's affection for the boy was shown in a letter from Gaye Legge to Lord Preston, dated 20 November 1682:

> His Majesty is extremely fond of My Lord Burforde, and seems much concerned in his education, and he being now of an age fit to be bred in the world hath resolved to trust him wholly in your hands; no impertinent body shall be troublesome to you, nor anybody but whom you approve of to wait on him.[24]

Legge went on to say that it was hoped that Preston's house would be big enough to accommodate the young earl and if not he was to move to a larger one. His education was all important. Preston was implored to provide masters for him, 'the best can be got of all sorts, but more particularly the King would have him study mathematics, and in that fortification, and that when the King of France moves in any progresses he constantly go with you to view all places in France &c.' Legge followed up his letter to Preston on 26 December 1682 saying that the boy will follow but with 'Nelly desiring he should be delayed for a little time in hopes of some settlement being made upon him.' No doubt the proximity of Master James's birthday added to Nelly's concern about her surviving son also journeying into France.

There was still the business of a dukedom for Master Charles to settle, a dignity that was afforded all of the king's natural sons, except Master James. Henry Jermyn, earl of St Albans, died on 2 January 1684. A minute taken to grant the title of duke of St Albans to Charles Beauclerk, earl of Burford, is dated 5 January. It was the last title to be granted by Charles II. Five days later Nelly was the mother of a duke (she would be full of 'My Lord Dukes'). The orange-seller had founded a dynasty.

Charles still revelled in the role of a father. He was often seen with his children, including Nelly's son. On 30 March 1684, Evelyn had listened to a sermon preached by the bishop of Rochester at Whitehall and noted that the king 'accompanied with 3 of his natural Sonns, (viz. the Dukes of Northumb; Richmond & St Albans, base sonns of Portsmouth, Cleaveland, Nelly, prostitute creatures) went up to the Altar.' He would later comment that St Albans, the son of Nelly ('the Comedian & Apple-woman's daughter') and Louise's son were 'both very pretty boys, & seeme to have more Witt than [most of] the rest.'[25]

Master Charles was appointed to the offices of the master falconer of England and the registrar of the court of Chancery, both of which were to be made hereditary to the young duke on the death of the current holders which occurred in 1688 and 1698 respectively. More importantly these offices would be worth about £1,500 a year.

From Burford House, Windsor, on 14 April 1684, Nell dictated a letter to Frances Jennings 'over against the Tub Tavern, in Jermin Street, London'. It is likely that this was Lady Frances Jennings, mother of Sarah who would marry John Churchill and become the duchess of Marlborough. It is worth transcribing in full as originally written:

Madam,

I have receiv'd y^r. Letter, & I desire y^u would speake to my Ladie Williams to send me the gold Stuffe, & a Note with it, because I must sign it, then she shall have her Money ye next Day of Mr Trant; pray tell her Ladieship, that I will send her a note of what Quantity of Things I'le have bought, if her Ladieship will put herselfe to ye Trouble to buy them; when they are bought I will sign a Note for her to be payd. Pray Madam, let ye Man goe on with my Sedan, & sent Potvin and Mr Coker down to me, for I want them both. The Bill is very dear to boyle the Plate; but Necessity hath noe Law. I am afraid M^m. you have forgott my Mantle, which you were to line with Musk Colour Sattin, & all my other Things, for you send me noe Patterns nor Answer. Monsieur Lainey is going away. Pray send Word about your Son Griffin, for his Majestie is mighty well pleasd that he will goe along with my Lord Duke. I am afraid that you are so much taken up with your owne House, that you forgett my Businesse. My service to dear Lord Kildare, & tell him I love him with all my Heart. Pray M^m. see that Potvin brings now all my things with him: My Lord Duke's Bed &c. if he hath not made them all up, he may doe that here for if I doe not get my Things out of his Hands now, I shall not have them until this Time Twelve-month. The Duke brought me down with him my Crochet of Diamonds, & I love it the better because he brought it. Mr

Lumley, & everie Body else will tell you that it is the finest Thing that ever was seen. Good M^m. speake to Mr Beaver to come down too, that I may bespeake a Ring for the Duke of Grafton before he goes into France.

I have continued extream ill ever since you Leaft me, & I am soe still. I have sent to London for a Dr. I believe I shall die. My Service to the Dutchesse of Norfolk, & tell her I am as sick as her Grace, but doe not know what I ayle, although she does, which I am overjoyed that shee goes on with her great Belly.

Pray tell my Ladie Williams, that the King's Mistresses are accounted ill-pay-Masters, but shee shall have her Money the next Day after I have the Stuffe.

Here is sad Slaughter at Windsor, the young Men's taking ye. Leaves & going to France, & although they are none of my Lovers, yet I am loath to part with the Men. Mrs Jennings I love you with all my Heart, & soe good by.

E.G.

Let me have an Answer to this Letter.

As with her letter to Laurence Hyde, we get a real sense of Nelly from this. Despite being ill ('I believe I shall die'), she retains a gossipy liveliness. Lady Williams (who had married a Dorset baronet, and who had been a mistress to the duke of York) was to be reassured that Nelly would pay promptly for her 'gold stuffe' (possibly ornaments that Nelly had taken a fancy to) regardless of the reputation of the mistresses. Nelly was obviously experiencing some more financial problems and was having to melt down some of her precious metals ('Boil the plate') to raise money. And yet there she is buying more: it's easy to see how she accrued her debts. Some of the characters mentioned in the letter can be identified: John Poietevin (Potvin) was a fashionable upholsterer and obviously well employed by Nelly as he also appeared as a witness to her granting of the power of attorney to James Fraser; Mr Coker may well be the silversmith John Coques; Griffin was probably Lady Jennings's son-in-law Edward Griffith; Lord Kildare lived in St James's Square and was to marry Lady Elizabeth Jones, who it is thought was the king's final mistress; 'My Lord Duke' was Nelly's son; Mr Beaver was probably a jeweller; the duke of Grafton was Henry Fitzroy, one of the king's natural sons with Barbara; Mary Mordaunt, duchess of Norfolk, whose 'baby' was seemingly not born, was a woman of her time and it was at her notorious divorce case in 1692 that Nelly's evidence was submitted. The identities of Messrs

Trant, Lumley and Lainey are unclear.

Nelly's mounting debts could not have been helped by Ireland once again becoming a problematic source of income for her. The treasury lords wrote to the earl of Arran, lord deputy of Ireland on 27 November 1682 reminding him that a previous letter dated 8 August desired Arran 'to take care to provide the monies due to Madame Gwynne and her sister Mris Forster and Mris Willoughby' and to obtain it from the farmers.[26] Arran responded by writing to the duke of Ormonde on 5 December saying that a letter from the lords of the treasury (through the king's orders) had instructed him 'to take the suspensions off Mrs Gwyn's and several others' pensions, which I will do.'[27] The treasury records show that, in 1681, Nelly (variously called M^ris Nelly, M^ris Eleanor Gwynn, M^ris Elianor Gwynne, M^ris Elea. Gwyne, M^ris Ellen Gwynne and M^ris Eleanor Gwynne) received £7,000; in 1682 some £9,750; in 1683, £8,750; and in 1684, £9,000. So her last four full years of payment yielded her £34,500, which amounts to the equivalent of over £2.6 million pounds today. In addition to this, she was to have income on the customs paid on logwood, although the figure is not given. She received two further pension payments in January 1685 amounting to £1,750 – her last payments before the death of the king.

An historian of Lincoln's Inn claimed that Nelly left 'a benefaction of oysters that the masters of the Bench enjoy to this day'.[28] Unfortunately, although the benchers are traditionally served with oysters before each council meeting, this seems once again to be apocryphal. Nelly, as far as official records tell us, never visited Lincoln's Inn, although she used to live nearby. However, she was almost certainly one of the actors who received £20 for a special performance of Dryden's *The Mayden Quene* at the Inner Temple in 1668. She visited again as a guest on Thursday 12 January 1682, where the inn accounts include an entry 'ffor sweet-meats for Madam Gwin £1.'[29] Interestingly, it appears that she was invited not by the masters of the Bench but by law students, which rings true. Records show that 32 'gentlemen [were] in commons this Christmas', but do not relate how many joined Nelly at the dinner. The night also included music, dinner, dice, wine (probably about 30 bottles' worth), 'coffe', and chocolate. All of that and Nelly? It must have been quite a night.

— 22 —

All in the Dust

The glories of our blood and state
Are shadows, not substantial things.
There is no armour against fate;
Death lays his icy hands on kings.

Contention of Ajax and Ulysses, James Shirley 1659

How will succeeding story blush to tell
What this Great Britain's monarch e'er did well?
What did he well? Why nothing but one thing,
He lov'd his whores, & dy'd a famous fucking king.

'*The Lady of Pleasure*', anonymous, c. 1687

Charles had been a man with a 'vigorous and robust constitution' and in general good health. However, he suffered his first bad illness in 1679 and was never the same man again. In 1680, he suffered badly from ague. In 1682, he had a slight stroke. By the start of 1685, he had an infuriatingly painful heel that prevented him from taking his beloved saunterings. He would, however, still insist on taking the air and was carried around in a calash – a light carriage with low wheels.

January was cold. The Thames may have been frozen but Charles relaxed in the warmth of his mistresses. Evelyn witnessed 'such a sceane of profuse gaming, and luxurious dallying & prophanesse, the King in the middst of his 3 concubines...'[1]

Following another similar night in the company of mistresses, gambling, song and wine, Charles took his leave. Thomas Bruce, Lord Ailesbury, as gentleman of the bedchamber, lit Charles's way to his rooms as usual. As he passed the candle to the page of the backstairs, the flame blew out although there was no draught. In a highly superstitious court such an omen was not good. Ailesbury recorded that Charles bantered with him for a while in his rooms, talking animatedly about his palace at Winchester. It was then that he uttered the ominous words, 'I shall be most happy this week, for my building will be covered with lead.' Within a week his dead body would be lying in a lead coffin. That night Charles, unusually, slept uneasily, tossing and turning. Ailesbury was unable to sleep at all, being kept awake by a combination of the big coal fire, the king's restless spaniels and the quarter chimes of Charles's many clocks none of which seemed to chime at the same time. Charles was immune to such discord.

On waking, Charles rose and walked to his closet. He looked pale and remained silent. When he did try to speak he stopped mid-sentence as if he had forgotten what he was going to say. He sat down as usual for his morn-ing shave 'with his knees against the window'. As his barber placed some linen on one side, with a cry Charles fell from his chair into the arms of Ailesbury. Luckily, physicians were in the room (they had come to attend to his heel) and they removed 16 ounces of blood from Charles, which helped revive him. Soon all Charles's personal physicians were arriving hurriedly. At one time there would be 14 of them attending him.

Interestingly, it is recorded that 'the night before he was taken ill [the king] was to visit the dutchesse of Portsmouth'.[2] But, according to Nelly's supposed horoscope, that day would have been her birthday. And yet no mention is made of this. Charles was known to enjoy celebrating birthdays – his own, his children's and his mistresses. It suggests strongly that 2 February was not Nelly's birthday at all.

Charles had pioneered an open monarchy and now, finally, this meant that even his death had to be a public performance, his bedchamber being full of lords, privy councillors, surgeons, bishops and servants. His head was shorn, his body bled, purged, cauterised, clystered and blistered in a vain attempt to control the fits, fevers and convulsions. But, in truth, his doctors were clueless. They ventured combinations of potions, compounds, cordials, draughts, tonics, emulsions and brews but returned to what they knew best: purges and bleeding. Such ignorance, rather than instilling caution, merely inspired them to greater energy. One purgative was supplemented with an enema made up of a pint of common decoction for clysters, one ounce of powder of sacred bitter, two ounces of Buckthorn, $^1/_2$ drachm of rock salt and two ounces of orange infusion of the metals.[3]

The hysterically griefstruck queen was unable to watch Charles suffer and had repaired to her rooms. She sent a message that the king should forgive her for not being able to stay with him. 'Alas! Poor woman!' cried Charles, 'she asks my pardon? I beg hers with all my heart.' In a somewhat ironic twist, with the exception of the queen, no women were permitted into the king's bedchamber. However, this did not stop a grief stricken Nelly trying. Lady Mason said Nelly 'roared to a disturbance and was led out and lay roaring behind the door'.[4] From the moment of his sudden attack, none of the mistresses saw him again.

James, meanwhile, as heir to the throne was taking no chances. The guards were doubled at Whitehall and all the chief ports were sealed to prevent a message getting to Monmouth that Charles was dying, thus signalling an opportunity to sail for England to claim the throne. The lord mayor, aldermen and lieutenants of London pledged their support to James in case of any disturbances.

Despite his worsening condition, Charles was hanging on. But everyone feared the worst. Fearful that Charles had not yet sought absolution, the bishops sent for Thomas Ken, bishop of Bath and Wells, whom they knew the king was fond of and who might be able to persuade Charles to comply. Ken said that Charles need not confess but need only to say that he was sorry for his sins. Charles did so and Ken pronounced him absolved. But Charles declined to take the sacrament, saying that there was time enough for that to happen.

About this time, Barrillon found Louise 'in great grief':

But instead of bemoaning her own sad and altered position, and her impending fall, she took me into a little room and said: Monsieur l'Ambassadeur, I am now going to tell you a secret, although its public revelation would cost me my head. The King of England is in the bottom of his heart a Catholic, and there he is surrounded with Protestant Bishops! There is nobody to tell him of his state or speak to him of God. I cannot decently enter his room. Besides the queen is there constantly. The Duke of York is too busy with his own affairs to trouble himself about the king's conscience. Go and tell him that I have conjured you to warn him that the end is approaching, and that it is his duty to save without loss of time, his brother's soul.[5]

Barrillon's homage to Louise's altruism may be sincere, but it's true enough that to effect a conversion would certainly stand the soon-to-be-ex-mistress in good stead with the very Catholic soon-to-be King James II. Indeed, within an hour of Charles's death, James would visit Louise and assure her of his friendship and protection.

Barrillon, charged with Louise's holy quest, met James and impressed upon him the urgency of the situation. James 'seemed as though roused from a dream. "You are right," said he, "there is no time to lose: I would rather risk everything than not do my duty on this occasion."'[6] James went to the king and ordered everyone out of earshot and spoke quietly with Charles. Those in the antechamber only heard the king say 'With all my heart' over and over. James cleared the room of all but the trusted earls of Bath and Feversham. However, they were both Protestant and this helped soften the naturally aroused suspicion. James dispatched Chiffinch to bring in Father Huddlestone who had helped the king escape after the battle of Worcester. On seeing him arrive, Charles said that the man who saved his body had now come to save his soul. Within an hour Charles had converted to Catholicism, had received absolution and taken the sacrament. Evelyn had certainly heard the rumours of the king's Catholic conversion: 'Hurlston the Priest, had presum'd to administer the popish Offices; I hope it is not true; but these busie emissaries are very forwarde upon such occasions.'

With people now back in the room; Charles received all his sons, Monmouth excepted, and blessed each one of them. Charles asked his brother to forgive the hardships he had occasionally forced on him and wished him a prosperous reign. He then spoke of his mistresses and is famously attributed with saying 'Let not poor Nelly starve.' So famous that it even rates inclusion in the *Oxford Dictionary of Quotations* and numerous other similar collections. But did he actually say it or is it more myth? The evidence, happily for once, is conclusive: Four separate eyewitness accounts include its mention. Evelyn wrote:

> He gave his breeches & Keys to the Duke, who was continualy kneeling by his bed side, & in teares; he also recommended to him the care of his natural Children, all except the D: of Monmouth, now in Holland, & in his

displeasure...He spake to the Duke to be kind to his Concubines the DD: of Cleveland, & especialy Portsmouth, & that Nelly might not sterve.[7]

Bishop Burnet confirms it:

> At last he gathered all his strength together to speak his last words to the Duke, and everyone was attentive to them. He expressed great kindness to him, and that he now delivered all into his hands with joy, recommending to his care, over and over again, Lady Portsmouth and her son, the Duke of Richmond, and desiring him to be kind to his other children, and not let poor Nelly starve.[8]

The dispatches of Bartillon and the Dutch ambassador, Van Citters also confirm the quote.

As death slowly and painfully tightened its icy grip, Charles still managed to display his characteristic wit. He apologised to all around him for taking such 'an unconscionable time in dying'. Earlier he had been encouraged not to talk to save energy: such a command, he replied, would be the death of his friend Harry Killigrew. At six o'clock on 6 February, he asked that the curtains be drawn back that he might see for the last time the sunrise light up an English morning. As he witnessed his final dawn, he suddenly remembered that one of his eight-day clocks needed winding that day or else it would run down and asked that it be done for him. At seven o'clock, he suffered breathlessness. At eight-thirty, his speech began to fail him and by ten o'clock he slipped into unconsciousness. Just before noon, King Charles II was dead.

Reflecting on his death, Evelyn cast his mind back to the previous Sunday:

> I am never to forgett, the unexpressable luxury, & prophanesse, gaming, & all dissolution, and as it were total forgetfulnesse of God (it being Sunday Evening) which this day sennight, I was witnesse of; the King, sitting and toying with his Concubines Portsmouth, Cleaveland, & Mazarine: &c: A french boy singing love songs, in that glorious Gallery, whilst about 20 of the greate Courtiers and other dissolute persons were at Basset round a large table, a bank of at least 2000 in Gold before them, upon which two Gent: that were with me made reflexions with astonishment, it being a sceane of utmost vanity; and surely as they thought would never have an End: six days after was all in the dust.

The playwright Aphra Behn wrote the official 'Pindarick on the death of our late Sovereign'. Two lines reflect the shock at the unexpected demise of Charles:

> And no dire warning to the world would be given
> No hurricanes on earth! No blazing fires in heaven!

An autopsy was carried out on Charles's body next day, after which the body was embalmed. A wax mask of his face was taken and can still be seen today as part of the effigy in Westminster Abbey, although its original clothes have been replaced. However, at the time ceremony was stood down and Charles's funeral was one of the greatest royal non-events. The Windsor herald, John Dugdale, wrote that 'we know nothing, only discourse is that it will be exceeding private, not so much as a footman of ye King's put in mourning.'[9] Charles's body was taken to the princes' chamber on 12 February and lay in state until Saturday evening. That evening, after dark, the funeral took place. Nelly and the other mistresses were not permitted to attend. There was to be no state funeral. There are probably two reasons for this: first, James knew that Charles had converted to Catholicism and therefore a state Protestant funeral was inappropriate: even James knew that he couldn't declare publicly Charles's conversion and therefore could not sanction a Catholic funeral; and second, the state could ill afford the expense of a state funeral. So, despite the natural and sincere grief of the people, the nation was not given a chance to mourn. Such was the ignominy of his end that Charles's body was interred in a new vault which for 200 years did not even bear his name.

Rumours raged that the suddenness of the king's death could mean but one thing: poison. People love a good suspicion of poisoning. It was suggested that any one of the queen, duke of York and Louise (all Catholics, so natural prime suspects) had carried out the dastardly deed. Louise had apparently either poisoned his chocolate or his eggs, whereas, somewhat bizarrely, the queen was accused of poisoning a jar of dried peas. However, it seems that Charles's death was caused by a chronic granular kidney disease. But at the time it was, as most things seemed to have been, reckoned to be apoplexy.

Nelly, excluded from it all, could only mourn in private. Protocol, which must have been wearing thin for Nelly, also forbade her and the other mistresses to put their houses in mourning. On 17 February, Sir Cyril Wyche wrote to the duke of Ormonde: 'Nell Gwyn has been forbid to put to put her house in mourning, or to use that sort of nails about her coach and chair which it seems is kept as a distinction for the Royal Family on such occasions, and had else been put on by her command.'[10]

Within six years she had lost her mother, son and lover. If the death of Master James had broken her heart, the death of Charles ripped out her spirit. And a spiritless Nelly was no Nelly at all. On 6 February 1685, to all intents and purposes, Nelly died with her king, her man, her lover, her best friend, her Charles III.

— 23 —

He Was My Friend

Thus we in short have all the virtues seen
Of the incomparable Madam Guyn;
Nor wonder others are not with her shown:
She who no equal has, must be alone.

'A Panegyric', 1681

However, 'twere as the old women say:
Her time was come & then there's no delay,
So down into the Stygian lake she dropt
To meet the prince she had so often fopt.

'The Lady of Pleasure', anonymous, *c*.1687

James took the mantle of kingship seriously and looked to break with the dissolution of Charles's merry court. It did not look to be a happy time for mistresses, including the new king's. Luttrell related that 'His Majestie hath discharged Mrs Sedley to see her no more since his comeing to the crown.' She was richly compensated by being created countess of Dorchester. One in the eye for poor Nelly.

The London Gazette, 5–9 February, reported that following Charles's death, James called the privy council and told them: 'Since it hath pleased Almighty God to place me in this station, and I am now to succeed so good and gracious a King, as well as so kind a brother, I think it fit to declare unto you, that I will endeavour to follow his example, and most especially in that of his great clemency and tenderness to his people.' However, not much of that clemency or tenderness exposed itself in the summer of 1685 following Monmouth's doomed rebellion.

Monmouth returning to England, landed near Lyme Regis, declared himself the lawful king and pronounced his uncle James a usurper. He was crowned at Taunton, raised an army of mostly peasant locals, but when the crunch came, he chose not to attack Bristol and retreated westwards, losing many recruits on the way. Instead he gambled on a surprise night attack at Sedgemoor. It was an awesome blunder. With the game up, he scarpered, leaving his poor, deluded followers to be massacred for the cause. The military mastermind was later captured in the New Forest, hiding pitifully in a ditch. Despite pleading desperately for his life, and having Catherine of Braganza speak for him, James II was not about to pardon this symbol of Protestantism. Monmouth was sentenced to death.

The surviving rebels felt the uncompromising cruelty of Judge Jeffreys – and his openly sardonic enjoyment of it. The judge, obviously keen to impress James, was sent to the western circuit and presided over his infamous 'Bloody Assize'. Records are unclear but the best estimates suggest that between 120 and 300 people were executed, with up to a further 800 finding themselves on a one-way passage to the West Indies. The opening case set the tone. Lady Alice Lisle was accused of harbouring a traitor against which she protested her – very probable – innocence. She was the widow of John Lisle, the old Cromwellian and regicide, who had been assassinated by Royalist supporters in Switzerland in 1664. This family connection would do little to bolster her defence and she was, inevitably, found guilty. Jeffreys, surely not wishing to influence the loaded jury, declared, 'Had she been my own mother, I would have found her guilty.' She was sentenced to burning at the stake, which was later commuted to beheading. She was over 70 years old. The king made the faithful Jeffreys a baron and appointed him lord chancellor.

Monmouth was executed on 15 July 1685 on Tower Hill. He confessed to the rector of St Martin-in-the-Fields, Dr Thomas Tenison, whom he had requested to be with him at the end, that 'I dye very penitent'. He looked at the executioner, Jack Ketch, and asked, 'Is this the man to do the business? Do your work well.' Monmouth then, in a brave act of theatricality, felt the edge of the axe and said 'I fear it is not sharp enough.'[1] However, as 'the executioner proceeded to do his office' either Monmouth was right about the blade, or wrong to trust that Ketch would do the job well. After the third swipe he threw down his axe complaining 'I can't do it.' Compelled to try again, he tried two more blows before deciding to finish the job with a butcher's knife, hacking Monmouth's head from his body. Ketch was so notorious and seemingly so woefully inept – he also bungled the execution of Lord Russell after the Rye House Plot, defending himself by saying that Russell 'moved' – that it's incredible that his name became synonymous with executioners or hangmen. Or maybe that was the point. John Wesley, the founder of Methodism, wrote about 'a kind of jack-catch, an executioner general'. Perhaps, however, only Mrs Ketch believed her husband was any good at his job: 'A man may be capable,' wrote John Dryden, 'as Jack Ketch's wife said of his servant, of a plain piece of work, a bare hanging; but to make a malefactor die sweetly was only belonging to her husband.'

As mistress to the king, credit had been easy, endless and unworthy of a thought. All such perks were as sweet and clear as the breath drawn by Charles at his beloved Newmarket. Following Charles's last breath, the air of credit staled and suffocated.

Deprived of heart and soul, Nelly's body felt like a bare carcass being attacked by the vultures of credit, all scavenging for the best they could get before the others. She was desperate. Creditors feared they wouldn't get their money and outlawed her for debt. This could mean that, like her father, she could end up in debtors' prison. She needed money and had only one real option. She needed to approach the king; she made contact with Richard Graham, who met her to discuss her situation. She then wrote to James. The letter, although unsigned or dated, is thought to have been sent in April or May 1685:

> had I sufered for my God as I have don for y^r brother and y^u I shuld not have needed either of y^r Kindnes or iustis to me.
> I beseech you not to doe any thing to the setling of my busines till I speake wth you and a poynt me by Mr Grahams wher I may speake wth you privetly God make you happy as my soule prays you may be, y^{rs}

It's clear from this letter that Richard Graham had received agreement from James to help sort out Nelly's immediate problems ('settling my business'). However, Nelly felt it important to speak to James privately.

Perhaps she hoped that a title might still be forthcoming. However, James would not see Nelly. Graham, along with Nelly's then steward, James Booth, listed Nelly's debts. The schedule of the secret services receipts and payments between 1679 and 1688 is fascinating.[2] An entry dated 22 September 1685 reads: 'To Richard Graham, Esq for excise by him payd over to Severall Tradesmen Creditors of Mrs Ellen Gwynn in satisfaction of their jobs for which the said Ellen stood outlawed – £729.2.3.'

More immediately, on 21 April 1685, Henry Guy, the secretary to the treasury, ordered Alderman Charles Duncombe, cashier and treasurer of the excise, to 'forthwith upon sight hereof advance £500 to Mris Gwynne.' She received her money exactly two months later. In July, Laurence Hyde tried to help. He issued a warrant to the 'Custom Commissioners to order the collectors of the outports to forthwith give account to Mris Ellen Gwynn of the receipts of the Customs on logwood, alias blockwood since 1677, Michaelmas…'[3] Nelly had not received any income from logwood for eight years and it's not clear that she ever saw any. The accounts of her executors include two payments 'Recd of the Farmers of Logwood' of £500, but not made until 15 October 1688 and 17 October the following year.

On hearing that financial help was underway, Nelly wrote again to James, dictating to her secretary Bridget Long. She begins by saying that the love she had for Charles and James was for them as the people they were and not what she could get out of them:

> Sr
>   This world is not capable of giving me greater ioy and happyness than y[r] Ma[ties] favour not as you are King and soe have it in y[r] power to doe me good having never loved y[r] brother and y[r] selfe upon that account but as to y[r] persons

She then describes what Charles had promised her and what he meant to her:

> had hee lived hee tould me before hee dyed that the world shuld see by what hee did for me that hee had both love and value for me and that hee did not doe for me, as my mad lady woster, hee was my frind advise me and tould me who was my frind and who was not.

That 'the world may see by what he did for me' may be a reference to Charles's supposed plan to create Nelly Countess of Greenwich. 'Lady Woster' was Margaret Somerset dowager marchioness of Worcester, who petitioned the king for the restoration of the £91,500 she reckoned her husband had spent in the king's service in exile. She went insane in 1679 and was known as 'the mad marchioness of Worcester'. The reference may well be that Charles believed that Nelly deserved to be financially settled for life. Most movingly, though, is her simple comment that Charles was her friend. She loved and trusted him. In a world of deceit, intrigue and selfishness, the tender honesty and simplicity of her devotion to him touches the heart. To love and be loved by your best friend: it doesn't come much better than that.

She concludes her letter:

> Sʳ the honour yʳ Ma:ᵗⁱᶜ has don me by Mʳ Grahams has given me great comfort not by the present you sent me to releeve me out of the last extremety, but by the Kind expressions hee mad me from you, of yʳ Kindnes to me wᶜʰ to me is above all things in this world having God Knows never loved yʳ brother or yʳ selfe interestedly, all you doe for me shall be yours it being my resolution never to have any interest but yʳˢ, and as long as I live to serve you and when I dye to dye praying for yᵘ.

Once again, Nelly emphasises her love of people not positions (never loving Charles or James 'interestedly'). On 25 December 1685, the following two consecutive entries are made in the secret services accounts:

To Ellinor Gwynn bounty	£500
To said Ellinor Gwynne, more	£500

As well as settling her most immediate debts, and donating gifts amounting to £1,000, James also settled a pension on Nelly of £1,500 a year. The accounts record payments out of the customs to Mr Gwynn – possibly the unrelated Francis Gwyn (although coincidentally he married an Eleanor) – who would act as a trustee. However, the accountants obviously knew who the real beneficiary was as a bracketed 'Mris Nelly' appears alongside Mr Gwynn's name. The amount she now received was a lot less than she had enjoyed previously, but it would ensure that bills could at the very least be part paid and food would make it to the table.

The aloof, humourless man, who rejected, Falstaff-like, his and the court's past life, respected his brother's dying wish: he did not let poor Nelly starve. Dismal Jimmy became her unlikely saviour. He would never see her again – mistresses not being part of his crafted image of kingship – but he never deserted her and certainly never forgot her.

Indeed, James went further and paid £3,774.2s. 6d. to redeem the mortgage on Bestwood Park on 16 October 1687. He also paid a further £1,256.0s. 2d. to settle Bestwood 'upon Mrs Ellen Gwynn for life and after her decease upon the Duke of St Albans and his issue'. Actually the payments to redeem the mortgage were paid in the first instance by Sir Stephen Fox. The hugely wealthy Fox often had a handy supply of cash (or rather such was his reputation that he was able to obtain it from banks) to conduct business. He would then be repaid by the treasury or, as in this case, from the secret services accounts.

Summers were usually spent at Windsor, but the energy and the company were gone. Her illness in 1687 kept her at Pall Mall. Seeking comfort, she probably hugged memories of better times. Chiffinch's secret services accounts reveal that at Windsor, between 19 May and 1 August 1674, Nelly spent £394.14s. on food alone. At today's equivalent that amounts to over £400 a day. Another bill amounted to £287. 5s. 8d. 'for diet for Mris Gwyn at Windsor and £1,15s.3d. for oringes, lemmons etc for her and £24.4s.8d. for goods bought for her use…'[4] No such luxury danced in her lap now.

Although she had withdrawn from public life, her notoriety kept her name grinding through the gossip and rumour mills. James II created Thomas Watson bishop of St David's on 26 June 1687. Some said he got the nod because he was backed by Baron Dover, others that he had bought the see, and others that Nelly had used her influence to secure it because he was said to have entertained her at his chambers in Cambridge. The reality was, at that time, Nelly was having trouble influencing her bowel movements let alone appointments to bishoprics.

A number of satires published in the 1680s are very critical of Nelly's looks. References were made to 'old Nelly' (*The Vindication, Part ye 2^d*, 1686); 'ugly fac'd Nelly' (*On the Ladies of Honour*, 1686) and the earlier and probably just spiteful 'Your haggard carcass yields no delight' (*Portsmouth's Return*, 1682). Time was not benevolent towards looks in the late seventeenth century. The average life expectancy was as low as 35. If you managed to survive beyond that there was usually a price to pay. The ravages of illnesses, smallpox and sexual diseases and their ilk did their damnedest to scar and deface. Only a very few managed to retain their looks beyond their twenties – Nelly and, in particular, Hortense retained a freshness of youth. However, Nelly was ill many times during this period and perhaps this debilitating experience aged her. Of course, the satires could just be vindictive, but that would be self-defeating. One other libel even noted that 'folks complain that her breath stinks of onyon'.

In March 1687, Nelly was very ill and appears to have suffered a paralysis down one side of her body. Contemporary letters tell the tale. On 20 March: she was 'dangerously ill and her recovery is much in doubt'. On 22 March, Alice Hatton reports that 'Mrs Nelly is dying of an apoplexy.'[5] John Verney had informed his father on 24 March 1687 that 'Mrs Eleanor Guin lies a–dying'.[6] On 26 March, Alice Hatton wrote to her brother that 'Tis said Nell Guin is dead.'[7] Finally, on 29 March, Sir Charles Lyttelton wrote: 'Mrs Nelly has bine dying of an apoplexie. She is now come to her sense on one side, for ye other is dead of a palsey.'[8] Nelly was now being attended by full-time nurses.

Nelly's doctor had been the Protestant Cornishman Richard Lower, whose Celtic origins would have pleased her. He was, in 1675, thought of as 'the most noted physician in Westminster and London' but had fallen from grace at court because he sided with the Whigs. Lower, who would try and claim the credit (erroneously) for inventing blood transfusions, was replaced by Dr Christian Harrell in July. Harrell had met Charles during his exile and became one of his physicians on his restoration. Nelly was also attended by a Dr Harrold and two court physicians, Dr Le Febre and Dr Lister, the last two along with both Harrell and Lower had attended Charles at his deathbed. Things were not looking good.

Around this time, if not sooner, Dr Tenison, who arrived at St Martin-in-the-Fields in 1680, began visiting a sick Nelly at Pall Mall. He may well have made his acquaintance through his friend Dr Lower. Bishop Kennet said, 'I have heard Dr Tenison . . . say often of him that Dr Lower was his special friend.' Lower told Tension that he would chat with Nelly 'and would pick out of her all the intrigues of the Court of Charles II'.[9] Nelly's own chaplain from the church, John Warner, was also visiting.

More bad news arrived in the form of the death of Buckingham. He had retired, riddled with debt, to Yorkshire and died from a chill after trying to dig a fox out of a hole. He was, however, unlike his childhood friend Charles, given an extraordinarily lavish funeral at Westminster Abbey. Around May or June 1687, Nelly had been forced to move out of her house in Pall Mall while her roof was being repaired. It seems that she didn't move back to her own house. She moved in with her friend and neighbour, Hannah Grace. The house was, according to rates records, four houses down from Nelly's and about a quarter of the size. It was registered in the name of Hannah's husband, Austin Grace, who apparently was away at the time. Hannah Grace received a payment of £26 on 17 March 1688, which may have been by way of board. A day later Mrs Edline received £13, which may be a payment for nursing Nelly during that time. Nelly must have felt the end approaching and in July drew up her will. It began:

> In the name of God, Amen. I, Ellen Gwynne, of the parish of St Martin-in-the-Fields, and county of Middlesex, spinster, this 9th day of July, anno Domini 1687, do make this my last will and testament, and do revoke all former wills. First, in hope of a joyful resurrection, I do recommend myself whence I came, my soul into the hands of Almighty God, and my body unto the earth, to be decently buried, at the discretion of my executors, hereinafter named; and as for all such houses, lands, tenements, offices, places, pensions, annuities and hereditaments whatsoever, in England, Ireland or elsewhere, wherein I, or my heirs, or any to the use of, or in trust for me or my heirs, hath, have, or may or ought to have, any estate, right, claim, or demand whatsoever, of fee-simple or freehold, I give and devise the same all and wholly to my dear natural son, his Grace the Duke of St Albans, and to the heirs of his body...

We can be sure that the houses left to her dear son included Pall Mall, Burford House (which had been leased to James II's nephew, Prince George of Denmark from October 1686 at an annual rent of £260) and Bestwood Lodge. The first two would not stay in the family long, but Bestwood, where members of the family including the tenth and eleventh dukes are buried, remained so until 1940.

Nelly also asked that her 'jewels, plate, household stuff, goods, chattels, credits and other estate' be held for her son in trust by her executors. She nominated four executors; Laurence Hyde, earl of Rochester; Thomas Herbert, now earl of Pembroke; the king's attorney-general Sir Robert Sawyer, who had prosecuted the perpetrators of the

Rye House Plot, although Burnet thought him 'a dull fat man'; and, strangely, Henry Sidney, the same-aged uncle of earl of Sunderland, whose diary shows him to have been very much with Louise. Nelly also provided that each of them should receive '£100 a-piece or lawful money, In consideration of their care and trouble herein'. The will was witnessed by five people: Nelly's close friend Lucy Hamilton Sandys, whom Rochester called 'the Good Lady Sandys'; Edward Wyborne; her chaplain, John Warner; William Scarborough and James Booth.

Nell issued a codicil to her will on 18 October 1687. She requested her son to ensure the following:

1. I desire to be buried in the church of St Martin-in-the-Fields.
2. That Dr Tenison may preach my funeral sermon.
3. That there may be a decent pulpit-cloth and cushion given to St Martin-in-the-Fields.
4. That he [her son] would give one hundred pounds for the use of the poor, of the said St Martins and St James's Westminster, to be given into the hands of the said Dr Tenison, to be disposed of at his discretion, for taking any poor debtors of the said parish out of prison, and for cloathes this winter, and other necessaries, as he shall find most fit.
5. That for showing my charity to those who differ from me in religion, I desire that fifty pounds may be put into the hands of Dr Tenison and Mr Warner, who, taking to them any two persons of the Roman Religion, may dispose of it for the use of the poor of that religion inhabiting the parish of St James's aforesaid.
6. That Mrs Rose Forster may have two hundred pounds given to her, any time within a year after my decease.
7. That Jo, my porter, may have ten pounds given him.

My request to his Grace [her son] is, further

8. That my present nurses may have ten pounds each, and mourning, besides their wages due to them.
9. That my present servants may have mourning each, and a year's wages, besides their wages due.
10. That the Lady Fairborne may have fifty pounds given her to buy a ring.
11. That my kinsman, Mr Cholmley, may have one hundred pounds given to him, within a year of this date.
12. That His Grace would please to lay out twenty pounds yearly for the releasing of poor debtors out of prison every Christmas-day.
13. That Mr John Warner may have fifty pounds to buy a ring.

14 That the Lady Hollyman may have the pension of ten shillings per week
    continued to her during the said lady's life.

Oct. 18 —87. This request was attested and acknowledged in the presence of
us,

> John Hetherington.
> Hannah Grace.
> Daniel Dyer.

The influence of Dr Tenison over the dying Nelly shows itself clearly in
this codicil. The request for him to preach her funeral sermon must have
been agreed by him before, not least because of the controversy it was
bound to cause. But to his credit, he complied with her request. The
nature of the will also dismisses the view that she might have converted
to Catholicism, as Charles had done and, of course, to seek James's
favour. Evelyn noted that 'Dryden the famous play-poet & his two sonns,
& Mrs. Nelle (Misse to the late...) were said to go to Masse; & such
purchases were no greate losse to the Church.'[10] None the less, Nelly
being Nelly, showed 'her charity to those who differ from me in religion'
by bequeathing £50 to poor Catholics.

It seems that of all Charles's natural children, it was Nelly's son that
James rounded on in the hope of securing another convert to
Catholicism. Alice Hatton, in her letter to her brother in March 1687,
when she thought Nelly was dead, confirmed James's wish for the young
duke's conversion: 'Y^e King has seazed on hir estate and jewles for hir
son, but, unless he will change his religion, he's not to have anything, w^ch
he is yet very unwilling to.'[11] The pressure put on Nelly is thought to
have taken its toll on her health. Nelly was reputedly told by James that
her son

> must be of the religion his father died in if she is expected that he should take
> care of him, and that...the Duke's governor or tutor, a French Protestant
> who has been long in England, must be removed because he was a heretic and
> he would place another, and has placed...a very fierce, active, discursive
> Papist who Harry Killigrew told the King would syllogize the Duke to
> death...All agree that it was an inexpressable grief to her that first brought
> her distemper upon her, and continued upon her heart till her death that a
> Papist...was made a tutor to her son...[12]

Despite all the overbearing influence, the young duke remained
Protestant and even became a Whig.

The poor languishing in debtors' prison were never far from Nelly's mind or heart, remembering perhaps not only her father but her own recent near-experience. Her sister, who had been almost a constant companion over the past year, was left £200, although Nelly had told her several times that she would 'get a good legacy'. Typically, Nelly left a year's wages to all her remaining servants, but granted a bonus £10 to Jo (John Berry), her loyal porter of at least 12 years. The £10 was clearly in gratitude for his devotion and long service. The widowed Lady Margery Fairborne, whose husband, Sir Palmes Fairborne, was governor of Tangier when he was killed in a siege in 1680, was a friend and regular visitor to Pall Mall. It has proved so far impossible to identify Nelly's mysterious kinsman, 'Mr Cholmley', or the Lady Holyman who received the pension.

Nelly was doing well to survive. The candles of her life were burning out and death's pale smoke was circling her soul. Nelly's visitors in the last few days said that she had made various promises to people: Rose could have her 'silver tissua mantua' (a rich silver cloak); a housemaid claimed Nelly said she could have 'my clothes or the best of my clothes which will be worth £500 more and my tippett' (a scarf-like wrap).[13]

On 14 November, her chaplain, John Warner, called to see her. Although struggling to talk and frequently reaching for breath, she said, 'I am glad you are come, I have something to say to you.' She asked Warner to get pen and ink and called everybody else in the house to act as witnesses. These were her friend Ann Edline, Dr Le Febre, Dr Harrell and his nephew 'Mr Derek', Hannah Grace and her maid, Margaret Bentley, Bridget Long who helped prop Nelly up, and the housemaid, Bess. Unable to find any fresh paper, Warner made notes on the back of a letter he had received from his sister Elizabeth. Nelly then in great pain and with great difficulty dictated a second codicil to her will. Afterwards she said, 'It's very well, now I shall die in peace.' She then called on Warner to 'Come let us hear what you have wrote.' He read it back out and then said, 'Madam, I will go into the next room and write it fair.' The second codicil provided:

> The said Mrs Ellen Gwinne did give and bequeath to Mrs Rose Forster, her sister, the sum of two hundred pounds over and above the sum of two hundred pounds, which she gave to her the said Rose in her former Codicil.
>
> To Mr Forster, husband of the said Rose Forster, a ring of the value of forty pounds or forty pounds to buy him a ring.

To Dr Harrell, twenty pounds.

To Mr Derrick, nephew of the said Dr Harrell, ten pounds.

To Dr le Febre twenty pounds respectively to buy them rings.

To Bridget Long, who had been her servant for divers years, the sum of twenty pounds of lawful money of England yearly during her natural life.

To Mrs Edling a new gown.

And Mr John Warner, her Chaplain, was present with others at the declaring thereof, and that a little before the declaring of the same she being of perfect mind and memory did order or desire the said Mr Warner to put into writing what she should then declare. And that said legacies were wrote and read to the deceased and by her approved as part of her last Will and Testament as by the proofs I made and sentences given in the said Cause do appear.

Hannah Grace said that Nelly was most pleased that she had doubled her bequest to Rose. Later that afternoon, she became concerned that she might not be able to afford her donations, worried that they might unduly 'prejudice my Lord Duke'. Warner told her that everything would be fine and she felt reassured and slept for a while.

The next day, still in pain and short of breath, she struggled through the day. Her woman, Bridget Long, sat with her. Nelly thanked her for her service and said that if only time would allow she would have used her more kindly. It was the last thing she said. At about ten o'clock on Monday night, 14 November 1687, the most famous woman in England bequeathed her final breath. Poor Nelly was dead.

Final Accounts

Not heaven itself upon the past has power
What has been, has been, and I have had my hour.

Translation of Juvenal, John Dryden.

With charming themes no more to be supply'd
For wit and beauty with Laurinda dy'd.

Her cheerful looks the winter's rage beguil'd
Her smiles made summer and she always smil'd.

'Laurinda, A Pastoral on the lamented death of the incomparable Madam Guin',

Anonymous, *c*.1687

Despite being swept off centre stage by the nation's new management, the faded star still made news. Dr William Denton, in a newsletter to Sir Ralph Verney, wrote on 16 November 1687 that 'Lord Langdale hath Plymouth's regiment, and I hear that Nell is dead.' Although mistaken about her place of death, Henry Muddiman, in a newsletter dated 15 November 1687, wrote: 'On the 14th, about ten o'clock, Madam Ellen Gwyn, after a long and wasting sicknesse died at her house in Pall Mall, whither her son the Duke of St Albans is now removing from his lodgings in Whitehall.'[1] The death register shows Nelly was one of six funerals that day 17 November 1687 and records her passing simply: 'Elinor Gwin, w.' The 'w' stood for 'woman'.

The elegy writers were ordering more ink. One typically anonymous verse, called *An Elegy in Commemoration of Madam Eleanor Gwynne*, concentrated on her quiet charity, and her natural modesty:

> ...some may cast objections in and say
> These scattered praises that we seek to lay
> Upon her hearse are but the formal way.
> Yet when we tell them she was free from strife,
> Courteous even to the poor, no pride of life,
> E'er entertaining, but did much abound
> In charity, and for it was renowned;
> Not seeking praises, but did vain praise despise,
> And at her alms were heard no trumpet noise;
> And how again we let them further see
> That she refused and hated flattery,
> And far from her dessemblers did command,
> We may have hopes her fame for this will stand.

Nelly's funeral was not overly ostentatious, she had, for example, asked to be placed in a plain black coffin which was to be left open. However, it was still appropriately extravagant, costing £375 (equivalent to about £28,500 today). The treasury accounts record that the money was taken out of Nelly's pension that would have been due had she lived: '1688, January. To Roger Hewitt, upon the like sume that would have become due at Xtmas last to Mrs Ellinor Gwynn, dec'd, on a pencion of £1500 per ann. in the name of Francis Gwynne, Esq., to reimburse so much money paid by Sr. Stephen Fox for the funeral of the said Mrs. Gwynn, £375.' As Melville said, 'So as she lived, so she died, at the country's expense.'[2] Nelly's final costs were paid in the first instance by Sir Stephen Fox. Fox was the man who, while at the treasury, had authorised Nelly's first ever payment from Charles on 5 December 1674 – nearly 13 years previously: 'Sir Stephen Fox to pay £500 to Mrs. H.G.' The circle was complete.

As requested in her first codicil to her will, she was buried at St Martin-in-the-Fields, very possibly next to her mother. Subsequent rebuilding of the church has meant that Nelly's tomb and that of her mother's have been dug up and lost. It very probably lies under the present-day National Portrait Gallery, which doesn't seem too inappropriate. One source cites that an American 'some years back [was] trying to prove that her remains had been re-interred in St Martin's graveyard in Camden Town in the 19th Century.'[3]

Tenison, also as requested, preached her memorial sermon. Apart from the threats to his clerical career, he also had to face opposition from his own parishioners who objected to Nelly being buried in the crypt. Tenison is said to have offered his own reserved grave for her if necessary.[4] He went on to become archdeacon of London (1689), bishop of Lincoln (1691) where he succeeded Bishop Tillotson, who had also been a curate at St Martin-in-the-Fields and, ultimately in 1694, he became archbishop of Canterbury, remaining so until his death in 1715. He crowned both Queen Anne and her successor George I.

Clearly, his support for Nelly did his career scant damage. However, it was used against him when he was being touted as a possible archbishop of Lincoln. The earl of Jersey was promoting the cause of his friend Dr Scott, rector of St Giles-in-the-Fields (where Catharine Sedley was baptised and where Andrew Marvell and Godfrey Kneller are buried). When Queen Mary II spoke of Dr Tenison with respect, Jersey reminded her that Tenison was the man who had delivered a notable funeral sermon in praise of Mrs Eleanor Gwynne, one of Charles II's concubines. The queen replied, 'What, I have heard as much. This is a sign that that poor unfortunate woman died penitent, for if I can read a man's heart through his looks, had she not made a truly Christian and pious end, the doctor could not have been induced to speak well of her.' A letter sent to Sir George Etheredge, then envoy at Ratisbon, by 'Wigmore' confirmed Nelly's contrition: 'She is said to have died piously and penitently, and, as she dispensed several charities in her life, so she left several legacies at her death.' Colley Cibber asserted that a solid authority told him that 'her repentance in her last hours appeared in the contrite symptoms of Christian sincerity.' However, the Egmont Papers, held at the British Library include a curious character sketch of Nelly. They say that a 'Dr Garth comforted a dying courtezan in despair by telling her on his honour there was neither God nor future state.'

Tenison spoke 'much to her praise' to the packed congregation, with crowds outside lining the streets. Although the sermon appears lost, it is thought that Tenison based it on Matthew, Chapter 18:

For the Son of Man is come to save that which was lost. How think ye? If a man have an hundred sheep, and one of them be gone astray, doth he not leave the ninety and nine, and goeth into the mountains, and seeketh that that which is gone astray? And if so be that he find it, verily I say unto you, he rejoiceth more of that sheep than of the ninety and nine which went not astray.

The lost lamb was found again. However, a renegade transcript of his sermon was published to his disgrace. Tenison had to respond. A notice was placed in his own newly published pamphlet on the Catholic controversy. It read: 'Advertisement. Whereas there has been a Paper cry'd by some Hawkers, as a sermon preached by D[octor] T[enison] at the funeral M[adam] E[leanor] Gwynn, this may certify that the paper is the forgery of some mercenary people.'[5]

As far as Nelly's business was concerned, it was a case of winding up the estate. As ever, there was speculation as to the worth of the ex-mistress of a king. Luttrell recorded that 'Mrs Ellen Gwyn was buried the 17th of November at St Martins; she hath left a considerable estate to her son, the Duke of St Albans.'[6] Sir Charles Lyttelton wrote at the time that Nelly was 'thought to be worth £100,000; £2,000 in revenue and the rest in jewels and plate.' This was a generous estimate. Nelly's nurse thought her worth about £5,000.

Her houses were worth a considerable amount, although some of Nelly's biographers have lacked caution, valuing Pall Mall at £10,000. Burford House was thought to be worth more, but the sale realised only £4,000. Pall Mall had cost about £1,400 in 1667. Prices were remarkably stable in Restoration London, only inflating by about $12^1/_2$ per cent over 30 years. Even allowing for a celebrity bonus, Pall Mall was probably worth about £2,000. However, after that there really wasn't a great deal left. Her silver was held by her bankers, Child & Co (today at 1 Fleet Street, London as they have been since April 1673), as a guarantee for her overdraft. She had sold the famous 'Ruperta pearl necklace' to meet debts. Her plate (there was 14,443 oz of it) raised £3,791.5s. 9d. The accounts of the executors took four years to be wound up. In the end the duke of St Albans 'pursuant to a decree in Chancery' paid in £3,355.7s. to close the account on 20 July 1692.

The delay, although perhaps not too unusual, probably concerned verification of many small creditors and the dispute that arose over the second codicil. Thomas Herbert, earl of Pembroke, one of Nelly's executors, had gained the consent of the 17-year old duke of St Albans to the first codicil only (apparently unaware of the second one's existence) and presented it to the Prerogative Court. It was proved in the first instance (in common form) in December. It was during the second presentation, to have the codicil proved in solemn form (which would mean the will could never be disputed) that John Warner, armed with a £40 bribe from Rose, produced the second codicil.

The executors disputed the authenticity of the second codicil, and thus a number of witnesses were called: the 30-year-old John Warner, a graduate of New College; Anne Edline, the widowed friend of Nelly's who was lodging with her son in Jermyn Street, and who probably nursed her; the 20-year-old Elizabeth Leverett, Nelly's housemaid for her last nine months; Christiana Murray, a nurse living in Charles Street; and the doctors who last attended her – Joshua Le Febre and Christian Harrell. Their evidence, unsurprisingly, since four of them stood to gain from the proving of the second codicil, was broadly consistent. One witness noted that Nelly wished to include the doctors 'for their extraordinary pains in watching with her'.

Warner, in the writing of his 'fair copy', added some other requests that he claimed to have remembered Nelly making at other times. She asked that Jo[hn] her porter be made a yeoman of the guard; that Harry [Henry Kent], her footman, be made a grenadier; Mrs [Frances?] Jennings was to have £25 for a mourning ring; Warner, himself, was to have her tea table, tea pots and dishes – undoubtedly all silver; and five pounds was to be given to 'Orange Nan', perhaps a seller at the theatre or a local legend, or even a friend from old days. The second codicil, with the exception of Warner's additions, was proved on 19 July 1688.

The archives of Child's Bank show a receipt from Dr Christian Harrell for £109 'paid in full of all remedies and medicins delivred to Mrs Ellin Gwyn deceased.'[7] Nelly's biographers have believed that this was paid three days after her death. However, it seems that they have misread the accounts. At that time it was customary for the new year to start at the end of March rather than January. So, what we would call January 1687 would have been written either as January 1686 or as January 86/87. However, just to confuse the issue; from 1690 the accounts revert to January as the calendar year start. I am confident however, that the good doctor only received his money one year and three days after her demise. The accounts of the executors of 'Madam Eleanor Gwynne' show that other doctors did well out of Nelly's illness.

Doctors Le Febre, Harrold, and Lister picked up £60 each, while Dr Lower collected £50. Mr Chase, an apothecary, had a bill for £26.9s. paid on 8 January 1689. Thus, her final illness cost her £365.9s. slightly less than her funeral. Dying always has been an expensive business.

All the payments laid out in both codicils were made. 'Guy Foster Esq and his Wife' (Nelly's sister) received £200 on 31 December 1687 and a further payment of £240 was 'Paid Mr Guy Foster and Rose his Wife' on 4 January 1689. The accounts credit the payment in January 1688, but this is clearly wrong as the court did not approve the second codicil until July 1688, and which wasn't solemnised until December 1688 (a bill was paid for 'Proveing the Will' of £7.14s.10d. on 24 December). So, the 1689 date must be the accurate one. One can also imagine Rose and Guy demanding their money as quickly as possible from the executors, and Pembroke clearly did not delay in paying out.

Lady Holyman received her weekly pension of 10s., which was paid quarterly (£6.10s. each time) around each of the English quarter days, just as Nelly herself had been. Her secretary, Bridget Long, also received her pension. However, the executors obviously decided that to maintain both pensions would be against theirs and the young duke's interests. So, it appears both pensions were bought out in March 1692: Lady Holyman's annual £26 pension was cashed in for £225.10s. (or eight years and eight months' worth); Bridget Long, apparently not as shrewd as her ladyship, received £150 for hers (settling for seven and a half years' worth).

Sir Stephen Fox once again appears in Nelly's financial affairs. He paid £2,300 into her account a month after her death to help settle debts. He received his money back again on 23 March 1688. Tenison received his £100 for the poor of the parish on 31 December 1688, and along with John Warner received the £50 for the Catholic poor on 25 January 1689. Mr Warner also got his £50 for his ring, and we can only hope that that's what he bought with it. Intriguingly, Warner's name appears once more: he collected the £100 for Nelly's 'kinsman' William Cholmley. It's hard not to suspect Warner of foul play given his role in the second codicil. Perhaps Cholmley never got his money. The request that her son gave £20 each Christmas was seemingly ignored with the exception of a payment on 20 January 1690 of £4.1s.10d. The extra £4.1s.10d. may well have been for the 'decent pulpit-cloth and cushion'.

Nelly's staff appear to have got their annual wages as promised. Henry 'Harry' Kent received £6, as did Nelly's housemaid Elizabeth Leverett.

Jo the loyal porter, set to receive a year's salary and a £10 bequest, only received £8. Her nurses, Mrs Edline and Elizabeth Hawkes both got their ten pounds. Her cook, 'Mr Lambe', who had once been of service to Charles II and was taken in by Nelly after Charles's death, received a whopping £29. Good chefs, clearly, have never come cheap.

Other interesting payments include: £11 to Mr Fuller, a 'Seedsman', perhaps reflecting Nelly's love of her gardens; £90 to Godfrey Kneller, although we do not know for which pictures, and there must have been at least two of them for that money; £31 was also paid to Mr [Peter] Cross, 'picture drawer'; Nelly's wine merchant, the suitably French-sounding Mr Gaultier had his bill of £39 (reassuringly over £3,000 at today's prices) paid – ill or not the poor girl loved a glass; Lord Pembroke hired a lawyer, Richard Grigson, to carry out the day-to-day work of settling debts, and he was rewarded with £20 per year for his pains; and finally, Nelly's haber-dasher, Henry Robins, who provided her with all her elegant lace and ribbons, had his outstanding bill settled 'in full' by payment of £68, Grigson extracting one last, final discount. That would have pleased Nelly. Henry Robins, like so many others, we can be sure was going to miss her.

Many thousands of people have lived worthier lives in British history, having won respect, admiration and appreciation. But very few actually endear us. Sentimental as it may be, we like to respect but we prefer to love. And Nell Gwynne was loved by those who knew her and was loved by those who didn't; indeed, those who didn't know her somehow felt they did. We still feel we know her today. She didn't direct wars, paint, sculpt or write, build bridges or invent stuff. She is not a serious bit of drama. She's a tart with a heart from a rags to riches story: she's a full-blown, smash-hit musical. It's the stuff of romance itself. Some may turn up their noses, but her name is up there in the nation's psyche with Henry VIII, Queen Elizabeth, and Cromwell – flashing in glorious Technicolor. From her own time, with all its abundant characters, it's her name and not, for example, Dryden's that is best known. Perhaps only Pepys and the merry monarch himself come even close. She may only be an edited footnote on the pages of history, but when it comes to affection, she's on the cover: knowing, confident, pretty, smiling, and with a gorgeous glint of mischief in her eyes. She was honest, loving, loyal, modest, charitable and caring. She also had that rare gift to put a smile on your face. Some achievement. Some woman.

— 25 —

Loose Ends

Methinks, I see the wanton hours flee,
And, as they pass, turn back and laugh at me.

Buckingham

Inevitably, when stories are told, some characters pass in and pass out, touching or being touched by the life of your central character. Our story ended with the death of Nelly, but some of those people who have shaped the story lived on. Here's what happened to them.

Louise de Keroualle, duchess of Portsmouth

Although in England through much of James II's reign, Louise would spend most of her life in France. Her famous apartments and many of her treasures perished in 'a dismal' fire at Whitehall which 'burnt violently for several hours'. Luttrell tells us that the fire began in the 'lodgins, late those of the Duchess of Portsmouth, occasioned (as said), by the carelesnesse of a maid in burning of a candle . . . the losse is very considerable in goods, plate, furniture &c, besides the buildings.' Indeed, the loss was considerable, for with the exception of Inigo Jones's Banqueting House, the whole rambling palace of Whitehall was destroyed. Most of Louise's later life was unhappy. Her only real consolation was writing to her son and her three grandchildren: Louise,

Anne and Charles Lennox, the last named coincidentally sharing Charles II's birthday, 29 May. Voltaire visited her in her dotage and he thought her to be still beautiful. Curiously, 'Madam Carwell' died in Paris on the very same day as Nelly, 14 November, only 47 years later in 1734. She was 85 years old.

Barbara, duchess of Cleveland

Barbara, gratifyingly, simply grew old disgracefully. Controversy was never more than a kiss away. She took up with the player Cardell Goodman, even though he had been convicted of conspiracy to poison her two sons. According to some accounts she had a son by him – Goodman Cleveland in March 1686 in her forty-fifth year. Her stooge of a husband, Roger Palmer, died on 21 July 1705. Four months later, aged 64, she married the notorious gambler Major-General Robert 'Beau' Fielding at St James's, Westminster. Soon after, Fielding was imprisoned for threatening and maltreating Barbara, only for it to be discovered that he was already married. The marriage was nullified on 23 May 1707.

In July 1709, she suffered with dropsy which caused her to swell to 'a monstrous bulk' and died on 9 October that year. She was buried in Chiswick parish church in an unmarked tomb.

Hortense Mancini, duchess Mazarin

Hortense carried on much as before. She moved to Chelsea in 1694 and her house 'was the constant resort of people of fashion who were attracted by her *converfaziones*, her basset table and her concerts.'[1] With the faithful Saint-Evrèmond ever attentive, she toyed with her pets and teased the lovesick men and women that her beauty, wit and tale attracted. Her nephew, the Chevalier de Soissons, fell so deeply in love with her that he fought a duel with and killed her lover, the Swedish Baron Banier. As she grew older, her circle of friends diminshed and she took to drinking absinthe and whisky. She died on 2 July 1699, having never paid any parish rates on her Chelsea home.

And yet her death does not end her story. Transported back to France, her decidedly unstable husband received her body, but refused to inter it. Instead he decided to tour his estates in Vincennes, Bourbon, Brittany and Alsace, taking Hortense's open coffin with him. This macabre progress became legendary: peasants would place their rosaries in the now saint-like Hortense's coffin and bring sick children to touch her for cures. Several months later she was laid to rest in the vault of the College des Quatre Nations next to her uncle, the Cardinal Mazarin. But even that wasn't to be final. During the French Revolution of 1789, the vault was stormed, the coffins opened and her remains thrown on to a bonfire.

Catherine of Braganza

Catherine mourned deeply Charles II and was bedridden with grief for two months after his death. She remained mostly at Somerset House, but later found relations with William III difficult. She left England – the country in which it is said she popularised tea drinking – to return to Portugal in 1692 and never came back. She acted as regent for her brother King Pedro and died of colic in 1705.

James II

Although single-minded in his belief that James was, without question, the heir to the throne, Charles knew his brother well and, prophetically, feared the worst: 'I am much afraid that when he comes to wear the crown he will be obliged to travel again. And yet I take great care to leave my kingdoms to him in peace, wishing he may long keep them so. But this hath all my fears, little of my hopes and less of my reason.'

Although popular on his accession, it didn't take long for James to reverse the feeling with his poor decisions, bad management and obstinate character. Within four years he had been replaced by the co-monarchs, his daughter Mary and her husband William of Orange. In 1690, he made his one serious attempt to regain his throne with the aid of French troops, but was defeated at the battle of the Boyne. He lived in exile in St Germain, France, where Louis XIV bestowed a pension on him, until his death in 1701. By this time although physically energetic, he had become senile. His son, James Edward, became known as the Old Pretender, and in turn, his eldest son became the Young Pretender, or more familiarly, Bonnie Prince Charlie.

Charles Beauclerk, duke of St Albans

After her death, Nelly's £1,500 pension, was transferred to her son. Remarkably, he also received a £2,000 a year pension from the dowager

Queen Catherine, which she maintained until her death in 1705. This act surely reflects the esteem in which the young duke was held and the quiet generosity of Catherine. But, perhaps it also reflected that, of all the king's mistresses that the queen had so stoically suffered and tolerated, she knew that at least Nelly loved Charles for who he was – faults and all – just as she herself had done. Her gift must have been as much in appreciation of Nelly as in her son.

St Albans moved into Pall Mall, but was forced to sell it to his creditors in 1694. He married the celebrated beauty Diana de Vere in the same year. Unfortunately, she didn't turn out to be quite the heiress Charles II had anticipated when he matched the pair some years before. She was the second daughter and eventual sole heir of Aubrey de Vere, twentieth and last earl of Oxford, and bore her husband 12 children. Clearly, Master Charles had inherited his father's virility.

He seemingly also inherited from his father his looks, his love of sport and his sexual magnetism. Macky described Charles St Albans as being 'of a Black Complexion, not so tall as the Duke of Northumberland, yet very like King Charles . . . a Gentleman in every Way, de bon naturel, well bred . . . is well-affected to the Constitution of his Country.' He, like his father and mother, enjoyed horse racing. Indeed, when Queen Anne initiated a new racecourse near Windsor – Ascot Common – the duke's horse 'Doctor' won the very first race held there. That old French stager, Saint Evrèmond, described the 27-year-old Duke as 'a young cavalier who has the art of pleasing all our ladies.'[2] Charles Beauclerk, duke of St Albans, died on or about 10 May 1726 in Bath and was buried in Westminster Abbey. Diana, who became first lady of the bedchamber, and lady of the stole to Caroline, princess of Wales (afterwards queen consort), died on 15 January 1742 and was buried in St George's Chapel, Windsor.[3]

St Albans travelled to France at the end of 1697 as an envoy for William III who thought highly of him. However, the duke's companion, Lord Portland, wrote back home to the king that St Albans 'has left debts unpaid in the shops, and borrowed £150 from Lord Paston to avoid having his baggage seized. He promised to pay when he got home, and has forgotten both.'[4] This story tends to support a character description that he 'doth not love business', and that he was also constantly in hock to his bankers. Debt ridden, no head for business, popular and pretty? He was then, after all, his mother's son.

Notes

Chapter One

1 C H Josten, ed. *Elias Ashmole (1617–92)*, The Clarendon Press, 1966.
2 Arthur Dasent, *Nell Gwynne*, Macmillan, London 1924, p.29.
3 Roy Gillett, April 2000.
4 'The Manager's Note-book, no XI, in *The New Monthly Magazine and Humorist*, Theodore Hook, ed., Part the Third, London, 1838, p. 87.
5 *Highfill's Biographical of Actors, Actresses, Musicians, Dancers, Managers & Other Stage Personnel in London 1660–1800*, London, Complete, p. 455.
6 Antonia Fraser, *King Charles II*, Mandarin, London 1996, p. 401; Ronald Hutton, *Charles II*, Oxford University Press, 1991, p. 400.
7 Fraser, p. 62.
8 Donald Adamson and Peter Beauclerk-Dewar, *The House of Nell Gwyn, 1670-1974*, William Kimber, London, 1974, p. 7.
9 Dasent, p. 23.
10 John Harold Wilson, *Nell Gwyn, Royal Mistress*, Pellegrini & Cuhady, New York, 1952, p. 7.
11 *Notes & Queries*, 4th series, vol. 1, 28 February 1885, p. 196.
12 Add MSS 32878 f282; 32896 f166l 32888 f285; 32933 f154; 32728 f79
13 *The Athenaeum*, 1 September 1883, quoted in *Notes & Queries*, 28 February 1885, p. 169.
14 Astrology software uses the Gregorian calendar date, although the contemporary Julian calendar date would be 2 February.
15 John Price, *An Historical Account of the City of Hereford*, Walker, 1796, p. 158.
16 John Duncumb, *Collections towards the History and Antiquities of the County of Hereford*, vol. 1, 1804, p. 334.
17 John Hutchinson, *Herefordshire Biographies*, Hereford, 1890, p. 48.

18 N Wharton, 'Letter XI' in *'Letters from a Subaltern in the Earl of Essex's Army ...'*, Archaeologia XXXV, 1853, pp. 331–3.

19 W Shaw, *The Organists and Organs of Hereford Cathedral*, 1988, pp. 28–9; W E H Clarke, 'Hereford Cathedral organ' in *'Transactions of the Woolhope Naturalists' Field Club'*, Hereford, 1921, pp. 41–8.

20 Horace Walpole, Letter to George Montagu, 22 October 1766.

21 Samuel Pepys, Diary, 29 July 1667.

Chapter Two

1 *Notes & Queries*, 2 January 1858, p. 9.

2 *Notes & Queries*, 3 November 1900, p. 350.

Chapter Three

1 Quoted in Liza Picard, *Restoration London*, Weidenfeld & Nicolson, London, 1997, p. 253.

2 Lord Chancellor's records (LC 5/188 f18).

3 Pepys, *Diary*, 2 November 1667.

4 John McPhee, *Oranges*, Heinemann, London, 1967.

Chapter Four

1 *A Perfect Diurnall of the Passages of Parliament*, number 12.

2 Allardyce Nicoll, *British Drama: an Historical Survey from the Beginnings to the Present*, George G. Harrap, London, 1925, pp. 215–18.

3 The Drury Lane patent, 1660.

4 *Pepys*, 13 February 1668.

5 'Tireing rooms' were changing rooms for actors.

6 The poet laureate was the poet of the royal household or court poet — so-called because distinguished poets in ancient Greece and Rome were awarded laurel wreaths in recognition of their status.

7 *Notes & Queries*, 20 May 1880.

8 H E Popham, *Quaint Survivals of Old London Customs*, Cecil Palmer, 1928.

9 John Downes, ed. Montague Summers, *Roscius Anglicanus*, Fortune Press, London 1928.

10 Pepys, 15 September 1668.

11 'Moone' was Major Mohun (it was pronounced 'Moon'), a celebrated actor, who had fought with the Royalists during the Civil War. He received a commission after he had been wounded and was billed as 'Major' on cast lists. He died in October 1684 in Brownlow Street (now Betterton Street), Drury Lane, and was buried in St Giles-in-the-Fields, London.

12 Censers – also known as thuribles, were small containers used mostly for burning incense, and cressets were iron containers.

13 *The Diary of John Evelyn, 18 October 1666*, Guy la Bedoyere, Headstart

History, Bangor, 1994.

14 Colley Cibber (1671–1757) was an actor, playwright and manager of Theatre Royal Drury Lane. He was created Poet Laureate in 1730. However, he is best known for his autobiography *Apology for the Life of Mr Colley Cibber, Comedian*, published in 1740.

15 Actresses were for the most part styled 'Mrs'. In Restoration times this signified 'mistress' and did not relate to their marital status. If you were labelled 'Miss' this was to signify that you were a kept mistress or (less commonly) a whore. Strangely, for us at least, when Nell became an official mistress of the king, she was at times billed 'Madam'.

16 *Roscius Anglicamus*, Downes, p. 2.

17 Quoted in Montague Summers, *The Playhouse of Pepys*, Humanities Press, New York, 1964, p. 84.

18 *Pepys*, 15 January, 1669.

Chapter Five

1 Downes, p. 2.

2 Downes, p. 16, and quoted in Cecil Chesterton, *The Story of Nell Gwyn*, Foulis, 1911, p. 22.

3 Thomas Rymer, *Tragedies of the Last Age Considered and Explained*, Augustus M Kelley, 1970.

4 Downes, p. 16.

5 Pepys, 7 May 1668.

6 *The Life of the Late Famous Comedian*, Jo Haines, 1701.

7 Downes, p. 39.

8 John Aubrey, *Brief Lives*, ed. Richard Barber, Boydell Press, 1982, p. 189.

9 Gerard Langbaine, *An Account of the English Dramatic Poets*, 1691.

10 'The Lady of Pleasure', 1681.

11 'Iantha' is how Pepys refers to Mary Saunderson, a fine actress who for him defined the role of Ianthe in *The Siege of Rhodes* – hence the use of the character name to refer to her – a common trait for playgoers.

12 The younger Marshall was Rebecca 'Beck' Marshall who, along with her elder sister Ann (or Nan), were actresses attached to the King's House.

13 John Dryden, dedication in *The Rival Ladies*, Herringman, London, 1693.

14 Nicoll, p. 221.

15 Richard Garnett, *The Age of Dryden*, London, 1907, p. 93.

16 Pepys, 23 February 1663.

17 Pepys, 4 August 1664.

18 Pepys, 15 January 1669.

Chapter Six

1 Clifford Bax, *Pretty Witty Nell*, Chapman & Hall, London 1932, p. 55.

2 Evelyn, 28 August 1665.

3 A halbert, or halberd, was a combination of spear and battle-axe, consisting of a sharp-edged blade ending in a point, and a spear head, mounted on a handle five to seven feet long.

4 Quoted in appendix to Daniel Defoe, *A Journal of the Plague Year*, Everyman, 1963, p. 284.

5 Quoted in Sutherland Ross, *The Fire and Plague of London*, Faber & Faber, London 1965, p. 14.

6 Pepys, 20 Sept 1665.

7 Defoe, p. 287.

8 Evelyn, 29 January 1666.

9 Pepys, 28 January 1666.

Chapter Seven

1 'Then have ye one other lane called Rother Lane or Red Rose Lane, of such a sign there, now commonly called Pudding Lane because the butchers of Eastcheap have their scalding house for hogs there, and their puddings, with other filth of beasts, are voided down that way to their dung boats on the Thames.' From Stow's *Survey of London*, first published in 1598.

2 Evelyn, 2 September 1666.

3 Quoted by Clifford Bax, *Pretty Witty Nell*, Chapman & Hall, London, 1932, p. 75.

4 Pepys, 6 September 1666.

5 Lady Burghclere, *George Villiers. Second Duke of Buckingham 1628–87*, John Murray, London, 1903, p. 154.

Chapter Eight

1 Quoted in Judith Milhous and Robert D Hume, eds. *A Register of English Theatrical Documents 1660–1737*, Vol 1, Southern Illinois University Press, 1991.

2 Pepys, 12 February 1669.

3 Judith Milhous and Robert D Hume, eds.

4 ibid.

5 Pepys, 2 February 1669.

6 Anthony à Wood, *Diary*.

7 The women's shift was the large changing room for the actresses who didn't have their own changing room.

8 Bryan Bevan, *Nell Gwyn*, Robert Hale, London, 1969, p. 50.

9 *The New Monthly Magazine*, Part the Third, 1838, pp. 87–95.

10 David Bond, *Nell Gwyn's Birthdate in Theatre Notebook 40*, 1986 pp. 3–9.

11 Thomas Betterton, *History of the English Stage from the Restauration to the Present Time*, Curll, London, 1741.

12 Downes, p. 24.

13 Bax, p. 129.

14 Pepys, 14 January 1668.

15 '*The Lady of Pleasure, or The life of Nelly truly shown from Hopgard'n Cellar to the Throne till into th' grave she tumbled down*', c. 1687.

Chapter Nine

1 Quoted in Bevan, p. 132.

2 Evelyn, 18 October 1666.

3 Pepys, 24 January 1669.

4 Philip Henry, *Diaries and Letters of Philip Henry*, ed. M H Lee, 1882.

5 A mark was valued at two-thirds of a sterling pound, that is 160 pennies or 13s. 4d. Thus Sedley's fine for drunkenness would amount to about an appropriately staggering £101,500 today.

6 Pepys, 7 April 1668. Some editions wrongly attribute this to be Jacob Hall, the rope dancer, with whom she did have an affair also. However, Hall was never part of the King's Company.

7 Quoted in Summers, *The Playhouse of Pepys*, p. 170.

Chapter Ten

1 Pepys, 29 July 1667.

2 Barbara Castlemaine was created Duchess of Cleveland in August 1670.

3 Rawlinson MS, held at the Bodleian Library, Oxford University. D790.

4 Mrs Knight – the singer Anna Maria Knight, a minor mistress to Charles II; Old Rowley – a nickname for Charles II, after his horse; 'tarse' and 'pintle' are words for penis.

5 Quoted in John Harold Wilson, *Mr Goodman The Player*, University of Pittsburg Press, 1964, p. 35.

6 Downes, p. 39.

7 Anthony Hamilton, *Memoirs of Count Grammont*, The Bodley Head, London, 1928, p. 246.

8 Colbert to Lionne, 17 November 1669 and 26 January 1670, quoted in Henry Forneron, *Louise de Keroualle*, London, 1897, p. 51.

9 John Harold Wilson, *Nell Gwyn, Royal Mistress*, Pellegrini & Cuhady, New York, 1952, p. 91.

10 Quoted in *The London Encyclopaedia*, Ben Weinreb and Christopher Hibbert, eds, Macmillan, 1985, p. 459.

11 Pepys, 10 February 1664.

12 Quoted by Summers in Downes, p. 130.

13 James took the name of his guardian, Lord Crofts.

14 Quoted in Bax, p. 134.

Chapter Eleven

1 Wood's *Life and Times*, p. 192.
2 Quoted in Lucy Norton, *The Sun King and his Loves*, The Folio Society, London 1982, p. 24.
3 Pepys, 22 November 1660.
4 Vincent Cronin, *Louis XIV*, Collins, London, 1969, p. 119.
5 F R Harris, *The Life of Edward Montagu, First Earl of Sandwich*, Murray, London, 1912, p. 207.
6 Mignet, *Negociations*, iii, p. 51.
7 *Calendar of Treasury Books*, vol. 3, Introduction pp. lxiv–lxvi.
8 Downes, p. 29.
9 Colbert de Croissy to Louis XIV, 16 June 1670.
10 Boussuet, *Oraison Funebre de Madame*, quoted in Forneron, p. 60.

Chapter Twelve

1 Quoted in Maurice Ashley, *Rupert of the Rhine*, Purnell, London, 1976, p. 1.
2 Historical Manuscripts Commission, Rutland MSS, fourteenth report, appendix IX.
3 Arthur Bryant, *Samuel Pepys, The Years of Peril*, The Reprint Society, 1952, London, cp p. 325 notes 5–7, p. 111.
4 ibid. p. 288.
5 Evelyn, 10 February 1671.

Chapter Thirteen

1 Anthony Aston, *Brief Supplement to Colley Cibber Esq., his Lives of the late Famous Actors and Actresses*, c. 1747.
2 OUP, *The Oxford Companion to the Theatre*, ed. Phyllis Hartnoll,1951, p. 77.
3 J M Scott, *The Book of Pall Mall*, London, 1965, p. 27.

Chapter Fourteen

1 Pepys, 20 October 1662.
2 Evelyn, 4 November 1670.
3 Rochester, *A Satyr on Charles II*, 1674.
4 HM Margoliouth, *Marvell's Poems and Letters*, Oxford University Press, 1952, p. 315.
5 Cham is an obsolete term for 'Khan' – a lord or prince.
6 'A Panegyric', 1681.
7 *'Dialogue between the Duchess of Portsmouth and Madam Gwin at Parting'*, anonymous, quoted in Lewis Melville, *Nell Gwyn – The Story of Her Life*, London, p. 283.

8 *Notes & Queries*, 15 March 1890.
9 Charles Lord Buckhurst, '*A Faithful Catalogue of Our Most Eminent Ninnies.*'
10 Julia Cartwright, *Sacharissa*, London, 1901.

Chapter Fifteen

1 *The Works of Andrew Marvell*, Ware, Wordsworth Poetry Library, p. 189.
2 Frances Stweart was yet another beauty – hence the soubriquet 'La Belle' – to bedazzle Charles. Despite writing her love poetry and having her model as Britannia for the new coinage, she remained unconquered.
3 *Historical Manuscripts Commission*, seventh report.
4 Bryan Bevan, *Charles the Second's French Mistress*, Robert Hale, London 1972, p. 43.
5 Evelyn, 10 October 1671.
6 Colbert to Pomponne, 30 January 1673.
7 WD Christie, ed, *Letters to Sir Joseph Williamson*, Camden Society, 1874, vol 1, p. 184.
8 Quoted in Lewis Melville, p. 306.

Chapter Sixteen

1 *Calendar of State Papers – Venetian*, 1673–5.
2 Quoted in Forneron, p. 108.
3 Ibid.
4 Francis Fane, *Commonplace Book*,
5 Historical Manuscripts Commission, second report, 4 March 1675.
6 Julia Cartwright, p. 222.
7 Arthur Capel, Earl of Essex, *Letters written in the year 1675*, Dublin 1773, p. 334, quoted in Moody, Martin and Byrne, eds. *A New History of Ireland*, vol. 3, p. 442.
8 Antonia Fraser, *King Charles II*, London, 1993 edition, p. 373.
9 Stowe MS 211, f330.
10 Lorna Weatherill, *Consumer Behaviour and Material Culture in Britain 1660–1760*, Routledge, London, 1958.
11 *Calendar of Treasury Books*, 1676–1679, HMSO.
12 *Calendar of Treasury Books*, 1672–1675, HMSO.
13 A chaldron is a unit measurement for coal equalling 16 bushels. An imperial bushel used in Britain contains 2218.19 cubic inches.
14 H M Margoliouth, ed. *Marvell's Poems and Letters*, second edition, Oxford University Press, London, 1952.
15 Roy McGregor-Hastie, *Nell Gwynne*, London, 1987, p. 113.
16 Evelyn, 4 February 1668.

17 Evelyn, 24 January 1682.
18 Evelyn, 10 September 1675.
19 Evelyn, 4 October, 1683.
20 John Lacy (possibly), *A Satyr*, 1677.
21 *Memorials of Nell Gwynne*, Brotherton Library, Leeds University.
22 Liza Picard, *Restoration London*, Weidenfeld & Nicolson, London, 1997, p. 68.
23 *Memorials of Nell Gwynne*, Brotherton Library.
24 Household bills held at Army & Navy Club.
25 *Calendar of Treasury Books*, 1676–1679.
26 Household bills held at Army & Navy Club.
27 WD Christie, ed. p. 109.
28 *Notes & Queries*, 4 January 1873, p. 24.
29 Thornbury, *Old and New London*, quoted in Melville, p. 216.
30 *Notes & Queries*, 17 September 1871, p. 236.
31 *Notes & Queries*, 4 April 1885, p. 275.
32 *Notes & Queries*, 20 January 1883, p. 54; *Notes & Queries*, 22 May 1869, p. 479.
33 A L Rowse, *Windsor Castle*, Book Club Associates, London, 1974, p. 113.
34 Quoted in Tighe and Davis, *Annals of Windsor*, p. 442.
35 J H Wilson, *Nell Gwyn, Royal Mistress*, New York, 1952, p. 161.
36 Gladys Scott Thomson, *Life in a Noble Household 1641–1700*, Knopf, London, 1937, p. 118.
37 Historical Manuscripts Commission, second report.
38 Kept at the Army & Navy Club, London; Brotherton Library, Leeds University and Ohio State Library.
39 Quoted in Bevan, *Nell Gwyn*, p. 93.
40 Colley Cibber.

Chapter Seventeen

1 J H Wilson, ed. *The Rochester-Saville Letters*, 1671–1680, p. 56.
2 Quoted in Forneron, p. 66.
3 Narcissus Luttrell, *A Brief Historical Relation of State Affairs from September 1678 to April 1714*.
4 Henry Sidney, *Diary of the Times of Charles the Second*, 8 January 1680, London, 1843.
5 C P Hill, *Who's Who in Stuart Britain*, St James Press, London, 1988, p. 225.
6 Hester W Chapman, *Great Villiers*, Secker & Warburg, London, 1949, p. 85.
7 Add. MSS 27872, f18, quoted in Bryan Bevan, *Nell Gwyn*, London, 1967, p. 117–18.

8 Add MSS 27872, f20, quoted in Bryan Bevan, *Nell Gwyn*, London, 1967, p. 118.
9 H M Margoliouth, ed. *Marvell's Poems and Letters.*
10 J H Wilson, ed. *Rochester-Savile Poems and Letters 1671–1680.*
11 Ronald Hutton, p. 344.
12 *Calendar of Treasury Books, 1676–1679.*
13 Graham Greene, *Lord Rochester's Monkey*, The Bodley Head, London, 1974, p. 114.
14 *Calendar of Treasury Books, 1676–1679.*
15 Brice Harris, *Charles Sackville*, New York, 1972, p. 83.
16 Evelyn, 18 August 1649.
17 In George Bernard Shaw's play *In Good King Charles's Golden Days*, although not one of his finer moments, it does include a capital exchange between Charles and James, the latter bemoaning of Monmouth that 'there is not a plot in the kingdom to murder either of us that he is not at the bottom of'. To which Charles replies, 'He is not deep enough to be at the bottom of anything.' Constable, London, 1939, p. 53.
18 Henry Sidney.
19 Sir John Reresby, *Memoirs and Travels of*, Kegan Paul Trench Trubner, London, 1904.

Chapter Eighteen

1 Quoted in Clifford Bax, p. 167.
2 Evelyn, 6 September 1676.
3 Quoted in Bryan Bevan, *Charles the Second's French Mistress*, p. 87.
4 Quoted in Forneron, p. 162.
5 Quoted in Forneron, p. 168.
6 Quoted in Bryan Bevan, *Charles the Second's French Mistress*, pp. 91–2.
7 Quoted in Forneron, p. 177–8.
8 Quoted in Bryan Bevan, *Charles the Second's French Mistress*, p. 113.
9 *Historical Manuscripts Commission*, seventh report.

Chapter Nineteen

1 Anthony Hamilton, *The Memoirs of the Count Grammont*, The Bodley Head, London, 1928, pp. 122–3.
2 *An Essay of Scandal*, 1681.
3 Evelyn, 22 July 1670.
4 Rawlinson MS D861.
5 Evelyn, 9 October 1671.
6 Evelyn, 19 October 1671.

7 Pepys, 4 January 1664.
8 Henry Sidney.
9 Baronne d'Aulnoy, *Memoirs of the Court of England*, G D Gilbert, ed. London, undated, p. 314–15.
10 Ibid., p. 289.
11 Quoted in *Games and Gamesters of the Restoration*,
12 Theophilius Lucas, *Lives of Gamesters*, London, 1714
13 Evelyn, 8 January 1668.
14 Evelyn, 7 and 19 July 1664.
15 Theophilius Lucas.
16 Ibid.
17 David Ogg, *England in the Reign of Charles II*, vol 1, OUP, 1963, p. 331.
18 Historical Manuscripts Commission, second report, appendix, p. 22.
19 Quoted in Judith Milhous and Robert D Hume, eds.
20 William Van Lennep, *Nell Gwyn's Playgoing at the King's Expense*, Harvard Library Bulletin, vol 4, no. 3, 1950, pp. 405–8.
21 Narcissus Luttrell, *A Brief Historical Relation of State Affairs from September 1678 to 1714*, Oxford University Press, 1875.
22 R B Beckett, *Lely*, Routledge, London, 1951.
23 Quoted in C H Collins Baker, *Lely and the Stuart Portrait Painters*, Phillip Lee Warner, London, 1912, vol 1, p. 172.
24 Pepys, 21 August 1668.

Chapter Twenty

1 *Historical Manuscripts Commission*, Seventh report.
2 *Memorials of Nell Gwynne*, Brotherton Library.
3 *Historical Manuscripts Commission*, fourteenth report, appendix IX, Laing MSS.
4 *Calendar of Treasury Books*, vol. VII, 1681; 13 January 1681.
5 Arthur Bryant, *Samuel Pepys – The Years of Peril*, The Reprint Society, London, 1952, p. 111.
6 Ibid., p. 288.
7 Arthur Bryant, *Samuel Pepys – The Saviour of the Navy*, The Reprint Society, London 1953, p. 140.
8 LC5/16, p. 97, quoted in the Register of Theatrical Documents.
9 Pepys, 26 December 1662.
10 *Harley MS* 7319, f135.
11 R Ham, *Otway and Lee*, 1931.
12 Pepys, 19 February 1669.
13 Captain C G T Dean, *The Royal Hospital Chelsea*, Hutchinson,

London, 1950, pp. 20–1.

14 Anonymous, *The Memoirs of the Life of Sir Stephen Fox*, kt, J Roberts, London, 1727.

15 *Historical Manuscripts Commission*, seventh report.

16 Edward Walford, *Old and New London*, vol 5, p. 70.

17 H M Imbert-Terry, *A Misjudged Monarch*, Heinemann, London, 1917, p. 343.

Chapter Twenty-one

1 Quoted in Bryan Bevan, *Charles the Second's French Mistress*, p. 125.

2 Henry Sidney.

3 Ibid.

4 Quoted in Bryan Bevan, *Charles the Second's French Mistress*, p. 118.

5 Ibid., pp. 141–2.

6 Narcissus Luttrell.

7 Sir John Reresby, 22 January 1682.

8 Calendar of State Papers (Domestic), 24 April 1683.

9 Evelyn, 24 January 1682.

10 Sir John Reresby, 11 January 1682.

11 Calendar of State Papers (Domestic), 1683, p. 76.

12 Sir John Reresby, October 1683.

13 William Durrant-Cooper, ed., *The Savile Correspondence*, Camden Society.

14 Ibid.

15 Edward Maunde Thompson, *Letters of Humphrey Prideaux*, ed., p. 101.

16 William Durrant-Cooper, ed.

17 Henry Sidney.

18 Lady Rachel Russell, *Letters*, quoted in Bryan Bevan, *Charles the Second's French Mistress*, London, 1972, p. 149.

19 E H Plumptre, *A Life of Thomas Ken*, John Murray, London, 1890, p. 158.

20 Ibid., p. 178.

21 Historical Manuscripts Commission, fourteenth report, appendix IX, Bath MSS

22 A I Dasent, *Private Life of Charles II*, quoted in Bryan Bevan, *Nell Gwyn*, p. 139.

23 *Historical Manuscripts Commission*, seventh report.

24 Quoted in Lewis Melville, p. 242.

25 Evelyn, 23 October 1684.

26 *Calendar of Treasury Books*, vol. VIII, 1681–85, 27 November 1682.

27 *Historical Manuscripts Commission*, fourteenth report, appendix IX,

Ormond papers
28 Sir Gerald Hurst, *A Short History of Lincoln's Inn*, Constable, London, 1946.
29 F A Inderwick, ed., *A Calendar of the Inner Temple Records*, London, 1901, p. lxi and 184.

Chapter Twenty-two

1 Evelyn, 25 January 1685
2 Narcissus Luttrell.
3 Raymond Crawfurd, *The Last Days of Charles II*, Oxford, 1909, p. 70.
4 Quoted in Antonia Fraser, *King Charles II*, Madarin, London, 1996, p. 447.
5 Quoted in Forneron, p. 284.
6 Raymond Crawfurd, p. 37.
7 Evelyn, 6 February 1685.
8 Bishop Burnet, *History of My Own Time*, London, ed. Thomas Stockhouse, Everyman, pp. 218–19.
9 Raymond Crawfurd, p. 50.
10 *Ormond MSS*, quoted in Lewis Melville, p. 304.

Chapter Twenty-three

1 *An Account of what passed at the execution of the late Duke of Monmouth*, 1685.
2 Rawlinson MSS D872.
3 *Calendar of Treasury Books*, XII. p. 361–8.
5 *The Ellis Correspondence*, George Ellis, ed., London, 1829, vol 1, p. 202.
6 Quoted in Lewis Melville, p. 308.
7 *The Hatton Correspondence*, The Camden Society, vol 2, pp. 66.
8 Ibid.
9 Quoted in Bryan Bevan, *Nell Gwyn*, London, 1969, pp. 164–5.
10 Evelyn, 19 January 1686.
11 *The Hatton Correspondence*, pp. 66.
12 Quoted in Donald Adamson and Peter Beauclerk-Dewar, *The House of Nell Gwyn, 1670–1974*, William Kimber, London, 1974, p. 13.
13 Jane Hoare, 'The Death of Nell Gwynne', in *History Today*, June, 1970, p. 103.

Chapter Twenty-four

1 Quoted in Notes & Queries, 10 September 1932, p. 195.
2 Lewis Melville, p. 309.
3 John Richardson, *Covent Garden*, New Barnet, 1979, p. 103.

4 E F Carpenter, *Thomas Tenison*, SPCK, London, 1948.
5 Dr Thomas Tenison, *A True Account of a Conference*, London, 1687, p. 100.
6 Narcissus Luttrell, vol 1, p. 420.
7 Quoted in Bryan Bevan, *Nell Gwyn*, London, 1969, pp. 166–7.

Chapter Twenty-five

1 Daniel Lysons, *The Environs of London*, 1810.
2 Quoted in Donald Adamson and Peter Beauclerk-Dewar's, *The House of Nell Gwyn – The Fortunes of the Beauclerk Family, 1670–1974*, p. 19.
3 For a history of Nelly's descendants, read Donald Adamson and Peter Beauclerk-Dewar's *The House of Nell Gwyn – 1670–1974*.
4 Calendar of State Papers (Domestic) 1698, pp. 138, 149.

Bibliography

Adamson, Donald &   *The House of Nell Gwyn, The Fortunes of the*
Beauclerk-Dewar, Peter   *Beauclerk Family 1670–1974*, (William Kimber, London, 1974)

Airy, Osmund   *Charles II* (Longman, London, 1904)

Allentuch, Harriet Ray   *Madam de Sevigne: A Portrait in Letters* (Johns Hopkins, Baltimore, 1963)

Anonymous   *Memoirs of the Life of Sir Stephen Fox, kt* (J Roberts, London, 1727)

Anonymous   *The Life, Amours and Exploits of Nell Gwyn, the Fortunate Orange Girl* (Fairburn, London, 1820)

Arber, Edward (ed)   *The Rehearsal by George Villiers* (Alex Murray, 1868)

Ashley, Maurice   *Charles II* (Panther, St Albans, 1973)

Ashley, Maurice   *Life in Stuart England,* (Batsford, London, 1964)

Ashley, Maurice   *Rupert of the Rhine,* (Purnell, Abingdon, 1976)

Ashley, Maurice   *The England of Charles II* (Longman, London, 1934)

Barber, Richard (ed)   *John Aubrey: Brief Lives* (Boydell, Woodbridge, 1982)

Bax, Clifford   *Pretty, Witty Nell* (Chapman & Hall, London, 1932)

Beaurline, L A &   *John Dryden, Four Tragedies* (University of
Bowers, Fredson   Chicago, 1967)

Beckett, R B   *Lely* (Routledge, London, 1951)

Bedford, John   *London's Burning* (Abelard-Schumann, London, 1966)

Betterton, Thomas	*History of the English Stage from the Restoration to the Present Times* (Curll, London, 1741)
Bevan, Bryan	*Charles the Second's French Mistress* (Robert Hale, London, 1972)
Bevan, Bryan	*Nell Gwyn* (Robert Hale, London, 1969)
Braybrooke, Lord	*Pepys Memoir & Diary* (Frederick Warne, London, c. 1 870)
Brett-James, N G	*Growth of Stuart London* (George Allen & Unwin, London, 1935)
Browne, Eric Gore	*History of the House of Glyn, Mills & Co* (Glyn, Mills & Co, London, 1933)
Bryant, Arthur	*Postman's Horn* (Longmans, London, 1936)
Bryant, Arthur	*Samuel Pepys - Saviour of the Navy* (Collins, London, 1953)
Bryant, Arthur	*Samuel Pepys - The Man in the Making* (Collins, London, 1949)
Bryant, Arthur	*Samuel Pepys - Years of Peril* (Collins, London, 1948)
Bryant, Arthur	*The England of Charles II* (Longman, London, 1934)
Calendar of State Papers (Domestic)	
Calendar of State Papers (Venetian)	
Calendar of Treasury Books, 1672–89	
Carpenter, E F	*Thomas Tenison* (SPCK, London 1948)
Carswell, John	*The Porcupine - The Life of Algemon Sydney* (John Murray, London, 1989)
Cartwright, Julia	*Madame* (E P Dutton, New York, 1901)
Cartwright, Julia	*Sacharissa, Some Account of Dorothy Sidney, Countess of Sunderland, Her Family and Friends 1617-1684* (Seeley & Co, London, 1901)
Chapman, Hester W	*Great Villiers - A Study of George Villiers Second Duke of Buckingham,* (Secker & Warburg, London, 1949)
Chapman, Hester W	*Privileged Persons, Four 17C Studies* (Jonathan Cape, London, 1966)
Chapman, Hester W	*The Tragedy of Charles ll* (Jonathan Cape, London, 1964)
Chesterton, Cecil	*The Story of Nell Gwyn* (Foulis, London,1911)
Christie, W D (ed)	*Letters to Sir Joseph Williamson* (Camden Society, London,1874)
Christie, W D (ed)	*Letters to Sir Joseph Williamson* (1874)
Cibber, Colley	*An Apology for the Life of Mr Colley Cibber, Comedian* (John Watts, London, 1740)

Clark, A (ed)   *The Life and Times of Anthony Wood, antiquary, at Oxford, 1632-95,* (Oxford Historical Society, Oxford, 1891-1900)

Clark, George   *The Later Stuarts 1660-1714* (Oxford University Press, 1964)

Collins Baker, C H   *Lely and the Stuart Portrait Painters* (Phillip Lee Warner, London, 1912)

Cooper, William D (ed) *Savile Correspondence* (Camden Society, London, 1858)

Coote, Stephen   *Royal Survivor A Life of Charles II* (Hodder & Stoughton, London, 1999)

Crawfurd, Raymond   *Last Days of Charles ll* (Oxford University Press, 1909)

Cronin, Vincent   *Louis XlV* (Collins, London, 1964)

Cunningham, Peter   *Story of Nell Gwyn* (Bradbury & Evans, London 1852)

Cunningham, Peter   *Story of Nell Gwyn,* Goodwin, G (ed), (John Grant, Edinburgh, 1908)

Cunningham, Peter   *Story of Nell Gwyn,* Wheatley, H B (ed) (Hutchinson, London, 1892)

Dasent, Arthur   *Nell Gwynne* (Macmillan, London, 1924)

Dasent, Arthur Irwin *The Private Life of Charles II* (Cassell, London, 1927)

De Beer, E S, (ed)   *The Diary of John Evelyn* (Oxford University Press, 1959)

De La Bodoyere, Guy, (ed) *The Diary of John Evelyn,* (Headstart History, Bangor, 1994)

Dean, C G T   *The Royal Hospital Chelsea* (Hutchinson, London, 1950)

Defoe, Daniel   *A Journal of the Plague Year* (Everyman, London, 1908)

Delpech, Jeanine   *The Life & Times of the Duchess of Portsmouth* (trans. Ann Lindsay, 1953)

Dent, Alan   *My Covent Garden* (Dent, London, 1973)

Dictionary of National Biography

Doran, John   *Their Majesties Servants* (Lowe, R (ed), 1887)

Drinkwater, John   *Mr Charles, King of England* (Hodder & Stoughton, London, 1926)

Dryden, John   *The Rival Ladies* (Herringman, London, 1693)

Duncumb, John   *Collections Towards a History and Antiquities of the County of Hereford* (Hereford, 1804)

Ellis, George (ed)   *The Ellis Correspondence* (Henry Colburn, London, 1829)

Falkus, Christopher — *Life and Times of Charles II* (Weidenfeld & Nicolson, London, 1972)

Fane, Francis — *Commonplace Book* (Shakespeare Library)

Fielding, Henry — *Tom Jones* (Everyman, London, 1998)

Forneron, Henri — *Louise de Keroualle* (Swan Sonnenschein, London, 1887)

Fraser, Antonia — *King Charles II* (Mandarin, London, 1996)

Garnet, Richard — *The Age of Dryden* (Bell, London, 1907)

Genest, John — *Account of the English Stage 1660–1830* (1832)

Gilbert, G D, (ed) — *Memoirs of the Court of England in 1675 by Marie Catherine Baronne D'Aulnoy,* (The Bodley Head, London, 1913)

Gray, Robert — *The King's Wife* (Secker & Warburg, London, 1990)

Greene, Graham — *Lord Rochester's Monkey* (The Bodley Head, London, 1974)

Hadley, William (ed) — *Selected Letters of Horace Walpole* (Dent, London, 1963)

Ham, Roswell Gray — *Otway and Lee: a Biography from a Baroque Age* (Greenwood Press, New York, 1969)

Hamilton, Anthony — *Memoirs of the Count de Grammont* (Swan Sonnenschein, London, undated)

Harbage, Alfred (Revised by S Schoenberg) — *Annals of English Drama 975 - 1700* (Methuen, London, 1964)

Harris, Brice — *Charles Sackville* (Lemma, New York, 1972)

Harris, F R — *The Life of Edward Montagu, First Earl of Sandwich* (Murray, London, 1912)

Hartmann, Cyril Hughes — *Charles II and Madame* (Heinemann, London, 1934)

Hartmann, Cyril Hughes — *The King My Brother* (Heinemann, London, 1954)

Hartmann, Cyril Hughes — *The Vagabond Duchess,* (Routledge, London, 1926)

Hartmann, Cyril Hughes (ed) — *Games and Gamesters of the Restoration by Charles Cotton* (Kennikat, Port Washington, 1971)

Hartnoll, Phyllis — *A Concise History of the Theatre* (Thames & Hudson, London, 1974)

Hartnoll, Phyllis, (ed) — *The Oxford Companion to the Theatre* (Oxford University Press, 1951)

Heckethorn, C W — *Lincoln's Inn Fields and the Localities Adjacent: their Historical and Topographical Associations* (Stock, London, 1896)

Hibbert, Christopher	*London* - The Biography of a City (Penguin, London, 1969)
Hibbert, Christopher	*The Court of Windsor* (Longman, London, 1964)
Hibbert, Christopher	*The English, A Social History* (Paladin, London, 1988)
Highfill, P *et al.* (eds)	*Biographical Dictionary of Actors, Actresses, Musicians, Dancers, Managers and Other Stage Personnel in London 1660-1800* (Southern Illinois University press, 1973)
Hill, C P	*Who's Who in Stuart Britain* (Shepheard Walwyn, London, 1988)
Historical manuscripts Commission Annual Reports	
Holme, Thea	*Chelsea* (Hamish Hamilton, London, 1972)
Home, Gordon	*Epsom: its History and Surroundings* (SR, York, 1971)
Hook, Theodore (ed)	*The Manager's Note-Book* (1838)
Hopkirk, Mary	*Queen Over the Water, Mary Beatrice of Modena Queen of James II* (John Murray, London, 1953)
Hurst, Sir Gerald	*A Short History of Lincoln's Inn Fields* (Constable, London, 1946)
Hutchinson, John	*Herefordshire Biographies* (Jakeman & Carver, Hereford, 1890)
Hutton, Ronald	*Charles II* (Clarendon, Oxford, 1989)
Imbert-Terry, H M	*A Misjudged Monarch* (Heinemann, London, 1917)
Inderwick, F A	*A Calendar of The Inner Temple Records, Vol III* (London, 1901)
Jameson, Anna	*Memoirs of the Beauties of the Court of King Charles the Second* (Samuel Bentley, London, 1838)
Josten, C H	*Elias Ashmole, 5 vols* (Oxford University Press, 1967)
Lamb, Jeremy	*So Idle a Rogue - the Life and Death of Lord Rochester* (Allison & Busby, London, 1993)
Langbaine, Gerard	*An Account of the English Dramatic Poets* (1691)
Latham R & Matthews W (eds)	*The Diary of Samuel Pepys, 10 vols* (Harper Collins, 1995)
Lennep, William van, *et al.* (eds)	*The London Stage, Part One 1660-1700* (University of Illinois Press, 1961)
Lindsay, Philip	*Hampton Court - A History* (Meridian, London,

1948)

Loth, David	*Royal Charles* (Routledge, London, 1931)
Luttrell, Narcissus	*A Brief Historical Relation of State Affairs from September 1678 to April 1714* (Oxford University Press, 1857)
Lyons, Paddy & Morgan, Fidelis,	*Female Playwrights of the Restoration* (Everyman, London, 1997)
Lysons, Daniel	*The Environs of London* (Caddell-Davis, London, 1810)
MacGregor-Hastie, Roy	*Nell Gwyn* (Robert Hale, London, 1987)
MacQueen-Pope, W	*Theatre Royal Druly Lane* (WH Allen, London, (1945)
Margoliouth, H M (ed)	*Marvell's Poems and Letters* (Oxford University press, 1952)
Marvell, Andrew	*The Works of Wordsworth* (Ware, 1995)
Masters, Brian	*The Mistresses of Charles II* (Blond & Briggs, London, 1979)
McPhee, John	*Oranges* (Heinemann, London, 1967)
Melville, Lewis	*Nell Gwyn, The Story of her Life* (Hutchinson, London, 1923)
Melville, Lewis	*The Windsor Beauties* (Hutchinson, London, 1928)
Milhous, J & Hume R (eds)	*A Register of Theatrical Documents 1660-1737* (Southern Illinois University Press, 1991)
Milhous, J & Hume R	*Roscius Anglicanus* (The Society for Theatre Research, London, 1987)
Moody, Martin & Byrne (eds)	*A New History of Ireland* (Clarendon, Oxford, 1976)
Nicol, Allardyce	*British Drama: an Historical Survey from the Beginnings to the Present* (George G Harrap, London, 1925)
Norman, Charles	*Rake Rochester* (WH Allen, London, 1955)
Norrington, Ruth (ed)	*My Dearest Minette* (Peter Owen, London, 1996)
Norton, Lucy	*The Sun King and His Loves* (Folio Society, London, 1982)
Ogg, David	*England in the Reign of Charles II, 2 vols* (Clarendon, Oxford, 1963)
Ollard, Richard	*Pepys - A Biography* (Hodder & Stoughton, London, 1974)
Parker, Derek	*Nell Gwyn* (Sutton, Stroud, 2000)
Pearson, Hesketh	*Charles II - His Life and Likeness* (Heinemann, London, 1961)
Picard, Liza	*Restoration London,* (Weidenfeld & Nicolson,

	London) 1997
Pike, Clement Edwards (ed)	*Selections from the Correspondence of Arthur Capel Earl of Essex 1675-1677* (Camden Third Series, London, 1913)
Pinto, V de Sola	*Sir Charles Sedley 1639-1701* (Constable, London, 1917)
Plumptre, EH	*The Life of Thomas Ken, 2 vols* (Isbister, London, 1890)
Popham, H E	*Quaint Survivals of Old London Customs* (Cecil Palmer, London, 1928)
Porter, Stephen	*The Great Fire of London* (Sutton, Stroud, 1996)
Price, John	*An Historical Account of the City of Hereford* (Walker, Hereford, 1796)
Reresby, Sir John	*Memoirs of Sir John Reresby* (Kegan Paul, Trench & Trubner, London, 1904)
Richardson, John	*Covent Garden* (New Barnet, London, 1979)
Ross, Sutherland	*The Plague and the Fire of London* (Faber & Faber, London, 1965)
Rowse, A L	*Tower of London* (Weidenfeld & Nicolson, London, 1973)
Rowse, A L	*Windsor Castle* (Weidenfeld & Nicolson, London, 1974)
Royal Bank of Scotland	*Child & Co - The First House in the City* (RBS, 1992)
Rymer, Thomas	*Tragedies of the Last Age Considered and Explained* (Augustus M Kelley, 1970)
Sackville-West, V	*Knole and the Sackvilles* (Lindsay Drummond, London, 1948)
Saintsbury, George (ed)	*John Dryden* (Ernest Benn, London, 1947)
Sargeaunt, John	*The Poems of John Dryden* (Oxford University Press, 1910)
Scott, J M	*The Book of Pall Mall* (Heinemann, London, 1965)
Sergeant, Philip W	*My Lady Castlemaine* (Dana Estes, Boston, 1911)
Shaw, G B	*In Good King Charles's Golden Days* (Constable, London, 1939)
Sheffield, John	*Buckingham's Miscellanea* (Haworth Press, London, 1933)
Sheppard, Francis	*London - A History* (Oxford University Press, 1998)
Sidney, Henry	*Diary of the Times of Charles the Second*, ed. Robert W Blencowe, 2 vols (Coburn, London,

1843)

Smith, David Nichol (ed)	*Characters of the Seventeenth Century* (Clarendon, Oxford, 1918)
Stackhouse. Thomas, (ed)	*Bishop Gilbert Bumet History of His Time,* (Everyman, London, 1979)
Stow, John	*Survey of London, Strype's edition* (Whitaker, London, 1842)
Summers, M (ed)	*Roscius Anglicanus by John Downes* (Fortune Press, London, 1928)
Summers, Montague	*The Playhouse of Pepys,* (Humanities Press, New York, 1964)
Summers, Montague	*The Restoration Theatre* (Macmillan, London, 1934)
Taylor, John Russell (ed)	*Penguin Dictionary of the Theatre* (Penguin, London, 1966)
Thompson, Edward Maunde (ed)	*Correspondence of the Family of Hatton, 2 vols* (Camden Society, London, 1878)
Thompson, Edward Maunde (ed)	*Letters of Humphrey Prideaux* (Camden Society, London, 1835)
Thomson, George Malcolm	*The First Churchill* (Secker & Warburg, 1979)
Thomson, Gladys Scott	*Life in a Noble Household 1641-1700* (Jonathan Cape, London, 1937)
Tighe, R & Davis, J	*Annals of Windsor* (Longman, London, 1858)
Treglown, Jeremy	*Spirit of Wit – Reconsiderations of Rochester* (Blackwell, Oxford, 1982)
Turner, E S	*The Court of St James's* (Michael Joseph, London, 1960)
Vieth, David M, (ed)	*The Complete Poems of John Wilmot, Earl of Rochester* (Yale University Press, New Haven, 1979)
Warrington, John (ed)	*The Diary of Samuel Pepys, 3 vols* (Everyman, London, 1953)
Weinreb, B & Hibbert, C (eds)	*The London Encyclopaedia* (Macmillan, London, 1983)
Wheatley, H B	*Historical Portraits* (Bell, London, 1897)
Williams, H Noel	*Rival Sultanas* (Hutchinson, London, 1915)
Wilson, John Harold	*All the King's Ladies - Actresses of the Restoration* (University of Chicago Press, 1958)
Wilson, John Harold	*Mr Goodman the Player* (University of Pittsburgh Press, 1964)
Wilson, John Harold	*Nell Gwyn, Royal Mistress* (Pellegrini & Cuhady, New York, 1952)

Wilson, John Harold   *The Court Wits of the Restoration - An*
                           introduction (Princeton University Press, 1948)
Wilson, John Harold   *Rochester-Savile Letters 1671-80*, 1941
Winifred, Lady Burghclere *George Villiers, Second Duke of Buckingham*
                           (John Murray, London, 1903)

Contemporary material

British Library

Additional MSS
MS 21483 ff27-28: Nelly's letters to James II
MS 6914: Rochester's Satyrical Poems
MS 35280: Sketch of Nell Gwynne's house at Bagnigge Wells
MS 27872, f18: Letter carried by Nelly to release Buckingham from the Tower;
f20: Buckingham's letter to the king
MS 26683, f59 B: Nelly's coat of arms
MS 49459, f4; MS 21553, f9; Add Charters 28094, f54 & 15862-15864:
    Various receipts, leases and pension payments
MS 5847: Copy of letter
Sloane MS 161, f22: Prologue to *Cataline*
Stowe MS 212, fl76, fl78: Irish correspondence
Stowe MS 211, f330: Rochester's letter acting as trustee for Nelly
Verney MS M/636 - Letter mentioning Nelly
Harley MS 7319 A Collection of Choice Poems; *see also* Harley MSS 6913,
    6914, and 7317 for poems, elegies and satires
Trumbull 72596 newsletter on death of Nelly
True News, February 4-7, 1680
London Gazette, January 1678: reward for theft from Nelly's house.
London Chronicle, August 15-18, 1778: the goldsmith's story
Theatre Royal, Drury Lane, Vol I, part 1 – includes spurious opening night
    playbill
Calendar of Treasury Books
State Papers, Domestic
Historical Commission Annual Reports
State papers, Venetian

Bodleian Library, Oxford University

Rawlinson MSS
D872: Secret Service payments (including James II settling Nelly's debts and
    buying her mortgage of Bestwood Park)
D861: Letter concerning illness of Charles Beauclerk

D809, f92: Witness statement
D790, f33: Fee farms grants - the king paying off Lord Buckhurst for Nelly?
Nelly's supposed horoscope

Public Record Office

CUST 109/10: patents, leases, warrants and excise 1683-90
Nelly's will and second codicil (PROB 11, 393: 1687, f64 1688 f162).

Domestic bills and receipts, patents, leases, warrants, satires, ballads and engravings are to be found in collections held at Morgan Pierpont Library, New York; State University of Ohio; Brotherton Library, Leeds University; The Army & Navy Club, Pall Mall, London; Crofton-Croker collection held by His Grace The Duke of St Albans at Child & Co, 1 Fleet Street, London; Yale University Library. Also Nelly's rate payments and burial register are at the Westminster Library Archive, London, Sir Frances Fane's Commonplace Book is at the Shakespeare Library, Stratford-upon-Avon, and the Ormonde papers are at the National Library, Dublin.

Index